THE ENTREPRENEURIAL BUSINESS FOR YOU

Other Books by Glenn Desmond

Handbook of Small Business Valuation Formulas and Rules of Thumb
Business Valuation Handbook
How to Value Professional Practices

THE *Ideal* ENTREPRENEURIAL BUSINESS FOR YOU

Glenn Desmond
Monica Faulkner

John Wiley & Sons, Inc.

New York • Chichester • Brisbane • Toronto • Singapore

To Martha

This text is printed on acid-free paper.

Copyright © 1995 by Glenn Desmond and Monica Faulkner
Published by John Wiley & Sons, Inc.

Library of Congress Cataloging-in-Publication Data

Desmond, Glenn M.
    The ideal entrepreneurial business for you / Glenn Desmond, Monica Faulkner.
      p.   cm.
    Includes bibliographical references and index.
    ISBN 0-471-11812-5 (cloth)   ISBN 0-471-11813-3 (paper)
    1. New business enterprises—United States.   2. Small business—United States.
  I. Faulkner, Monica.   II. Title.
    HD62.5.D47   1995
    658'.041—dc20   95-1373

Printed in the United States of America

10 9 8 7 6 5 4 3 2 1

Acknowledgments

This book would never have come to fruition without the help of literally hundreds of people. I'd like to give special thanks to the following: the good folks at Camden Harbor Enterprises—Paula Smith for her marketing acumen and enthusiastic teamwork, Dorothy Thatcher for her calm and competent organizational skills, and Serena Moon for her invaluable data-gathering; Mike Hamilton at Wiley for his support and confidence; the people at Impressions for their patience, attention to detail, and gentle nudging about deadlines; Ethan at Barnes & Noble, who graciously saved my co-author hours of research; Phyllis Loud at Drohan Mangement Group for her greatly appreciated database search; and the many business professionals whose experience and insights have contributed to these pages.

But the biggest thank you of all is to my patient and loving wife Martha, who had to constantly remind me that I was married to her and not to my computer.

Contents

CHAPTER 1

Introduction

Maybe you're among the hundreds of thousands of Americans whose traditional employment has disappeared. If so, your changes of finding another job in your old field may be limited. Or maybe you're a recent graduate and are starting to realize that the huge corporations that used to offer 30 years of job security seem to be going the way of the dinosaurs—leaving you wondering where to look to create a financial future. Or maybe you have a job but already see the handwriting on the wall and are thinking ahead to the day when you may be "technologized" out of a paycheck. Or maybe your job still has a good future, but you find yourself wondering what it would be like to work for yourself.

I thought about that a lot when I was younger. Twenty-eight years ago, I did something about it.

Now I'm at what is generally considered normal retirement age, and I could remove to my summer home on Lake Maguntacook in Maine (well, for six months of the year) and do little or nothing. However, I really don't want to retire. There's too much fun to be had. Too much to prove.

I thought about corporate layoffs and downsizing that are forcing people into early retirement and about the financial squeeze of unemployment, the decline of our defense-supported economy, and the many other forces that are shaping the ways we do business (and make money).

Who wants to retire when there are so many new opportunities to have fun making money? What I have to say about retirement goes for the unemployed or the person who is employed doing something he or she does not like but sees no way out. In this book, I'm going to show you the way out.

1

Let me tell you a little story about myself. Just 28 years ago last April, I quit a very secure, well-paying position as manager of my employer's largest and most profitable division, headquartered in Chicago, because I was not satisfied and longed to be independent.

I had previously contacted a potential client in New England (a government agency) to see if there was an opportunity for me to do subcontract work. I had been assured that there was plenty of work and that it would be available by April (just about four months away). I informed my employer of my decision to leave, giving about two months' notice. A new manager was selected to fill my position. I was at a point of no return.

However, within a few days of my scheduled departure, I was informed that funding for the project for which I had been assured subcontract work had been canceled. I had made no other contacts for work. I had very limited liquid resources, no job, and suddenly no client, in a depressed economy, in an area of the country where I was known only to a few government agencies that now had no money.

The one important asset I had was several years of experience as a real estate and business appraiser. I knew that experience and related education would assist me greatly down the line. But starting out on my own, in an area where I wasn't known and had to generate cash income quickly appeared not only difficult but perhaps impossible. Despite these circumstances, I decided to go. I was determined not to allow fear of the unknown to hold me back.

On a Monday morning in April, I was sitting in my car in a service station getting gasoline. I literally did not know where I was going to go to get started with my new nonexistent business. What I did know was that I would be in the business of doing business and real estate appraisals; that was what I enjoyed doing, and I wanted to do it in my own shop. I decided I'd let my intuition and common sense take over. I realized that the first step in my marketing plan should be to survey the kinds of people who might need my service.

And that is how I started. My intuition paid off immediately. In that single day I made three calls on appraisal users. I did not know the people I contacted, nor did they know me. By the first evening I had a car with out-of-state license plates, the YMCA as my home address, a month-to-month lease on a 100-square-foot office above an old grocery store, and enough verbal contracts for appraisal work for myself, a part-time research assistant, and a half-time clerical assistant.

Within three years I had a national company of about 70 professional and support employees with a New England headquarters. In addition

I had acquired a controlling interest in another established appraisal company with offices in Cincinnati, Minneapolis, Denver, and New York.

Why I Wrote This Book

What qualifies me to write *The Ideal Entrepreneurial Business for You*? The small-business start-up experience I've just recited? Or the fact that, along with successes, I've probably made lots of stupid mistakes, too? All of this probably helps.

But I think my most important qualification is the profession I've been in—the profession of valuing businesses, both very large ones and very small ones. I've found out what makes business value and what makes failure; what kinds of smaller start-up, or established, businesses have the best chance of success today; what are the riskiest and the least risky; what you should go after; what you should avoid; what businesses have the best chance of becoming multimillion-dollar operations in a relatively short time; and which ones have the most potential for failure in an even shorter time. Whether you want to start your own business, buy an existing business, or sell your own business and move on to something else, this book can help you.

I've lectured throughout the United States. I've written several other books. But all of this has been aimed at educating professionals—business appraisers, accountants, attorneys, financial consultants, and government agencies such as the IRS, the Department of Justice, state highway departments, and others. Now I think it's time to translate my unique knowledge into something useful to individuals who really need the information to use in making their own decisions.

People often ask me, "What's the best business to be in?" I usually answer, "One that balances your abilities and interests with your need to make a certain level of income—one that's right for this time, and one that makes *you* happy." By the time you finish reading this book, you'll be well on your way to answering that question for yourself.

As you read *The Ideal Entrepreneurial Business for You*, keep the following in mind:

- Have patience.

- Be focused on an objective that is well thought out and realistic. At the same time, do not allow this objective to prevent you from being flexible and seeing opportunities.

- Control your fear. Stick around just to see what happens; you're probably on the edge of something big and don't even know it.
- Have enough self-esteem to be able to sell yourself and your business or profession, whether you're buying, selling, or creating a new enterprise.
- Have a generally positive outlook. This is crucial no matter what your goals and purposes are.
- Don't let yourself be held back by a limited education. It's not what school you attended or what degrees you have that make success.
- Realize that the greatest source of ideas is within you; it's not "out there somewhere."
- Have the ability to listen to your own intuition and to others. Keep your mouth shut and your eyes and ears open.

Success in business, like all things in life, is an integral part of you, of how you think. This book is dedicated to giving you information of a kind that is not found anywhere outside you but that you must have if you're going to be able to effectively answer the questions, "What's the best entrepreneurial small business for me, and what types of businesses should I avoid and why?"

No matter who you are, if you've ever thought about going into business for yourself, you've probably also worried about risking the family farm. That's a valid concern—but the message of this book is that the world is so full of exciting entrepreneurial opportunities that there's no better time to make the move into self-employment—if you do it right!

What you need is a new way of looking at what's going on all around us. That's what you'll get from this book.

- It will open your eyes to the new world of entrepreneurial opportunities that will carry you well into the twenty-first century.
- It will alert you to the lowest-risk, highest-return, greatest-growth business opportunities in today's economy—many of which are being overlooked.
- It will offer a guide to your best and worst risks if you want to buy an existing business.
- It will give you state-by-state information about the small-business climate gathered from a unique national survey.

Think about what is said here. Read this book carefully, and take notes as you go along. Then, if you decide to take the plunge, I wish you the best!

GLENN DESMOND

CHAPTER 2

There's No
Open Prairie Left

Have you ever dreamed of being an entrepreneur? Does the traditional American Dream of being your own boss lure you? But has the precarious economic climate of the past few years scared you off because you don't want to jeopardize your financial security and your family's future? Maybe you've seen the statistics on small-business failure rates and have decided that working for yourself seems too risky. It's time to think again, because all you need is to go about it the right way.

This book will show you that there is a whole new world of unprecedented moneymaking opportunities as we approach the twenty-first century. And if you know where to look and what to look for, you can position yourself today to make your dream of financial and business success come true tomorrow—without risking everything you've worked so hard to get up till now.

Whether you're an aerospace engineer, welder, middle manager, or chief executive—no matter who you are, you may have already experienced the pain of losing the job you trained for and devoted your life to. What's worse, you may be realizing that your old job has disappeared, perhaps forever. You may be facing an uncertain future.

And suppose you're fortunate enough to be still working. Can you honestly say you've never lost a moment's sleep worrying about what would happen to you and your family if you lost your job? Or if both you and your spouse lost your jobs?

Even the most positive of us is bound to have such thoughts on occasion, if only fleetingly—especially when we look around us and see friends and neighbors out of work. Even born optimists would hardly be so foolish as to bury their heads in the sand in such risky economic times.

I believe that there will never be a better time to start exploring new opportunities in self-employment. Why? Because the very forces that are buffeting our society and making it so complex are also opening up a whole new world of entrepreneurial business opportunities—if you know what to look for and where to look! Also, being aware of the forces that are creating new business opportunities will help you identify businesses that may be riskier.

In the next chapter, I'll be discussing 13 of the most important Forces of Change affecting American society today. And their impact will continue well into the twenty-first century. After you've taken a careful look at this list, you'll understand that when I talk about going into business for yourself, I'm not talking about what your parents meant 30 or 40 years ago, or even just 15 years ago.

I'm not talking about the mom-and-pop convenience stores, or the necktie shop, or the laundromat, or the pizza kitchen. I'm not even talking about the newer wrinkles in small business like balloon delivery services and aerobics studios. These kinds of self-employment businesses can all be the right choices at the right time for some people. But from my standpoint, as someone who has seen thousands of small businesses succeed and fail over the years, they also have problems that make them high-risk choices in today's rapidly changing world.

For example, traditional home-based small businesses such as handicrafts, and faddish ventures such as balloon delivery services, may be easy to get into because they require very little start-up investment. But they also offer little in the way of long-term growth possibilities, so it's probably safest to think of them as limited activities at best. Oh, they can bring in a little extra income to your household, but don't expect much more.

What you really need to do is grab onto the coattails of the Forces of Change—not cling to the ways of the past. There are hundreds of new opportunities out there that can offer you a low-risk combination of minimal start-up investment, rapid positive cash flow, and long-term value—in short, the ideal entrepreneurial business for you. And this book will help you because it's a road map to this new world of businesses that make sense—the ones that will let you take control of your own life and create your own financial security.

Where Have All the Gunslingers Gone?

The small-business environment is dramatically different today from what it was in even the very recent past. It's no longer the place for gunslingers who succeed just because they're lucky or are the only shop in town. There's no open prairie left. The field is crowded with aggressive competition, and ways of doing business are changing faster than the gunslinger's speeding bullet.

But what do we usually think about when we use the terms "small business" or "self-employment" enterprise? The Small Business Administration classifies firms with fewer than five hundred employees as "small." A recent federal report on the state of small business estimated that there were about 22 million "small" businesses in the United States as of 1994. However, most small businesses actually have fewer than three employees, while more than half have no employees other than the owner—and many owners work only part-time at their business.[1]

We all tend to think of "business" as a structured form, such as an independent store or office, a franchise, or some other kind of enterprise. We think in terms of set hours of operation, of management and employees, of investment and cash flow, of location, and of a specific product or service. It's time to rethink this definition. In this new era, business can be much less structured and more free-form, and entrepreneurial small businesses are a matter of you coming up with an idea or concept and testing the waters in a given geographic area by making contacts with potential customers. Instead of being carved in stone at the outset, your service actually begins to take form in the early start-up period and changes as you begin selling it, bringing you a rapid positive cash flow with a minimal initial investment and minimal risk.

The Secret? Service!

The Forces of Change are transforming the ways we do business and will have a major influence on which ventures succeed and which go down in flames. *Traditional small businesses no longer offer the best opportunities for new entrants to self-employment and small business.*

This means that if you're thinking about going into business for yourself, you should be looking at the new opportunities being created because of the Forces of Change. This book will not only tell you about the best business opportunities available but will spark your own creativity and imagination so you can come up with your own "better mousetrap" that will have the world beating a path to your door!

But before I tell you more about this, I should mention that business brokers in our state-by-state survey (see chapter 8) report that most of their new small-business entrepreneurs have been looking for manufacturing or distribution operations.

In general, these potential investor-operators are seeking businesses that are seeing a positive cash flow and can be purchased for $500,000 or less. They're also hoping to make a cash down payment of no more than 25 percent with the owner taking back paper on the rest, or possibly getting SBA-guaranteed loan financing. The buyers also hope to obtain financing through banks, equipment manufacturers, or equipment leasing companies for the fixed assets involved in the purchase.

Good luck! Everybody wants the same thing. The owners of these businesses are besieged with suitors, and they're not about to give away their stores. The fact is, the demand far outstrips the supply, and the few that are available can command high prices.

Our surveys show that retail and food-service operations are among the least sought-after. There is an ample supply of these, but the majority offered are at best mediocre moneymakers and are more probably losers. These businesses face extensive competition, not only from other established small businesses but also from the growing numbers of discounters, superstores, and major chain operators, which are active in this as well as in almost every other field of retail endeavor.

If you have no choice other than food service or retail, your best option may be to join a franchise operation. But keep in mind that the investment required can be substantial ($100,000 to $200,000 is typical), profits are very often marginal, and it can be a long time before you see a return on your investment. Another factor to keep in mind is that running a successful franchise retail or restaurant business requires constant hands-on involvement that most people aren't used to, aren't trained for, and don't like. This book is for people who either don't have the hefty initial investment required to buy a franchise or who just don't want the risk.

The best new opportunities are primarily in the service area—not in products. These promising, potentially profitable, and interesting areas of small business make up my Ideal Entrepreneurial Businesses Master List, which is discussed in detail in chapter 5. Many of these types of businesses, which are being created due to the Forces of Change, can be carried out from your own home as a one-person operation.

Make no mistake about it—this type of entrepreneurship can be full-time and even more. But think of the flexibility. If you're working out of your home, you can go to work in your bathrobe or your sweats, or you can put on a coat and tie every morning, if you're crazy enough to want to. Or you can work in boots and Levi's if you're out in the country somewhere doing consulting or computer communications.

As you'll see in the next chapter, these businesses respond to the new needs and markets that are arising out of the Forces of Change. And as these forces play themselves out in the next several decades, they will create new opportunities for entrepreneurs who dare to take advantage of them.

Nothing's Risk-Free, but This Might Be As Close as You Can Get

I can't deny that everything involves some risks. So, what risks will you be running as you work to create the ideal entrepreneurial business for you? Your business risks will lie primarily in the time required to start from scratch until you attract enough customers. The other risk, perhaps the most important one, is that even these best businesses will require that you be able to sell yourself as well as your services. If you are going to keep your costs low, it just won't be practical to hire professional salespeople to sell your services, especially when you're just beginning.

The types of businesses where I see the greatest opportunities are primarily for "lone wolf" operators who begin with a relatively modest cash investment and who personally sell their product or service and who perform all other functions, at least initially.

Of the 246 businesses described in chapter 5, more than 100 can be started for less than $5,000 as an initial investment. Another 60 or so would require between $5,000 and $10,000, and another three dozen can be started for less than $25,000.

When I say start-up investment, that includes basic operating expenses, initial supplies or products, and a start-up marketing program. It does not include the cash necessary for your personal expenses during your start-up period, when you may see little if any positive cash flow.

But even the most modest self-employment business requires some start-up cash. Where will you get it? Your first thought may be, from your own savings. But think creatively. It could also come from the combined limits from several credit cards, or from Uncle Henry. Brokers in state after state have told us that bank loans for business start-ups are difficult to obtain unless you're buying a business with fixed assets for collateral. Or you might take out a home equity loan. But beyond that, don't expect much.

By the way, bank loans guaranteed by the Small Business Administration may often not be worth the hassle, paperwork, and loss of control that comes with them. As one specialist commented, "With the SBA, you must remember that you have to make it out the way the SBA says to make it out—not how your attorney or accountant wants to make it out. You must remember that this is the government, and they like things done a certain way. Their way!" Or as another broker put it more succinctly, "The SBA will stick their nose into the business and tell the new owner how to run it."

To sum up, these businesses are (a positive way to grasp the opportunities offered by the changing economic environment of the late 1990s.) We can meet the challenges of this new era with new activities which may at first seem so ephemeral that it's hard to put them in a box and say "This is a business" in the traditional sense.

The rest of this book will show you that these new forms of self-employment hold out the promise of growing into full-fledged small businesses—just as the lowly caterpillar eventually metamorphoses into a moth.

Endnote

1. *The State of Small Business: A Report of the President* (Washington, D.C.: U.S. Government Printing Office, 1992), 20.

CHAPTER 3

Ideal Entrepreneurial Businesses and the Forces of Change

It's always been tough to begin a new business venture, but in the economic climate of the late 1990s, the odds of surviving (not to mention succeeding) in traditional independent self-employment businesses such as convenience stores, laundromats, service stations, auto repair shops, animal kennels, fast-food restaurants, and video stores are worse than ever.

Why are things so different today, and why is entering a small business so dangerous? Well, just look around you. What are some of the obvious changes you see? How about discount superstores? The rapidly increasing crime rate in many cities and even in smaller communities? How about local, state, and federal regulations, which have increased to the point that it's no longer economically feasible to enter many types of business? How about the time it takes to get the needed permits, even when a business is feasible otherwise? How about the possible cost of a federal health care system? How about the cost of business liability insurance? How about the increases in costly lawsuits aimed at businesses? How about the astoundingly rapid advances in telecommunications and interactive video technology? How about the environmental crisis?

We are going through a period of drastic change in the ways we do business, and no one has a handle on what the end results will be. But if your objective in this period of transition is to find or create a low-risk self-employment business that will bring you a rapid positive cash flow and a quick return on your start-up investment, along with the potential for future value for your retirement, read this section very carefully. It should provide you with just the kind of direction you are seeking.

11

The business environment since 1990—the beginning of the most recent recession—has certainly been discouraging. You're probably reading this book because you've been directly affected by the many changes in our economy and ways of doing business, most of them seemingly negative. You're probably convinced that no one really knows what's going on or what to do about it—not the politicians, not the pollsters, not the economists, not anyone!

Instead of being discouraged and confused by these changes, take advantage of them! The opportunities today for self-employment are as great as ever—if you know where to look. We're talking about ground-floor opportunities. This book will take you through a process that will show you how and where to discover the scores of moneymaking situations that are waiting for you.

I've sorted out the primary causes for the changing business environment into what I call the Forces of Change. It's easy to think of these forces as negative, especially if you're trying to make ends meet or to find employment. However, we're going to discover that out of these seemingly negative developments come positive opportunities.

As a first step in this discovery process, we have to open our minds to accept change. We may have to accept doing things we never thought we could or would do. Some of the best moneymaking self-employment possibilities ever are out there right now, but they're hidden from us because of self-imposed biases about the social acceptability of certain activities, or because we lack the proper education, training, or financing, or because of any other limitations our minds may impose on us.

Please don't read any further until you ask yourself, "Is my mind really open to all new ideas?" and you can answer, "Yes!"

Now that your mind is wide open and ready to accept change, let's talk about the Forces of Change, which include the following:

1. Big government: the deficit, too many regulations, too many tax increases
2. New telecommunications and video technologies
3. Cutthroat competition by retail mass marketers and discounters
4. Changing consumer behaviors and lifestyles
5. Skyrocketing health care costs and the debate over national health insurance
6. Out-of-control litigiousness and the overburdened court system
7. Increasing crime rates
8. Overpopulation and traffic congestion, especially in urban areas

9. Deteriorating educational systems
10. Demographic changes such as an aging American population and a new influx of immigrants
11. The new interdependent world economy and the end of the Cold War
12. Corporate downsizing and layoffs
13. The environmental crisis

It's clear that we're in a fundamentally changing economy. It isn't just the corporate world that is downsizing; we are also having to downsize our individual expectations in our personal lives (smaller houses, lower educational levels, questions about the value of a college degree). Perhaps most important, we are being forced to downsize our income and our purchasing power, and we can no longer rely unthinkingly on our old notions of job security.

These days, it isn't just blue-collar workers who have to think about losing their jobs—it's everyone in corporate America, at every level, from the most menial to the most exalted. The great expectations and continually improving standard of living that characterized American life for the past five decades since the end of World War II seem to have come to an end.

One of the most fundamental changes going on today—and one that may be very dangerous—is that the corporate world, big business, is tending to consolidate more and more, while at the same time government is becoming more and more "socialistic," that is, more involved in what business is doing and in effect controlling it.

Government at every level is taking more and more wealth from businesses and individuals alike and is making it harder for people to accumulate wealth. However, the consolidation and conglomeration of the corporate world means that more and more wealth is being accumulated there too, especially with vertical and horizontal integration. For example, cable companies' production of programming is vertical integration, whereas AT&T's entry into the cellular phone business and cable business is horizontal integration.

Retailers are doing the same thing: Companies like Wal-Mart may not be their own manufacturer, but they can basically control the operations of the manufacturers that supply them because of their economic clout. In addition, the big retailers are squeezing out traditional wholesalers and distributors in every area, from groceries to lingerie.

So we have an enormous concentration of wealth; an increasing concentration of communications, which also controls what is offered as entertainment; and a greater concentration of superstores and chains, meaning that a decreasing variety of products is offered on the market as originality gets squeezed out—what I call the "McDonaldization" of the marketplace. (Except that people will always tire of sameness sooner or later and will always look for the unique and the creative.)

How do you, the small guy, compete against these forces? How do you fight the telecommunications and other giants? *The answer is: Don't fight them, join them—by serving them!*

Let's talk about the Forces of Change in more detail. Then we'll look at the new opportunities they offer.

1. Big government: The deficit, too many regulations, too many tax increases

How many times have you heard comments like these: "Government's gotten too big, and there's too much control." Federal, state, and even local governments seem to be overregulating and controlling society and small businesses. The laws and regulations that affect pricing, environment, delivery, and packaging not only control how small businesses operate but also take lots of time to comply with. Compounding the problem is government's shortage of money needed to adequately enforce regulations and laws. This results in unevenness of administration, loss of effectiveness—and yes, even unfairness.

The effects on small businesses are not only the cost and time involved but also frustration and discouragement. Certainly, in most instances the government's desire to regulate or control is considered to be in the interest of the public good, and indeed all of the laws and regulations come from some segment of society that is demanding this or that.

One problem is that the government is not a business and is not run like a business—and perhaps it can't be. Ideally, government is supposed to enforce laws on an evenhanded basis. However, not all businesses are the same; that is, not all businesses have the same requirements, the same costs, or the same management skills.

For example, a business using a chemical that is not really toxic might be forced to store and use it in the same manner as another business using a chemical that is indeed very toxic. Both are chemicals, broadly speaking, but they are different; nevertheless, both might be regulated in the same manner.

Here's another example: If a national health care program were adopted that required all employers to offer health insurance to their workers, it's evident that the costs of this care would be disproportionately burdensome for small businesses compared to larger ones.

A packaging firm in Texas estimated that an 8 percent health levy on its 220 workers would raise the company's total benefits burden (which includes workers' compensation, unemployment insurance, Social Security payments, and the costs of complying with government regulations) from 33 percent of its payroll to more than 41 percent. The company was considering replacing five workers with a $500,000 gluing machine that over the long run would cut costs enough to compensate the firm for the increased tax levies it foresaw, according to *Fortune.*[1]

Pricing controls also affect the small guy more dramatically than the large one. For example, independent check-cashing businesses serve an estimated 17 percent of U.S. families who do not have bank accounts, according to the *Los Angeles Times.*[2] Should the Federal Trade Commission step in to begin licensing these operations and sets caps on the fees that can be charged, as has been proposed by Congress, the profit margins of small operations could well decline to the point where they might not be able to operate any longer.

Then there's the federal deficit. The Deficit Reduction Act of 1993 includes a combination of reduced government spending and increased taxes on businesses—businesses that are already tax-burdened. And even though some smaller businesses may qualify for exemptions from the tax increases, it may not be worth the time and cost.

However, from the entrepreneur's perspective, all of these new laws, regulations, controls, and taxes—not to mention reduced government spending—create a myriad of new opportunities for small businesses. It's not enough to just label government regulation as "interference." In my view, the major opportunities for new small businesses will be found in privatization: first, by supplying private services to replace government programs that have been eliminated but are still needed, and second, by the sale of government properties to private parties.

For example, human welfare programs such as child care, education, lunch programs, care and education of people with disabilities, airports, harbors, and police and security services will have to be handled by somebody, and why shouldn't these areas offer opportunities for private businesses? Consulting services in all these areas will be needed, as will additional tax expertise, legal expertise, and other services. What's more, improved packaging and delivery services will be needed to supplement services that may be restricted as attempts are made to control traffic and street congestion in municipalities.

In short, the government services that will be cut or reduced, but that must be continued in some form, offer almost infinite opportunities for the imaginative entrepreneur.

2. New telecommunications and video technologies

New wireless and fiber-optic telecommunications systems are already giving us interactive video and other brand-new ways of using our televisions. We'll soon have computerized video in every household and business in this country and, before long, throughout most of the world. The easy availability of these technologies will change the way we live and the way we do business. The Industrial Revolution certainly changed the way people lived, too, but the inventions that emerged and caused those changes took the better part of a century. The high-tech changes we're about to experience will be seen in five to eight years, or even less. For example, look at the speed with which the fax machine has caught on. That one invention has had a mighty impact on the way businesses (and to a much lesser degree, households) communicate. But you ain't seen nothin' yet!

If you're seriously considering beginning your own small (or large) business, you'd best not think in terms of traditional methods of doing business. Tradition will be out and high-tech will be in—fast! Imagine that the cable TV converter box sitting on top of your set has been replaced with a new super-box. It may not be much bigger than the one you have now, and it probably won't cost you more than about $200, but its capabilities will be vastly different. It will be a high-powered computer capable of decoding hundreds of digital cable signals and allowing you to navigate your way through a true maze of services—shopping, movie selections, library selections, video games, and video-telephonic communications, to name only a few.

Also on the horizon are wireless devices that will allow us to communicate with our computers, our television sets, our appliances, and other electronic equipment not even thought of yet.

Fiber-optic systems will replace existing hardwired telephone and video systems. Fiber optics not only allow many more transmissions on a single strand but also permit two-way exchanges. The result is that our television sets will no longer be limited to one-way transmissions, whether direct or via microwave or satellite systems. And instead of just a few channels, there will be three to five hundred. Fiber optics will give us information superhighways direct to every household, every business, every vehicle, every school, and every government office.

Imagine the possibilities! Every schoolroom in the country—and every home—will have access to the very best education available. Any book in the finest library can be obtained with the mere push of a combination of buttons on your TV remote control.

Want to go to a concert two weeks from today? Just order the tickets right from the TV. How about a cruise to the South Pacific next February? Book your cabin directly through the television. Hungry for a special pizza and want to see what it looks like before it's delivered? Just push the right TV remote button. Want to see a certain movie? No need to drive to the video store—it's already available on your TV. How about calling your daughter and son-in-law in Portland, Maine—when you're in Portland, Oregon—and being able to see and talk to the whole family, including the grandkids, via the TV? There may even be services specifically designed to help you figure out what's on those three to five hundred stations!

Do you begin to get the idea of how dramatic the changes will be? Many forms of businesses that are common today, including small businesses such as video rental stores, may soon be gone altogether. Others will still be with us, but in a changed form. And many new types of businesses will emerge, most of which we can't yet even imagine, let alone adequately define. It's a pretty daunting picture to a lot of small-business owners who have trouble imagining how they'll fit into the new telecommunications picture.

But it also opens up a new world of ancillary services limited only by your imagination. For example, even if people can order goods instantaneously from television, those goods still need to be packaged and delivered. I expect that business-to-business services will continue to expand rapidly in the coming decades to support new forms of electronic marketing. It's even been predicted, according to the *Los Angeles Times,* that in 25 years QVC, the "Quality Value Convenience" shopping network, could be "the biggest retailer in the country," with cable shopping services resembling electronic malls in which specialty stores will serve as "anchors" and smaller specialty services will fill out the rest of the broadcast time."[3]

Another possibility would be for smaller retailers to compete by grouping together to share costs and to benefit from economies of scale the way the big guys can. (And the big guys will need packaging, delivery, and other services, too.)

This means new opportunities for you! Small businesses that can be carried out using telecommuting—working from home via computers, interactive video, fax, and modem—will play no small role in these developments. Telecommuting is an efficient way to do business because it cuts down on traffic congestion, air pollution, energy consumption, highway construction and repair, and traffic accidents. In addition, telecommuting offers flexibility—you can do business all over the globe without ever leaving your home.

Journalist David Lamb, writing in the *Los Angeles Times,* has dubbed these new entrepreneurs—freelance professionals, consultants, manufacturers' representatives, financial advisers, and analysts—"Lone Eagles." They can do what they're doing because the new technologies have "cut the ties that traditionally bound workers to cities," and now they have the best of both worlds: They can live in low-stress towns and rural areas but still do business with customers in metropolitan areas. According to this report, by 1993 more than 39 million Americans were working out of their homes, compared to only 6 million in 1974.[4] You may as well join that number, and the new technology will let you do it!

3. Cutthroat competition by retail mass marketers and discounters

In the America of the late 1990s, there are so many businesses and so much merchandise that every market seems to be oozing with competition—not just from a lot of other little guys, but also from the giant chain operations and discount superstores that now dominate almost every field of retailing.

Also, it's difficult to find a good retail location that hasn't already been taken. Our superhighway system has been built, and there won't be much expansion in the next few years. Therefore, unlike the 1950s, 1960s, and 1970s, new prime locations will not be created.

To be sure, new locations will appear as populations shift or areas become popular or unpopular. However, competition is so well established that it is difficult to find a place where your business would be the only player in the community unless you're very creative and develop something that is indeed new, or is perceived as new.

It's going to be harder and harder for small retailers to find a niche. For example, small toy retailers have been walloped by the "Big Five" (Toys R Us, Wal-Mart, Kmart, Target, and Kay-Bee), which were expected to pull in between $11 billion and $17 billion in 1993. The smaller retailers, like the smaller manufacturers and wholesalers, are surviving by steering clear of popular mass-market toys where they can be undercut, and they're specializing in higher-priced educational toys that the big discounters don't pick up. In fact, some manufacturers sell their toys only to the smaller stores, although these account for only about 5 percent of U.S. toy sales.

Business Week warns, "In category after category, giant 'power retailers' are using sophisticated inventory management, finely tuned selections, and above all, competitive pricing to crowd out weaker players."[5] The trend is for manufacturers to be drawn to the big retailers "in the hopes that huge volumes will offset slender profit margins," but the deal goes both ways because big retailers prefer big suppliers to small ones.

The "500-pound gorillas" like Wal-Mart also get to call a lot of the shots, and suppliers who fail to measure up to the giants' stringent demands for quality control and on-time delivery can find themselves shunted over to the sidelines. Just-in-time manufacturing schedules, which cut costs by avoiding production of excess inventories, use sophisticated point-of-sale electronics to get data on what customers want.

In fact, there is so much competition that the best new business opportunities lie in serving companies that are already competing with each other. In other words, look for ways to help established businesses cut their costs by improving efficiency and effectiveness. There are many businesses that can be created to serve this function.

Exporting, both overseas and to other regions in the United States, is another route small businesses are taking to compete in the world of giant discount superstores. The secret is to choose a business that will give you the flexibility to move with the transitions caused by the domination of the "big guys."

4. Changing consumer behaviors and lifestyles

Recent changes in consumer patterns are related to the pressures from superstore discounters, but other factors are involved as well. These changes create new problems and issues for small businesses and also open up new opportunities for businesses that can build on these changes.

It used to be that bargaining was the province of bazaars in Morocco, or in more recent times, Saturday swap meets. No longer is that true. In today's America, everyone, it seems, is on the hunt for the lowest price—but also for quality merchandise. And people are not afraid to ask, anywhere.

Consumers have been so squeezed by the recent recession that they tend to buy only on sale—and they'll wait to make their purchase until someone reduces the price, because they know that somebody is bound to. This means that consumers will do their shopping at several places if necessary, rather than just heading for the nearby regional mall.

People today want the best product at a real discount price, and they don't much care how fancy the premises are either. But cheap is not the only feature they're looking for either, if cheap implies poor quality. They want good quality. The operative term is value pricing.

Numerous other changes in consumer patterns have changed the face of small business and will continue to do so as we approach and enter the twenty-first century. As the 1992 federal report on small business puts it:

> An evolutionary process that began years ago, driven by technological changes, rising incomes and education levels, and changes in living arrangements, continues in force today. . . . Some changes [in new types of small businesses] seem unusual, but all represent what people do for a living and services that are demanded in the marketplace.
>
> A few examples: horse walking, pet sitting, asbestos removal, paint deleading, can crushing, newsletters, boat waxing, voice mail, faxing, copy machines, T-shirts, baseball cards (retail), pizza delivery, computer software (retail), tile stores, land trusts, aquarium setup, banquet booking, beauty consulting, bill paying, career counseling, cellular phones, yacht chartering, software installation, fishing charters, grant writing, land planners, magnetic resonance imaging, mail box rental, mediation services, automotive oil change services, pager rental, party planning, radon detection, staff leasing, audio and video tape repair, and waste management consulting.
>
> [These] changes tell a story of changing markets, technologies, ways of living, attitudes toward the environment, and use of leisure time. The shift to two-worker families is reflected in the many household support services. Health and environmental concerns are prominent, as are industries based on the emerging information technologies and new legislation. Virtually all of these represent new markets, new technologies, and new ways of living, with small business playing the major role in the delivery of such goods and services.[6]

5. Skyrocketing health care costs and the debate over national health insurance

As we saw during the 1992 presidential campaign and as soon as the Clinton Administration took office, a national health care program of some kind seems inevitable, although it may still be some years down the road.

From my viewpoint, it's not even clear whether a federal program is a good idea or not. Have government attempts thus far impeded or helped the health care industry? Well, one thing we can all probably agree upon is that our health care "system" is in such a shambles that it scarcely deserves the name. Both private and government-sponsored programs are under attack.

But whether you're for or against government becoming involved in the health care system doesn't matter much at this point. The fact is, the government is going to be involved, and an effort will be made to provide health insurance and care for virtually the entire population. This will be a costly program. It will also create a need to expand many existing services and will generate new opportunities for small businesses—everything from consulting on how to take advantage of available services, to cost control, to implementing the system, to opening special-care facilities.

6. Out-of-control litigiousness and the overburdened court system

Too many lawsuits! The U.S. legal system is based on the principle that all people are equal, but the system is also constantly evolving and being reinterpreted. In the past two decades, costly jury awards and time-consuming class-action suits have created barriers for businesses. The chances of stepping into some legal minefield have increased, raising the specter of expensive, lengthy litigation. Professionals of all sorts are subject to litigation. Some medical specialties—obstetrics, for example—are especially vulnerable to litigation, and the high costs of malpractice insurance are driving doctors out of their practices.

Civil-rights–related suits such as sexual harassment cases have also been increasing. Between 1987 and 1992, complaints filed by the Equal Employment Opportunity Commission (EEOC) doubled to 10,532, and *Fortune* has estimated that harassment cases could cost U.S. businesses $1 billion in fees and damages in the coming five years.[7]

In addition, manufacturing and other types of businesses are vulnerable to potentially devastating product liability suits. According to one report, the number of product liability lawsuits filed in U.S. federal courts increased 1,000 percent between 1975 and 1990, and filings in state courts increased between 300 and 500 percent. Average total liability costs for U.S. companies were running 15 times the costs in Japan and 20 times the costs in Europe.[8]

All of these factors, in addition to the delays and complications attributable to the increases in crime discussed below, are resulting in massive court congestion and clogging of the entire legal system. Lawyers are probably the only ones who really like litigation, but the fact is that litigation is with us, will probably remain with us, and may even continue to grow. Thus, there are bound to be new opportunities for small businesses as a result. Some examples include document storage, taking depositions on video, paging, research, consulting, court reporting, and other legal support services to lawyers, the courts, and everyone else involved in the legal system.

7. Increasing crime rates

In American society today, there are no more "new frontiers," and we don't do very well when we have to live all together. The massing of people together, especially when they come from different backgrounds, generally works well when there's a lot of room for people to create their own new "niches"—but we have to face the reality.

Exaggerated differences in income and cultural differences among people who are all living too close together results in crime and the drug scene. In addition, too many Americans feel trapped in unfulfilling work and as though there's "no way out" for them. This contributes to the mood of psychological distress.

Criminals have become more aggressive and fearless; the courts and jails are crowded; there are too few police and security forces—in other words, there has been a breakdown of an overburdened and underfunded system.

Crimes against both individuals and businesses dominate the news every night. We are more concerned than we have ever had to be before with the safety and security of our homes, our businesses, and our motor vehicles. Even our schools offer no refuge—increasing numbers of schools are installing metal detectors and other security measures to try to keep guns off the school grounds.

The crime situation may be the greatest deterrent to would-be entrepreneurs who are thinking of starting up or buying a small business, especially if they are interested in retail. Statistics cited in *Investor's Business Daily* show that robberies against retailers rose by 58 percent between 1984 and 1991, that employee theft, customer shoplifting, and vendor fraud accounted for 82 percent of all inventory losses.[9] U.S. Census Bureau data for 1992 indicate that retailers lost an estimated $30.7 billion that year from these three forms of crime. In addition, one research group reported that almost 20 percent of New York employers had employees who had reported being assaulted on their way to or from work.

But however threatening the crime situation is, it also opens the door to a wide array of new small business and self-employment opportunities. The costs of crime are mind-boggling, but so are the possibilities. Businesses that offer security systems, guard services, ways of guarding against fraud, and consulting in all these areas are just a few options. There may be great opportunities for such services as the videotaping of business and home possessions for insurance purposes, in case of theft or other damage or loss. Another potentially important example might be related to education: new trade schools that could help meet the basic demand for the creative in the midst of the mass-produced might well offer ways to free people from feeling trapped. Offering people more options for creativity, satisfaction, and value in their lives might be the best way to solve the crime problem.

8. Overpopulation and traffic congestion, especially in urban areas

Overpopulation and traffic congestion are causing many changes in our thinking about efficient ways to get from one place to another and how to receive services or products. Certainly, two-way television is going to allow us to order from our living room, and this is going to save us time, money, and frustration in traffic.

This ability to shop at home will in turn create new opportunities, such as the need for rapid delivery of merchandise or groceries. We may also see the rise of alternative transportation systems aimed at cutting a number of single-passenger cars that currently clog so many of our streets. Some small-business entrepreneurs have already come up with new ways to cope with congestion. For example, several companies nationwide have created services that fill in for working parents by ferrying children to and from after-school activities.

According to Jackie Christiansen, an executive director of Kearny Mesa Transportation Management Association of San Diego, California, traffic congestion—along with air pollution—could be cut by 20 percent if people would carpool to work just one day each week.[10] The telecommuting "Lone Eagles" referred to earlier are one group that is taking advantage of technology to avoid contributing to traffic congestion.

There is a multitude of small-business opportunities that can help individuals and other businesses cope with traffic congestion. For example, teleconferencing could cut the number of business trips in the U.S. by 13 million a year, according to one report.[11]

9. Deteriorating educational systems

Many factors have been blamed for the apparent decline of the U.S. educational system: the rapidly expanding population in some areas, which strains resources; governmental difficulties in balancing budgets and the resulting cuts in budgets for all educational purposes, including plants and facilities; the disruption of children's home lives because of family breakups and dual-career parents; and school violence and other issues that distract from effective education.

Perhaps the major problem is a lack of money to keep the basic educational infrastructure going. Whatever the causes, teachers are no longer respected and must too often play the role of security guard in their classrooms. The high rates of immigration to the United States in recent years have meant that the schools are filled with students from widely differing educational and cultural backgrounds who may not share a common language. All these pressures have become too strong for the schools to absorb.

Nonetheless, the deteriorating quality of education creates an abundance of opportunities for new small businesses serving almost every aspect of education. Cutbacks in the arts, music, athletics, and "enrichment programs" open opportunities for "privatized" replacement programs, possibly including small-scale tutoring programs for groups of children. This would be a service that could give people interested in education temporary or long-term tutoring assignments. One way to proceed might be to go into areas and look around and study what people are actually doing and producing. Then you might go to an enterprise and offer not only publicity but also a market for the products that might be generated.

10. Demographic changes such as an aging American population and a new influx of immigrants

Our population is becoming too big, particularly in confined metropolitan areas. The result is crime. We can't seem to live together. We attribute problems not only to increasing population from within but also to immigration. We have ongoing racial problems that too often result in crime or poverty. Generally, our population is becoming poorer, and the homeless are all around us.

We are also seeing an increase in the average age of the American population as the baby boom generation grows older. An aging population is not necessarily a negative, but businesses should be prepared to cope with these changes by modifying their products and services accordingly.

The U.S. Census Bureau has predicted that by the year 2050, Asians, Hispanics, African-Americans, and other nonwhite groups could represent 47 percent of the total U.S. population. In addition, the total U.S.

population could increase by 50 percent to 383 million, from 255 million in 1992; by 2050, 12 percent of the total population will be Asians and Pacific Islanders, and Hispanics, at 21 percent, will have long overtaken African-Americans as our largest minority group.[12]

There is no doubt that the debate over legal and illegal immigration has become increasingly acrimonious. The North American Free Trade Agreement (NAFTA) has heightened some of these concerns.

What the truth is depends on who you talk to and what axe they have to grind, but economist George Borjas of the University of California, San Diego, has calculated that although our 20 million immigrants have received about $1.1 billion more in cash welfare payments each year than they paid into the welfare system through taxes, they have also been contributing $5 billion a year to the economy by spending their earnings on food, rent, clothing, and other purchases.[13]

With reference to aging, the number of older Americans, and thus those needing the most in terms of health care, is expected to increase five-fold in the next 60 years. Ray Vagelos, chief executive of Merck & Co., predicts that by early in the twenty-first century, one in five Americans will be eligible for social security and medicare.[14]

Although our aging and increasingly diversified population creates many problems and pressures, it also opens up many new small-business opportunities for services that can supplement governmental programs—for the homeless, the aging, the infirm, and the incapacitated, among others. For example, immigration brings with it a diversity of languages, which means an increased need for translators or translating services and specialized educational services, including vocational services for recent arrivals.

With the increasing average age of the population, there will be the need for new products and services, as well as expanding existing ones that cater to this population group. Another approach is being taken by small businesses such as Denver's Senior Skills, which places older workers in companies that need office and technical support or middle management staff. This company started out with a pool of eight employees; it now has a pool of 2,000 and, in late 1993, was placing 250 workers a month in the Denver area.

11. The new interdependent world economy and the end of the Cold War

The increasing interdependence of the world's various economies will probably be one of the most important factors affecting our lives as the twenty-first century begins. The North American Free Trade Agreement

(NAFTA) will create the world's largest free trade zone among the 360 million people in the United States, Canada, and Mexico.

Another important international influence has been the end of the Cold War, which has precipitated a major transition from a defense-based economy to a peace-based economy. This means that there will be fewer traditional jobs and many new kinds of jobs. It's a time of transition. It's been at least 60 years since we've had a peacetime economy; we're now in a massive transition that is affecting a very large proportion of the workforce.

Cuts in the defense budget have already resulted in massive layoffs that have affected the economy and exacerbated the recession that began in 1990, which would have been shorter if we were still in our "normal" defense-related economic stance. Less emphasis on a war footing means less government spending. The massive deficit and debt related to the defense budget, especially in the 1980s, has meant that government has fewer resources to spend on overcoming the recession.

Some companies are already taking imaginative advantage of the increasing internationalization of business. For example, Warming Up, Inc., a small firm in Seattle, specializes in helping Japanese businesspeople and their families adjust to life in the United States by supplying them with informative books and videotapes.

12. Corporate downsizing and layoffs

As I pointed out in the previous section, a great deal of the unemployment we have seen in the past few years is related to cuts in the defense industry—fewer military forces, fewer NASA employees, fewer defense workers. Our government can no longer use national defense as an excuse for pumping money into the economy. Nondefense industries are also affected because of the ongoing recession, and they are seeing lower revenues, lower growth rates, and sometimes actual losses.

However, larger industries have been able to maintain profit levels by cutting their labor force. This has allowed corporate America to maintain reasonably high profit levels, and—ironically—the stock market has been reaching record levels.

Our economy has continued to be consumer-driven, but the recession has limited people's discretionary spending. Rising rates of unemployment have cut purchasing power and lowered profit margins. Small businesses suffer from the growing strength of mass retailers, which cut costs by offering low wages, minimal staffing, and less than full-time employment. The mass retailers are a major labor market for part-time workers, who don't get benefits.

However, this situation is also replete with new opportunities if you approach it with an open, optimistic perspective. The first thing to keep in mind is that these conditions won't last forever. Left alone, the economy will begin to find itself. Downsizing will have to stop at some point because it is as cyclical as the real estate market (in which construction falls off until existing spaces are filled and then picks up when the inevitable shortage occurs and demand increases again). Eventually, as unemployment declines, consumers will be able to spend again.

The longer-term outlook is positive; there are grounds for optimism. In the meantime, present conditions are creating a strong climate for temporary employment in all areas (such as education, clerical work, and manufacturing) because businesses will seek short-term temporary help, despite the expenses of agency fees, rather than add permanent workers to their payroll.

This trend is strengthened by government regulation of labor practices, the prohibitive costs of health care, and other factors. So services related to the growth of the temporary labor market have a bright short-term future. There are other imaginative opportunities available for new self-employment businesses, for example, tele-interviewing of prospective temporary and permanent employees, which can save both employers and employees time and money.

There are strong possibilities in the reeducation field, such as seminars, retraining courses, skills upgrades, placement services, tutoring, and any other services that help people find work.

Other promising areas are in serving employers who don't want to spend their time and resources dealing with regulatory and legal issues and in subcontracting to companies by supplying them with personnel ranging from computer experts to janitors.

13. The environmental crisis

Everyone is affected by the environmental crisis. And if you're thinking about starting a new business or buying an established one, environmental concerns should be an important consideration. Lots of traditional small (and large) businesses are dramatically affected by environmental laws. Many businesses that are successful and profitable are virtually not salable because of environmental impacts.

You are advised to avoid any business directly affected by the environmental crisis. The following are a few examples:

- Dry cleaning plants that use solvents and other cleaning materials. If older machinery is still being used, it will have to be replaced with very expensive, much less efficient equipment. There is no "grandfathering"; compliance requirements mean that sooner or later (and probably sooner) your shop must comply with the latest ordinances.

- Paint shops of all types. Whether a paint store, auto painting shop, or any other retail, commercial, or industrial user, you must have proper protection against possible contamination.

- Automotive and other businesses that use or dispense petroleum products are subject to new codes to protect the environment.

- Any product-oriented business you consider could have environmental impact. And don't stop with the business itself. Consider the real estate it occupies. Who has been there before you? What have been the uses of the property historically, all the way back to the first user? Who are the neighbors, what are their properties used for now, and what have those properties been used for historically?

If you are the owner of a business that has the potential to cause contamination, it will probably be virtually impossible to sell it—at least, to a prudent buyer. Although many existing businesses are caught in an unfortunate damned-if-you-do, damned-if-you-don't position, environmental concerns create loads of opportunities for small businesses in everything from cleanup to designing new concepts and preventatives.

Endnotes

1. Myron Magnet, "Small Business's Big New Worries," *Fortune,* 26 July 1993, 65–67.
2. "In Neighborhoods Overlooked by Banks, Check-Cashing Stores Flourish," *Los Angeles Times,* 8 August 1993, sec. D, p. 18.
3. Jill Gerston, "They Want Their QVC," *Los Angeles Times,* 11 June 1993, sec. E, p. 4.
4. David Lamb, " 'Lone Eagles' Flying from Cities to New Job Horizons," *Los Angeles Times,* 18 August 1993, sec. A, pp. 1, 17.
5. Wendy Zellner, "Clout! More and More, Retail Giants Rule the Marketplace," *Business Week,* 21 December 1992, 66–73.
6. *The State of Small Business: A Report of the President* (Washington, D.C.: U.S. Government Printing Office, 1992), 57–58.
7. Anne B. Fisher, "Sexual Harassment: What to Do?" *Fortune,* 23 August 1993, 84–88.
8. Susan Engeleiter, "Product Liability Laws: The Economy Is the Victim," *PR Newswire,* 24 July 1990.

9. Carl F. Horowitz, untitled column, *Investor's Business Daily,* 20 April 1993, p. 1.
10. Julie Cankler, "Filling the Transit Gap," *Nation's Business,* January 1993, 39.
11. Lauren Speeth, *Telecommuting Review: The Gordon Report,* May 1993, p. 9.
12. Brian Bremner, "A Spicier Stew in the Melting Pot," *Business Week,* 21 December 1992, 29–30.
13. Jacklyn Fierman, "Is Immigration Hurting the U.S.?" *Fortune,* 9 August 1993, 76.
14. Brian Bremner, "A Spicier Stew in the Melting Pot," *Business Week,* 21 December 1992, 29–30.

CHAPTER 4

Location and Risk

There is one factor that, more than any other, distinguishes successful businesses from those that are not as successful. That factor is *location*. All business ventures have at least some risk attached to them—some are just riskier than others. But in my experience, the factor that divides the unrisky from the risky is location.

Why Location Is Crucial

In the broadest sense, every business has to have a location of some sort. It may be your garage or den, a building at a highway intersection, a store in a shopping mall, or a freestanding building. It may be located in a small town or in a large metropolitan center.

However, some types of businesses *require* a specific location. Location may be the most important attribute of retail and service businesses that depend largely on walk-in trade and thus need exposure to pedestrian or vehicular traffic. For example, it is evident that a gasoline service station must be located along a major street or highway and have high visibility and a certain minimum population density within a two-mile radius.

Other kinds of businesses—and I argue that these are the best types of entrepreneurial businesses—can be operated from almost any location as long as customers can be reached. The more location-specific a business is, the harder it will be to find the location you need to succeed. Businesses that are not location-specific are less risky.

Impulse-purchase businesses such as ice-cream or cookie outlets in shopping malls are location-specific businesses. If you assume that any location inside a mall is probably good enough, you're wrong; not all locations are equal when it comes to customer drawing power. The success of your outlet will depend on the visibility and the amount of traffic that passes your particular spot.

Although it may seem obvious that finding a good location is the first step toward creating a successful retail business, location has many important implications for other types of businesses as well. Let's explore some of those issues.

First, assume you are considering buying an established business at a very favorable location. The attributes of that location are reflected in a good stream of revenue and cash flow. However, the business leases the location and does not own it. Therefore, although the business may be doing phenomenally well at the location, this is no assurance of continued success.

Why? Because the property is leased, and at some point in time, the lease will run out. And unless the lease contains provisions for long-term renewals (*at least* another 10 or 15 years) at specified rental rates, there is no assurance that the business will be able to continue at that location and therefore continue to prosper. Some leases contain options for extending or renewing, but those options often fail to specify rental rates and other important conditions—which makes them seem like better deals than they are. Basically, any business that has a super location but a lease with a remaining period of less than six or eight years has minimal value. I never fail to be surprised by how many people get hooked into buying businesses that are in good locations and have a history of success but are in leased premises with limited remaining terms.

One more point: Any business that benefits from a strong positive cash flow and a secure long-term lease is likely to carry a hefty price tag because the owner is going to be only too aware that he or she is sitting atop a little gold mine.

Let's consider a second scenario. Assume that the business in question owns the real estate where it is located or that the real estate can be acquired along with the business. This certainly is an answer to the risk created by having a short-term lease that lacks an adequate renewal option.

However, acquiring a good location and a successful business will be expensive. You need to determine what is really being acquired. Is it basically the business or the real estate? What are the long-term prospects for appreciation of the real estate and for continuation of the business? Also, given the substantial amount of money involved, if it is your goal to purchase a business that will generate a given level of income, your costs may be too high to let you reach that particular goal. However, if you wish to be partly in the real-estate business, and you see long-term benefits from that (and there are many long-term benefits to acquiring real estate at the same time you acquire a business), then the investment may prove to be just what you're hoping for.

Here is a third situation: Assume that you have decided to start de novo with a new business and a new location. Unless you are highly skilled at determining locations for location-sensitive businesses, the risk of making a mistake is extremely high.

Very few people really understand the intricacies and subtleties of location. Even the most experienced franchise operations, ones that have representatives who spend their entire career determining locations, can and do make mistakes when it comes to choosing locations.

In short, the real-estate agent's motto applies as much to business properties as to residential ones: "Location, location, location!"

But Is Location Enough?
Other Risk Factors

When businesses fail it is usually because the owners or buyers do something wrong. They enter the wrong business at the wrong time, in the wrong industry, at the wrong location, at the wrong price, and too often for the wrong reasons.

In other words, even if you manage to find a successful existing business in an unbeatable location, or a location that would be just perfect for the particular location-sensitive business you're dreaming of starting, there is always a possibility, and even a high probability, that you may not be particularly suited to that business. In my years as an appraiser, I've seen hundreds of businesses that have been extremely well located but have fared very poorly—not because of their location but because of their management.

Here are sixteen important factors (besides location) that you need to consider if you are thinking about starting or buying a business. The degree of risk you will run depends in large part on these factors.

1. Competition from chain stores and discount superstores

Many types of businesses, particularly retail, are being affected by competition from the growing number of chain and discount superstores and by the ever-increasing variety of goods and services they offer. This appears to be a long-term trend, and the impact on small retail businesses can be devastating.

If you are considering entering any retail business, be sure to research industry trends. Also, you must try to find out whether there is any possibility that a competing discount superstore may be planning to open in your market area.

2. Telecommunications and interactive video

Within the next few years, and certainly before the year 2000, it's likely that we will have access to hundreds of channels on our television sets. The technology is already being tested in some communities. Fiber optics, coupled with small digital supercomputer converters connected to our TV sets, will create an information superhighway allowing two-way communication for a vast range of product and service merchandising.

The widespread availability of this technology will create the need for many related businesses and services. The opportunities will be many and exciting, but these technological advances will also mean the displacement of many traditional businesses. Most types of retail business will have to adapt or disappear.

If the business in question will definitely benefit from this developing and expanding technology, it will be less risky. Some examples of such businesses are auctioneering, real-estate brokering, wedding planning, travel services, medical services, dating services, legal services, security services, employment services, educational services, interior design, architecture, and advertising and promotional services, to name just a few. Businesses like these should be able to take part in the new technology with only minor changes to their existing operations, or they should be able to readily add special activity centers to their existing operations.

This factor relates to outside technological developments over which a business has no direct control. It differs from adaptability (discussed later in this chapter), which refers to the ability of the business to adapt and take advantage of outside influences. The latter characteristic is much broader and is not limited to technology-induced changes.

3. Litigation

Of course, any business can be subject to lawsuits, but businesses that involve a great deal of contact with the public are more susceptible than others. For example, restaurants are especially vulnerable to nuisance suits. On the other hand, a home-based mail-order business would run a much lower risk of being sued—as long as the operator obeys the laws and delivers as promised.

4. Changing demographic and consumer patterns

Some businesses are more likely than others to be affected by shifts in age patterns, ethnic mix, disposable income, and similar factors. The increasing average age of the U.S. population directly affects businesses that depend on older persons for much of their patronage. Some examples are medical services and leisure-related activities.

5. Seasonality

Many types of businesses are considered seasonal even though they operate all year long. Businesses that depend on a single season for all or most of their revenue are riskier than those that experience little or no direct seasonal influence. However, the vulnerability of a business to seasonal swings may be offset by some significant advantage, such as an exceptional profit potential during that season.

6. Sensitivity to recession

Most businesses are affected by general economic downturns—in fact, that may be the very definition of "recession." But some are more vulnerable than others. Those that are recession-proof are obviously less desirable, while those that tend to benefit from recessionary conditions are clearly less risky.

Businesses that involve a heavy capital investment and high fixed overhead, such as food processing and clothing manufacturing, are highly recession-sensitive. Low-overhead businesses, on the other hand, are more flexible because they can retrench and use contract labor as needed when times are hard.

Also, businesses such as temporary staffing services, which can help another business cut its overhead, are likely to thrive during recessionary times. Tax, bookkeeping, and accounting firms are also recession-resistant because businesses must handle these matters regardless of the state of the economy.

7. Regulations

It's hard to think of any business that isn't affected by governmental or trade regulations of some sort. This is a given. However, some businesses thrive on regulations imposed by governmental codes, rules, laws, and regulations. For example, many soil-testing services exist primarily because of laws regarding soil contamination.

Businesses that are positively affected by these factors are more desirable, as are those that are not affected by any special regulations or where the relevant regulations are not unduly burdensome. Businesses are riskier if they are subject to so much regulation that would-be entrepreneurs are discouraged from starting them or if compliance cuts into profitability.

Some businesses are affected positively and negatively at the same time. One such example is employment services that specialize in providing personnel under contract and also handle all payroll taxes, workers' compensation insurance and claims, and other related items. Clients are attracted to such agencies because they can be relieved of much burdensome paperwork. Thus, the existence of laws and regulations is a positive influence on the business—but on the other hand, the agency must deal with the same burdensome duties for its own staff.

8. Salability

If you hope that your business will someday be valuable enough that you can sell it and end up with a retirement nest egg, you must take into account whether the type of business you choose is salable or not. The vast majority of small businesses are not salable. In most cases, a business dies when the owner leaves because it depends on the personality or particular abilities of the owner and it is not really possible to transfer the goodwill. A business must not be so dependent on the owner that it is little more than an extension of him or her. Some businesses are salable under certain conditions, and this makes them less risky. Businesses are more salable if they show positive revenue and cash flow trends.

Some businesses can be sold only under certain conditions, for example, if the seller agrees to remain with the business for an extended period after it has been sold. In some cases, a certain type of business is in demand and salable in one geographic area or during a particular time period, but not in other places or at other times.

Businesses that are rarely if ever salable are less desirable. This does not always mean that the business has not been profitable—indeed, many nonsalable businesses are quite profitable—but it may not be salable for a variety of reasons. For example, a business that requires specialized expertise may not be salable because a qualified buyer could easily, and with less expense, begin a new business. So there's no point in buying an established one.

9. Adaptability to changing market needs and ways of doing business

Businesses are less risky if they are able to readily adapt to changing market needs and ways of doing business. These are businesses that can flex with change—changing markets, changing ways of obtaining new business, changing government regulations, and so on. Riskier businesses are those that will probably have difficulty in adapting and thus run the risk of becoming obsolete.

For example, telephone answering services have generally been replaced with answering machines and, more recently, voice mail and electronic mail. And, as mentioned previously, the coming of interactive in-home television is likely to spell the end of today's video-rental stores unless they find a way to develop new markets or services. On the other hand, a gift-basket business can be quite flexible because you can easily change your mix of items, products, and offerings to meet changes in public demand.

10. Cash versus billing

Businesses that sell products and services for cash or through credit cards, or that sell on a billing basis but usually experience rapid collections of accounts receivable, are less risky. Businesses that make most of their sales on a billing basis or that tend to experience large outstanding accounts receivable or receivables losses expose an owner to greater risk.

11. Cyclical factors

Most businesses are cyclical to some extent; it's rare, if not unheard of, to find one that shows constant upward trends in sales and profits. Individual businesses usually follow the cyclical patterns of their industry. Typically, industrial cycles operate in four- to five-year patterns. The real-estate cycle is a good example: When housing demand is high, more builders are drawn into the market until finally construction exceeds demand, sales slow down relative to the inventory of houses available, and profits decline. The industry responds by attempting to cut costs and jobs. This pattern continues until another upturn in demand begins, when the cycle starts again.

Businesses that have a history of strong resistance to downturns, or whose troughs (the bottom of the cycles) are very short and whose growth lines are long, are less risky. Businesses that typically follow normal cyclical trends also run average risk in this respect, whereas those that experience exaggeratedly long or severe cycles are clearly riskier. Keep in mind that new entrepreneurs often overspend during rapid growth periods, and they often fail to adequately anticipate sudden declines due to cyclical factors.

12. Complexity

Complexity is relative, of course. It is linked to a multitude of factors, such as education, prior experience, new laws or regulations, the type of products or services being sold, and the marketing and sales methods that must be used, to name only a few. What seems complex to one individual is simple to another. Businesses that are relatively simple to operate with products that are fairly simple to manufacture or services that are fairly simple to market are generally less risky. Simple businesses usually have a narrow product or service line, and they can usually be operated by the owner alone or with a very limited number of associates.

Businesses that are unusually complicated, even for the most experienced entrepreneur, are less desirable. These types of businesses usually require special skills and education along with extensive prior experience.

13. Permits and licenses

All businesses require some form of permit in order to operate legally. Businesses that require only a minimum number of permits, such as a local business license, are less risky, whereas those that require many licenses or permits that may take a long time to obtain expose an owner to greater risk.

14. Competition from similar small businesses

Obviously, businesses that experience limited competition are less risky. This means they are in a strong competitive position, either because there is high demand for the service or because the existing competition is inadequate or incompetent. Businesses that have substantial competition are clearly riskier. This does not mean there are no opportunities left for a new kid on the block, but it does mean that a product or service must be exceptional or have other attributes that give it an edge over the established competition.

15. Failure rate

Businesses that historically experience an unusually low failure rate are less risky, whereas those that experience relatively high failure rates obviously expose an owner to greater risk.

In recent years, the risks of failure have become less predictable. The recent wave of corporate downsizing has motivated people to start their own businesses—but an oversupply of any service can lead to a saturated market and a greater risk of failure. This does not mean that opportunities are diminishing, but rather that great personal commitment in terms of follow-up, customer service, flexibility, and patience are more important than ever.

Success and failure are related to management and the adequacy of capital, which are internal factors. But external forces such as market saturation are also crucial.

16. Prospects for overall long-term stability

This factor is related to a business's prospects for relative stability over time. If there is ever a point at which a business can be said to have achieved stability, the rule of thumb is three years from start-up, by which time the business should have achieved more or less stable growth. Any business that is breaking even or showing a profit after the first three years is likely to have a life over the longer term as well, so long as the owner's energy, commitment, and patience don't waver.

CHAPTER 5

Your Winner's List of Ideal Entrepreneurial Businesses

I've kept you in suspense long enough. It's finally time to give you the profiles of the very best entrepreneurial businesses—the ones that will have a future in the year 2000 and well beyond. Now don't get me wrong—I'm not suggesting that you wait until the century turns over before starting up or buying into one of these gems. Start ASAP! This highly selective list of businesses offers you the best opportunities to make good bucks—and you won't have to sell the farm to get started.

Remember, the goal of these business profiles is to help you select the ideal business for you! This section describes and lists more than 200 self-employment businesses that *you can start on your own with a relatively small initial up-front cash investment.*

These are opportunities for people who want to be independent and who don't want a boss, either in the form of an employer or a franchisor. Most of these businesses require no more up-front cash investment than similar franchise opportunities, and many require much less. And you don't have to deal with the restrictions imposed by franchisors or with high ongoing franchise fees.

These businesses are good bets because you can operate them on your own, or with the help of family members or friends, during your start-up period. Also, your initial investment is relatively modest—there is no need for you to enter into long-term financial commitments for expensive real estate leases, a staff of full-time employees, elaborate advertising, or expensive office furnishings and equipment.

These businesses make it easy for you to maintain control of your direction—you can easily suspend operations temporarily if conditions seem to demand it, or permanently if things just don't seem to be going right. In short, these types of businesses make it easy for you to become aware of problems and control any potential losses before they get out of hand. You should not have to lose the farm.

Winner's List Criteria

To make it onto our Winner's List, a business has to meet the following criteria:

1. These businesses can be fully operated, or at least headquartered, almost anywhere, including your home.

Almost all of these businesses can be operated from any location, including your own home, although I have included a couple of exceptions for opportunities that meet all the other criteria but require a nonresidential or even a specific location to be successful. These exceptions are discussed in detail in the profiles. As I've stressed previously, location-sensitive businesses require lots of special knowledge or just plain good luck. There's no need to take on the location problem if you can avoid it. Also, keep in mind that the importance of location will probably change for many businesses in the coming era of advanced business communications.

2. These businesses require a minimal up-front capital investment.

You can get into almost all of these self-employment businesses with less than $25,000, and some require as little as $2,500. These figures should cover your initial start-up expenses, such as small-scale advertising, buying and installing your telephone and fax lines, buying basic office furnishings, equipment, and supplies such as stationery, and so forth.

However, these initial capital investment figures do not include a salary for you or any payroll expenses. I've chosen these businesses precisely because you can operate them on your own, solo, during your start-up period. If you operate carefully, you should begin to see enough cash flow early on that you can gradually increase your operating expenses, including hiring temporary help as you need it. In addition to your up-front capital investment, you should have a savings account, reserve fund, or other easily accessible funds to cover your personal expenses during the start-up phase.

3. These businesses are direct outgrowths of the Forces of Change and stand to benefit from future trends.

These businesses are on the Winner's List precisely because they both meet existing demand and offer long-term growth potential within the context of the Forces of Change described in chapter 3. In most instances, these businesses should prosper even if there are further downturns in the U.S. economy or dramatic changes in how American businesses operate.

4. These businesses can generate positive cash flow within six to nine months or less.

In most instances, you should be able to cover all of your operating expenses, except your own labor, within three to six months. In some cases you'll be able to see a positive cash flow at the end of your very first month. However, you will have to plan carefully to reach this goal, paying particular attention to reaching your market.

As part of your initial planning, you should do lots of word-of-mouth promotion before you quit your present job. Also, spend lots of time studying who your potential customers are, and try to line up some who are willing to use your services immediately and pay you promptly as well.

However, do not plan to start drawing a salary for yourself until you are seeing a consistent, positive cash flow after you cover all of your operating expenses and until you've been able to pay back at least 50 percent of your initial capital investment.

If you used your own money to start up, put your early cash flow revenues into a reserve savings account. Pretend that this money belongs to someone else—don't use it for your own salary. Keep it in reserve for gradual expansion. And if you borrowed your start-up funds on your credit cards (see number 6 of this list), pay off that debt in full before you even think of drawing a salary for yourself.

5. These businesses can generate a full return on your initial investment within the first year.

Like number 4, this too requires careful planning. Think ahead before you make each business move. As Henry Ford reportedly said, "Use one hour to think for each one minute of action." Remember that in the early days, most of the money that comes into your company account or cash drawer actually belongs to the source you used for your start-up funds, even if that source was your own savings or retirement fund.

6. If you need start-up financing for one of these businesses, you may be able to charge much of it on your credit card(s).

Sounds good, doesn't it? But it's true. However, I recommend saying "Charge it!" only for purchases of capital items such as equipment and supplies—never for cash to cover your personal needs and expenses. It's vital that you keep a positive balance between your business revenues and your credit-card payments. And don't forget the interest charges. In fact, you'd do well to research which cards carry the lowest interest rates and most favorable conditions, and apply for those several months before you launch your business venture. You could save several hundred dollars a year in interest if you shop around.

7. These businesses require little or no special training.

Again, there are a few exceptions, which are discussed in the individual business profiles.

8. You can start these businesses as either a part-time or full-time activity, on your own or with a very limited staff that might include your spouse or kids.

For your own peace of mind, it's probably wise to hold on to your regular job—and your regular paycheck!—while you get your feet wet by starting your new business on a part-time basis. And, as I mentioned earlier, these businesses don't require a permanent staff, at least not at the start. You can turn to your spouse or kids for help, or hire temporary help as needed. These businesses give you learning time, and you won't feel you're going too far out on a limb right at the outset.

But suppose you're a recession victim and are out of work right now. You'd probably do best to try to find a job with an existing firm in your present field or a closely related one, bide your time, save your money, and start your own business part-time when you can.

Now let's look at the worst-case scenario—suppose you're really up against it and are fresh out of options. You've got to start generating some income on your own, ASAP. Well, you're reading the right book because this Winner's List was selected with you in mind. For one thing, the services offered by these types of self-employment businesses are in demand right now all over the country. They're also relatively easy to start, can be operated on a solo basis initially, and can grow into high-quality, permanent businesses—which leads right into my next point.

9. These businesses have the potential of developing into long-term companies that will create future value for your retirement or estate.

10. Finally, these businesses are viable because the market is not already saturated with similar operations in all geographic areas.

Your Winner's List of Ideal Entrepreneurial Businesses

1. Computer services
2. Education services
3. Health care support services
4. Information search and retrieval services
5. Janitorial, cleaning, and related services
6. Legal support services
7. Local delivery and transportation services
8. Money-saving services
9. Packaging, shipping, mailing, and related services
10. Records storage and retrieval services
11. Referral services
12. Security services
13. Specialized merchandising
14. Temporary employment and related services
15. Miscellaneous

Note: Wherever possible, trade and professional associations have been listed so you can obtain more information about businesses that may interest you. The addresses and phone numbers listed here are current as of the publication date of the book, but such information is of course subject to change. Also, some of these businesses are too new or too few in number to have established formal trade associations.

1. COMPUTER SERVICES

Of all the families of businesses described in this book, computer- and technology-related services probably offer the widest array of possibilities. Each day the media tell us about new developments that simply did not exist twenty-four hours earlier.

How can you as an individual entrepreneur get in on the continually shifting ground floor of these developments? If you already have the skills, or after you have gotten the necessary training, you can start out by approaching some large retailers or professional firms and offering your services as a consultant on a contract basis. Suggest a specific project, such as developing a customized program. After you finish that first project, you can use that company as a reference when approaching other clients, who should not be too difficult to come by.

Another option is to focus on planning, coordinating, and researching computer systems for potential purchases, whether for individuals or corporations. This is a consulting activity and could be as simple as generating accurate cost comparisons for different systems from the many publications and on-line services available today. In other words, you can do the research legwork for your clients, give them the data, and then arrange for the purchase.

You could even research the comparative costs of service and maintenance agreements—no small matter (and no small cost) given the complexity of today's home and office electronic equipment.

These types of businesses should provide a reasonable income level and could evolve into a larger service involving a more formalized business with good profit potential given sufficient time (three to five years).

Hottest Prospects

Computer consulting services

This service, which provides planning, advice, and design of the best computer set-ups as well as sources of equipment, software, and services to individuals and businesses, is a natural for computer professionals, but anyone who's computer-literate and willing to learn could get up to speed in a short time. Initial investment, $2,500–$5,000.

Independent Computer Consultants Association
933 Gardenview Office Pkwy.
St. Louis MO 63141
(314) 997-4633 or (800) GET-ICCA

Computer design services

These services cover numerous activities that can range from desktop publishing to CAD/CAM (computer-assisted design and computer-assisted manufacturing). The possibilities are limited only by your imagination, but one fruitful way to proceed is to think about unfilled market niches and services that can build on existing services. Initial investment, $2,500–$5,000.

National Computer Graphics Association
2722 Merrilee Dr., #200
Fairfax VA 22031
(703) 698-9600 or (800) 225-NCGA

Computer repair services

If you decide that this field appeals to you, you don't necessarily have to do the work yourself. Instead, think about setting up a company that hires experts to carry out computer repairs. You will, of course, have to be able to judge the competence and reliability of your subcontractors because computer downtime is an expensive proposition for any company. Initial investment, $5,000–$10,000.

National Association of Service Dealers
c/o National Association of Retail Dealers of America
10 E. 22nd St., #310
Lombard IL 60148
(708) 953-8950

Desktop video services or multimedia production

This kind of work could include desktop presentations, computer graphics, video production, and television commercials for local cable companies, as well as special-interest and corporate videos. Another possibility is creating visualization aids such as accident reconstructions and prototypes or walk-throughs of proposed buildings. In this area, the only limitations are technology and your imagination. Initial investment, $5,000–$10,000.

More Hot Prospects

- CAD/CAM systems and services; initial investment, $2,500–$5,000
- "Channel-surfing" services (designing custom TV services from offerings on interactive television and superhighway systems, for people who lack time to do it themselves); initial investment, $2,500–$5,000
- Computerized bill-paying and other services for the elderly; initial investment, $2,500–$5,000

- Computer and printer maintenance (selling clients on the desirability of regular preventive maintenance to avoid costly downtime due to breakdowns and malfunctions); initial investment, $5,000–$10,000
- Computer and peripherals rental and leasing; initial investment, $5,000–$10,000
- Computer cleaning services; initial investment, $5,000–$10,000
- Computer-designed renderings of landscaping for homes (service is sold to contractors, who show renderings to homeowners and share fees with the computer designer); initial investment, $2,500–$5,000
- Computer facilities management services; initial investment, $2,500–$5,000
- Computer games development; initial investment, $2,500–$5,000
- Computer services for children; initial investment, $10,000–$25,000
- Computer software systems analysis and design; initial investment, $2,500–$5,000
- Custom programs or systems software development; initial investment, $2,500–$5,000
- Computer time leasing and/or rental; initial investment, $2,500–$5,000
- Computer time-sharing; initial investment, $2,500–$5,000
- Database development; initial investment, $2,500–$5,000
- Database information retrieval services; initial investment, $2,500–$5,000
- Data entry services; initial investment, $2,500–$5,000
- Data processing consulting and services; initial investment, $2,500–$5,000
- Data verification services; initial investment, $2,500–$5,000
- Disk and diskette conversion services; initial investment, $2,500–$5,000
- Emergency standby services in case of breakdowns; initial investment, $5,000–$10,000
- Local area network (LAN) systems and services; initial investment, $5,000–$10,000
- On-line information retrieval services; initial investment, $2,500–$5,000

- On-line or interactive-television-based clipping services; initial investment, $2,500–$5,000
- Optical scanning data services; initial investment, $2,500–$5,000
- Planning and production of interactive conferences and other activities; initial investment, $5,000–$10,000
- Tabulating services; initial investment, $2,500–$5,000

2. EDUCATION SERVICES

During the coming decade, training and retraining programs of all kinds are likely to be in demand, in part because of the impact of corporate downsizing. Observers also believe that people will continue to be absorbed in self-development and will be willing to pay for seminars on a wide range of subjects. In addition, decreasing school budgets and cutbacks in programming open the door to private offerings of enrichment programs that used to be part of school curricula.

The United States continues to face what Nan Stone, managing editor of the *Harvard Business Review,* calls a "skills crisis":

> It is not the performance level of students that has declined. Rather, the demands of the external competitive environment have increased. Twenty years ago, U.S. companies could hire graduates who performed at this level without compromising their competitive capabilities. Today they cannot. The degree of competence that the averages reflect is too low to equip students to work successfully in self-managed teams or to use new technology to the fullest possible extent.[1]

Another significant crisis, unseen by the general public, is developing in our college and university systems: Costs are increasing so dramatically that many if not most of our higher educational institutions will become out of reach financially to many middle-class Americans. The increases in cost are due in part to the research emphasis that prevails in most institutions because research grants are a major source of revenue. This has always conflicted with the teaching function, and the situation is not likely to change unless the funding of higher education changes.

Fortunately for the imaginative and flexible businessperson, these issues create enormous opportunities in services ranging from private tutoring to seminars to development of specialized technical and vocational schools.

Hottest Prospects

Computer training for children

Although more and more computers can be found in schools, budget constraints also limit student access to the new technology. This opens the way for private computer training that could be offered after school and on weekends. Another possibility would be to offer computer training as an adjunct to language training for recently arrived immigrants. Or consider the elderly, who may feel intimidated by the new technology. Initial investment, $20,000–$50,000.

Futurekids
5777 W. Century Blvd., #1555
Los Angeles CA 90045
(310) 337-7006 or (800) PRO-KIDS

Technical and vocational schools

These special trade schools offer courses and training programs in a wide range of vocationally oriented fields ranging from electronics repair to real estate, computers, accounting, and so forth. Initial investment, $50,000 or more.

American Association for Vocational Instructional Materials
745 Gaines School Rd.
Athens GA 30605
(404) 543-7557 or (800) 882-4689

More Hot Prospects

- Computer tutoring and training services; initial investment, $10,000–$25,000

- Customized in-house training courses for executives, managers, and staff on particular topics such as leadership, cross-training, presentation skills, business basics, conflict resolution and negotiation, improving productivity, and so forth; initial investment, $2,500–$5,000

- Driver retraining and upgrading (for growing numbers of senior citizens and immigrants); initial investment, $10,000–$25,000

- Job training and retraining for senior citizens; initial investment, $10,000–$25,000

- Language schools; initial investment, $10,000–$25,000
- Literacy and basic skills training for immigrants (and even for the native-born who are still functionally illiterate because of poor education systems); initial investment, $10,000–$25,000
- Manufacturing skills training (all forms); initial investment, $25,000–$50,000
- Services that evaluate the long-term economic benefits of education programs; initial investment, $2,500–$5,000
- Vocational apprenticeship training services; initial investment, $25,000–$50,000

3. HEALTH CARE SUPPORT SERVICES

The American health care industry is rife with opportunities for supplementary services that will only increase if and when a national health care system is created. The intricacies of the plan, whatever form it eventually takes, will create a need for consulting services to aid both individuals and businesses. Also, health care providers will also probably need new support services and perhaps consulting to comply with the plan.

New opportunities will open up if home health care is emphasized as opposed to hospitalization, which is more costly. Any national plan's emphasis on cost controls in hospitals would create a need for independent auditing-related consulting and contract work. There might also be a role for managed-care professionals to monitor the performance of doctors, hospitals, and other providers for cost and quality control.

If a national plan were to encourage generalization rather than specialization, the need would arise for employment and networking services for pharmacists, physicians' assistants, nurse practitioners, and other nonphysician roles.

Hottest Prospects

Health care services

These personalized services offer assistance in hospitals, convalescent homes, or private residences. Usually workers in this field must be licensed. This type of work is not only personally satisfying but also provides a good, steady income. If this area interests you, opening an agency to offer these services is probably the best way to proceed. There is a fair amount of competition in this field, but demand will only increase. Linking yourself to one institution at the outset and building on that is a useful strategy for assuring a steady referral of clients. Initial investment, $2,500–$5,000.

Home health care services

Home health care is an alternative to sky-high hospital costs and offers many new opportunities for coordinating services. As mentioned above, this field may well be affected by any national health care program. Initial investment, $5,000–$10,000.

Medical claims processing and billing services

As our health care system has become more complex and specialized, it has also become more difficult for medical practices to devote staff time and resources to billing and submitting insurance claims. Claims processing and billing services take this burden from the doctors' and dentists' offices, and sometimes from patients as well. As in most businesses, specialization can result in increased efficiency and thus increased profit, especially in large urban areas. These emerging industries speed up the receivables process for doctors. Also, patients are assured that their claims forms are filled out correctly and that they are receiving all the benefits to which they are entitled.

Electronic claims processing is the coming trend. By the year 2000, up to 90 percent of claims are expected to be submitted electronically. These services can also provide comparisons of carriers, rates, and benefits. But this is secondary to the main thrust, which is acting as an extension of the clerical or processing arm of the employer. Developing a reasonable cash flow will require several large clients or a large number of small ones. The most likely candidates are smaller businesses, which may try to economize on payroll by farming out claims processing. Initial investment, $5,000–$10,000.

Medical Claims Processing Business Guide
Entrepreneur Magazine
2392 Morse Ave., Box 19787
Irvine CA 92713
(800) 421-2300 or (800) 352-7449 (California only)

Medical resources information and referral services

This type of service could go hand in hand with claims processing. It is in effect a consulting service that links up individuals or companies with qualified specialists in medical areas. One problem with this type of service is collecting from clients—continual follow-up is required. Once established, the cash flow can be excellent. The initial capital investment, other than the time and cost involved in start-up promotion and advertising, is minimal. Your typical clients would be doctors, medical centers, nursing homes, hospitals, university medical centers, and so forth—all easy to identify and reach. However, there is growing competition in this field. Initial investment, $2,500–$5,000.

Medical transcription services

There has been a shortage of medical transcriptionists, who produce transcribed notes from the audiotaped comments physicians dictate regarding their patients and cases. However, more and more people are moving into this field precisely because of the shortage. There is growing competition from other freelance transcribers and from agencies that specialize in this service as well as from in-house transcribing departments in hospitals and medical centers. But if you are skilled and can offer accuracy and speedy turnaround, you should be able to quickly develop a healthy flow of business. Transcription requires specialized skills and knowledge of medical terminology. If you already have these capabilities, you have the basis for an excellent cash flow business. Initial investment, $2,500–$5,000.

American Association for Medical Transcription
Box 576187
3460 Oakdale Rd., #M
Modesto CA 95357
(209) 551-0883

More Hot Prospects

- Insurance consulting services; initial investment, $2,500–$5,000
- Insurance research services; initial investment, $2,500–$5,000
- Medical insurance consortiums (managing groups of businesses that band together to get cheaper group rates on medical insurance); initial investment, $5,000–$10,000

- Mobile medical, surgical, or alternative health centers (vans equipped to do pediatric care, dental care, and so forth); initial investment, $50,000 or more

- Senior day care centers or services (provide supervision, leisure activities, and companionship to compensate for decline of extended family); initial investment, $25,000–$50,000

- Services related to long-term care (demand will grow as the U.S. population ages); initial investment, $25,000–$50,000

- Visiting nurse associations; initial investment, $10,000–$25,000

4. INFORMATION SEARCH AND RETRIEVAL SERVICES

There is a whole family of new high-technology research activities that use computers and the other electronic media available today to locate information, which is then organized and presented to clients who have ordered it. Sometimes the work takes more traditional forms, such as interviews and library research. These services help to fill the research gap for companies and corporations that need up-to-date research but do not wish to establish in-house departments.

An important element of such services is the ability to not just present masses of information, but to analyze it so your clients can use it. Information and data may be related to specific customer projects or to more general needs. The services you provide can thus cover a wide variety of consulting and interpretation services as well as factual data services. Gaining a reputation for reliability will take time, but profit margins can be reasonably good.

These services will benefit from almost all of the Forces of Change, but they're especially related to continued corporate downsizing, because downsized companies may no longer have in-house staff to perform these tasks. One way to start is by taking a look at your interests and knowledge. If you already have in-depth knowledge about some field, it will be easier to get started by specializing in what you already know. In fact, your main difficulty at the outset may be in defining what you really want your business to be and relating it to a specific market.

Speed and personalized attention are major selling points, and you should focus on them from Day One of your operation. When you begin, consider approaching professional firms such as law offices, medical offices, and accounting firms that are likely to have a continuing need for up-to-the-minute knowledge about developments related to their activities. Information services offer great flexibility and are ideal home-based businesses, but your initial investment in necessary hardware (computers, printers, modems, fax machines) and software (on-line bulletin-board systems, database programs) can be costly. You will also want to upgrade as new hardware and software come onto the market.

Association of Information Industry Professionals
PO Box 3189
Penack NJ 07666

National Federation of Abstracting and Information Services
1429 Walnut St.
Philadelphia PA 19102
(215) 563-2406

Society of Computer Intelligence Professionals
818 18th St. NW, #225
Washington DC 20006
(202) 223-5885

Special Libraries Association
1700 18th St. NW
Washington DC 20009
(202) 234-4700

Hottest Prospects

Information broker

Information brokers can provide a wide variety of consulting and interpretation services or services that specialize in obtaining, organizing, and analyzing factual data. You will need to become expert in the ever-expanding resources offered by computer services and databases. Gaining a reputation for reliability takes time, but profit margins can eventually be reasonably good. Initial investment, $5,000–$10,000.

Information management

These services provide records creation and record keeping. Advances in telecommunications and other electronics are creating an immense demand for information services of almost every type imaginable—information for video production studios, background research for lawsuits, research for new forms of education, and on and on. This type of service can be operated with minimal investment and can be done from home or a small office.

The primary requirement is having the necessary research skills and the ability to ferret out prospective clients who have an ongoing need for your services. If you carry out your business with your customers' needs regarding timing and quality in mind, these businesses can develop into good cash flow producers and have a potential for growing into a more extensive multi-employee company. Initial investment, $2,500–$5,000.

Association of Commercial Records Centers
PO Box 20518
Raleigh NC 27619-0518
(800) 336-9793

More Hot Prospects

- Abstracting and indexing services; initial investment, $2,500–$5,000
- Genealogical research services; initial investment, $2,500–$5,000
- Research services; initial investment, $2,500–$5,000
- Search services for books and periodicals; initial investment, $2,500–$5,000

5. JANITORIAL, CLEANING, AND RELATED SERVICES

During our latest national survey of the small-business scene, we heard many comments like this one, from a business broker in South Carolina: "The most promising opportunities currently available are in areas such as landscaping, house cleaning, window washing, and janitorial services."

He went on to say that buyers can do very well in these businesses because "there is very little risk and very little financial outlay. You can purchase an established business for one-and-a-half times the profit with one-third to one-half down and get that all back in less than a year." In short, these types of businesses are flexible and are also "the best growth areas, 20 to 40 percent a year."

The minimum investment you would need to reach a positive cash flow (not including your own salary) will average between $2,500 and

$10,000, but substantially more could be required to launch a full-range service. For example, parking lot maintenance could include striping for parking spaces, driveways, and so forth. This type of service requires expensive special equipment and ample storage for maintenance and repair. Also, because paints are involved, contamination control is an essential but added expense.

The average time required to begin generating positive cash flow, assuming full-time work on your part, is between two and four months, while average potential cash flow should be between $6,000 and $10,000 per employee, with you handling all customer contacts, marketing, and general management. For example, if you own a janitorial service with ten regular or contract employees, your annual cash flow should be at least $60,000 to $100,000 after all payroll and other normal operating expenses.

Whenever possible, maintenance services should be carried out on-site, not in a separately located business. This means that your only locational needs will be a place for telephone and other administrative activities and room to store supplies and equipment. You may also need room to park trucks or other vehicles, but these types of facilities are easy to lease and can be located in less expensive areas of your community.

There is a strong and growing need for all types of cleaning and janitorial services. Your primary problem is to take enough time to develop the business by word of mouth and with minimal advertising. You as owner should take a direct part in the business and be familiar with all its aspects. One way to break into this market is to focus on a few large projects by getting in touch with office and apartment managers and developing a strong reputation for dependability and quality of workmanship.

You can create the best advertising of all by being dependable, because these types of businesses are replete with individuals who are sloppy, careless, and generally undependable. This kind of competition opens the door to a truly professional-level service. If you start out as an individual who provides super service, this will become a strong foundation for expansion and good cash flow rewards. Quality control is essential. Your rule of thumb should be to operate this service as you would a professional practice. If you do, it will be hard to go wrong.

Another option is to create referral services in this area. Maid referral, for example, can easily be carried on from your home. There is a growing need for these services, given the continuing increase in two-income households, but there is also competition. With a referral service, you do not go out and do the service yourself. Rather, you become a center where people who want that kind of service place orders with you and you recruit workers to carry out what needs to be done. You might look for referrals through bankers, real estate brokers, and building managers as well as satisfied clients.

Society of Cleaning Technicians
3028 Poplar Rd.
Sharpsberg GA 30277
(404) 304-9941

Hot Prospects

- Asbestos removal; initial investment, $10,000–$25,000
- Acoustical tile cleaning; initial investment, $2,500–$5,000
- Air-duct cleaning; initial investment, $2,500–$5,000
- Apartment preparation services (cleaning, painting, repairing, and re-plastering before new tenants move in); initial investment, $2,500–$5,000
- Bird-proofing; initial investment, $2,500–$5,000
- Building maintenance (no repairs); initial investment, $2,500–$5,000
- Carpet and rug cleaning, care, and maintenance; initial investment, $2,500–$5,000
- Ceiling cleaning; initial investment, $2,500–$5,000
- Cemetery upkeep (independent); initial investment, $2,500–$10,000
- Chimney cleaning; initial investment, $2,500–$5,000
- Deodorizing restrooms; initial investment, $2,500–$5,000
- Disaster cleanup, especially for absentee homeowners of condominiums and other housing in resort areas; initial investment, $10,000–$25,000
- Domestic services of all kinds; initial investment, less than $2,500
- Floor cleaning and waxing; initial investment, $2,500–$5,000
- Furniture and upholstery cleaning on customers' premises; initial investment, $2,500–$5,000
- Home garage detailing (degreasing home garage floors; also school grounds, parking lots, service stations, and so forth); initial investment, $5,000–$10,000

- Garden maintenance and planting; initial investment, $2,500–$5,000
- Gas station restroom cleaning (perhaps specialized by brand or sponsored by major companies); initial investment, $2,500–$5,000
- Graffiti removal; initial investment, $5,000–$10,000
- Lawn care and maintenance (mowing, clipping, and raking services, possibly expanding into crew operation and use of chemical technology to care for lawns and eradicate pests; see also, organic lawn care); initial investment, $10,000–$25,000
- Lighting maintenance (bulb replacement and cleaning); initial investment, $2,500–$5,000
- Maid referral service (bonding and insurance would be the principal cautions here); initial investment, $10,000–$25,000
- Mini-blind cleaning service; initial investment, $2,500–$5,000
- Mowing highway center strips and edges (especially in smaller communities that may have limited public-works departments); initial investment, $25,000–$50,000 or more
- New home interior cleaning; initial investment, $2,500–$5,000
- Office cleaning; initial investment, $5,000–$10,000
- Ornamental bush and tree care (planting, pruning, bracing, spraying, removal, and surgery); initial investment, $10,000–$25,000
- Parking lot maintenance and striping; initial investment, $50,000 or more
- Registry services for cleaning, janitorial, and maintenance; initial investment, $5,000–$10,000
- Restaurant restroom cleaning; initial investment, $2,500–$5,000
- School custodian work; initial investment, $2,500–$5,000
- Seeding highway center strips and edges (especially in smaller communities that may have limited public-works departments); initial investment, $10,000–$25,000
- Service station cleaning and degreasing; initial investment, $2,500–$5,000
- Snowplowing services; initial investment, $50,000 or more
- Sweeping services for roads, airports, and parking lots; initial investment, $50,000 or more
- Swimming pool and spa cleaning and repair; initial investment, $5,000–$10,000

- Telephone booth cleaning and maintenance; initial investment, $5,000–$10,000
- Tree trimming for public utility lines; initial investment, $50,000 or more
- Turf installation (natural and artificial); initial investment, $25,000–$50,000
- Upholstery cleaning (customers' premises only); initial investment, $2,500–$5,000
- Vacuuming airport runways; initial investment, $50,000 or more
- Valet services; initial investment, less than $2,500
- Window washing; initial investment, $5,000–$10,000

6. LEGAL SUPPORT SERVICES

The ever-increasing number of legal cases being filed in our litigious society will require a corresponding increase in legal support services. Generally, the courts are so congested that the time is coming when they will no longer be able to handle everything efficiently.

Some services that are currently needed and will be needed on an increasing basis can be supplied by small businesses that specialize in legal support. If you are generally interested in the law and the courts, it may be well worth your time to get acquainted with judges, lawyers, or other members of the legal community to find out what the needs are in your area.

Hottest Prospects

Court reporting services

This business specializes in recording and transcribing trials, depositions, and other legal proceedings where detailed records are required. It requires special training and equipment. Initial investment, $10,000–$25,000.

Court and legal support services

These include services to attorneys and courts, including deliveries, paging, trial watching, subpoena services, and the like. Initial investment, $5,000–$10,000.

Legal document storage services (see also category 10, Records Storage and Retrieval, later in this chapter)

All documents and other forms of evidence used in court cases must be stored securely for possible future reference. This is an excellent potential business because the need is immense and growing. Cash flow can be substantial even though there is a great deal of competition. This business requires skills in making contact with people who have a need for these services. A check with the courthouse, preferably by seeing the clerk or secretary to the supervising judge, may give a clue as to how extensive the need is and if it is possible for you to provide a service for document and evidence storage and retrieval. You will have to invest in secure warehouse and storage facilities as well as trucks for pickup and delivery and a staff to operate the business and provide fast response to customer needs. Initial investment, $50,000 or more.

Association of Records Managers and Administrators
4200 Somerset, #215
Prairie Village KS 66028
(913) 341-3808

More Hot Prospects

- Accident prevention and liability seminars; initial investment, $5,000–$10,000
- Bankruptcy referee services; initial investment, $5,000–$10,000
- Consulting services regarding on sexual harassment and other laws and policies; initial investment, $2,500–$5,000
- Divorce filing services; initial investment, $2,500–$5,000
- Legal aid services; initial investment, $5,000–$10,000
- Mediation services; initial investment, $5,000–$10,000
- Paralegal services; initial investment, $5,000–$10,000
- Process serving; initial investment, $2,500–$5,000
- Product liability research and other types of research for self-employed inventors and marketers of new products; initial investment, $2,500–$5,000

7. LOCAL DELIVERY AND TRANSPORTATION SERVICES

As our cities become increasingly congested, the need for smaller-scale and specialized transportation services will only increase as well. However, this market is competitive, and therefore it is all the more important that you find or create your own special niche. You might consider offering automobile, van, or bus transportation to and from not just airports, docks, and train stations but also such everyday destinations as light-rail stops and bus stops.

You will have to plan on spending a relatively large amount on initial advertising and promotion and will also have to invest in vehicles on either a lease or purchase basis. Your best place to start is by getting in touch with organizations or agencies that require personalized transportation on a dependable, as-called-for basis. One starting point is housing facilities for the elderly. You could also offer home-to-market transportation for those who cannot drive or choose not to drive.

Off-premises dining, services that deliver complete restaurant meals to people's homes, may actually benefit from recessionary conditions and the fatigue engendered by the two-career rat race in that people may be too tired to go out to eat. They may well wish to have restaurant meals delivered for less than what it would cost them to go out. Also, delivery services of everything from baby supplies to groceries will also see an upsurge due to two-career households. Some supermarkets are already offering same-day shopping services in which people fax in their orders and the store fills and delivers them.

Hottest Prospects

Airport transportation services

These services provide automobile, van, or bus transportation to and from airports, train stations, and other destinations. This is just one example of many types of specialized transportation services that can take advantage of increasing traffic congestion in urban centers. Initial investment, $50,000 or more.

Bus charter services

This type of service, which provides chartered passenger transportation either within a single geographical area or over a broader region, requires the purchase or lease of vehicles. In addition, you must be prepared to advertise, emphasizing your availability, reliability, and other features. It can take a good deal of time to develop a steady flow of referrals and clientele, and in most areas there is a substantial amount of competition. Initial investment, $50,000 or more.

American Society of Transportation and Logistics
3600 Chamberlin La., Unit 232
Louisville KY 40241
(502) 425-1780

Food delivery services

Delivering prepared foods and meals from restaurants to homes and businesses will become more and more needed as working people seek the combination of eating at home without having to cook. You can begin developing this business by getting in touch with local restaurants and perhaps by taking out cooperative advertising in your target market area. It may take time to develop this service, but once it's going, word-of-mouth advertising should take over, and it could be reasonably profitable—provided that you play a major day-to-day role in your business and control every phase to guarantee consistent quality. Initial investment, $10,000–$25,000.

Entrepreneur Group
2392 Morse Ave.
Irvine CA 92714
(714) 261-2325

Postal and local delivery services

Like packaging, shipping, and mailing services (see category 9 later in this chapter), these services are best done directly at the customer's place of business. Your clients can be any small or large retailer that needs to ship merchandise sold to walk-in customers or through direct mail, video, or other means. Your service operates as an extension of the existing retailer, wholesaler, or even manufacturer and is in lieu of their hiring staff to perform these services. The selling point is that your customers pay only on a per-piece basis and thus should see a savings on their payroll. Developing this type of business takes time, but not a large capital investment except for vehicles. This type of service will be increasingly in demand, particularly with the advent of interactive video, where firms that can offer rapid delivery will have a greater competitive edge. Initial investment, $10,000–$25,000.

Taxi or independent cab operator

Very often these are franchised operations in cities, but they may also be independent cabs that work for an association of some sort. Usually, the driver owns or leases the vehicle, and the business is often regulated. There are security and safety concerns in this type of business. However, the major benefit is considerable independence. Initial investment, $25,000–$50,000.

More Hot Prospects

- Bicycle, motor scooter, and other small vehicle rentals and leasing (for quick commuting around downtown areas of cities and in smaller communities); initial investment, $5,000–$10,000

- Car pools and van pools on a subcontract basis for corporations or municipalities (especially smaller ones); initial investment, $25,000–$50,000

- Chauffeur service (providing drivers for clients' own cars); initial investment, $5,000–$10,000

- Children's cab service (offering transportation to dance classes, dentist appointments, and other activities when both parents are working; requires impeccable reputation and safety record); initial investment, $25,000–$50,000

- Designated driver services for parties and occasions when people drink; initial investment, $2,500–$5,000

- Executive transportation services (providing chauffeur-driven vehicles equipped with reading lamps and other amenities so executives can work while being transported from one location to another) or limousine services; initial investment, $50,000 or more

- Jitney and minibus or van services (offering customized transportation so people will be willing to leave their cars at home); initial investment, $50,000 or more

- Limousine services that find available limousines for clients; initial investment, $5,000–$10,000

- One-day-a-week carpool services (to match people for carpooling one or two days a week to cut traffic congestion; funding may come from city governments supplemented by corporate funding, or from a nom-inal fee paid by passengers); initial investment, $5,000–$10,000

- Shuttle services to and from movie theaters, concert halls, sporting events, day trips, and other events and activities; initial investment, $50,000 or more

- Transportation services to hospital appointments, physical therapy, and other locations for the elderly and disabled; initial investment, $25,000–$50,000

- Van pool operations; initial investment, $50,000 or more

8. MONEY-SAVING SERVICES

This category covers a wide and somewhat disparate group of innovative businesses, all of which focus on saving money for individuals or other businesses.

Hottest Prospects

Bill auditing services

The use of these services, which audit bills for mistakes or fraud, is growing rapidly. Bill auditing originated with utility bills and has ex-panded to telephone bills, property taxes, mortgages, and insurance and medical claims, to name just a few. Fees are usually a percentage of the amount saved. Government work at the local, state, and federal levels may be among the specialized markets that you could develop as a bill auditor.

These businesses have other advantages: They are not seasonal, and they are probably recession-proof because companies will always be in-terested in cutting costs even if they have to spend some money to do so. This is a specialized business in which there can be a fair cash flow. Your initial investment is minimal other than advertising and promotion. It will take time to develop a regular clientele, and you will have to have special knowledge and skills in analysis. One possible extension of au-diting services may happen in the telecommunications area.

As the information superhighway becomes established, there may well come a need for outside auditing of household and corporate bills for on-line data services as well as consumer goods and services such as pizzas and movies. Initial investment, $10,000–$25,000.

American Institute
American Institute Building, First Floor
7326 S.W. 48th St.
Miami FL 33155
(800) US-AUDIT

Bookkeeping and billing services

These services handle the finances of individuals or businesses. Qualified bookkeeping services, which provide updates on individual and business finances, are becoming more and more in demand due to the constant changes in U.S. tax laws. This type of business requires special education and skills. Bookkeeping services also face an immense amount of competition from several sources such as large chain operators who offer full- and part-time services to individuals, large international, national, and regional firms, and independents. Initial investment, $10,000–$25,000.

American Accounting Association
5717 Bessie Dr.
Sarasota FL 34233
(813) 921-7747

Collection agencies and services

These services help business owners collect outstanding accounts receivable and are likely to be in increasing demand in times of economic stress when cash-strapped individuals and companies delay paying bills. Some companies may use their own staff to follow up on receivables, but others may well prefer to subcontract this work to collectors.

It will take time to develop the word-of-mouth advertising you'll need for an adequate and acceptable cash flow, but your up-front capital investment is virtually nil, except for advertising in the Yellow Pages and other forms of direct solicitation. You'll probably be more successful in your collections if you use a problem-solving approach with debtors. You might want to specialize in a particular area, such as health care or day care center collections.

This is one business that requires a specific location. You should open an office where clients can visit if necessary. You can choose to operate from your home, but it's probably easier to project an image of success if you're based in an attractively furnished office space. Initial investment, $5,000–$10,000.

American Collectors Association
4040 W. 70th St.
PO Box 39106
Minneapolis MN 55439-0106
(612) 926-6547

Corporate relocation services

This type of service would carry out research for companies or self-employed individuals on relocation issues such as tax laws, licensing and regulations, real estate, crime rates, workers' compensation costs, and bank policies. Initial investment, $5,000–$10,000.

Credit consulting services

These services provide professional advice on how to manage personal and business finances and restore bad credit. This area requires that you establish relationships with credit companies, collection agencies, and lenders. You should also be familiar with federal and state laws regarding consumer credit. The increasing complexity of personal finance today makes this a promising field because the public realizes the need for expert assistance in these areas. This is a semi-professional service that can form a basis for an excellent long-term activity with good financial rewards. You must have the needed educational background and the patience to gain recognition among clients who are willing to refer other business to you. When you are starting out, you can contract out for specialized activities such as clerical help as needed. Initial investment, $5,000–$10,000.

American Consultants League
1290 Palm Ave.
Sarasota FL 34236
(813) 952-9290

Cross-cultural orientation services

These types of services offer classes about American culture for foreign businesspeople newly based in the United States as well as courses and training for U.S. businesspeople on cultural differences and the etiquette of doing business with members of other societies. Initial investment, $2,500–$5,000.

Financial advising services

These services offer professional advice on financial matters to both individuals and companies. These are consulting businesses that must be developed over a long period of time. You will need to create a reputation for professional service and success. You can start this business from your home, but this is one of the handful of businesses better suited to an office location. Your home may not offer the desired professional atmosphere unless it is very exclusive and is itself a place where potential clients would like to live or work. If you don't have that kind of home, an office is the best option. This type of business is difficult to develop on a part-time basis. Although it is possible during the initial start-up, your chances of success will improve if you can devote yourself to it full-time and if you have the patience and the capital to wait for a steady flow of clients and adequate cash flow. Initial investment, $25,000–$50,000.

Fund-raising consulting services

This type of business specializes in fund-raising under contract for organizations such as hospitals, schools, churches, and for special projects where funds are solicited from the public or other sources. If you're going to be working on your own, you had best think of this as a part-time business. Many institutions such as universities, colleges, and hospitals hire fund-raising consultants, but what will make you attractive to these institutions is your network of contacts or your ability to make contacts with the kinds of people who can make significant contributions. Initial investment, $5,000–$10,000.

American Association of Fund-Raising Council
25 W. 43rd St., #1519
New York NY 10036
(212) 354-5799

Income tax preparation services

This business specializes in income tax preparation and is a growing field because the tax laws are becoming more and more complex. Accordingly, it is a long-term business. You can operate it on your own or with employees. It does require special education and skills, but not of the level of a CPA or other certified accountant. If you wish to increase your credibility and the depth of service you can offer clients, it's helpful to have accounting and tax-planning credentials. This is an excellent business service for lawyers interested in a specialized focus or niche market. The cash flow potential is excellent although somewhat seasonal. Initial investment, $5,000–$10,000.

American Accounting Association
5717 Bessie Dr.
Sarasota FL 34233
(813) 921-7747

Leak detection services

These services specialize in detecting roof, water, and other types of leaks in business and residential buildings. Most companies tend to specialize; you will probably need some special equipment. One way to establish yourself and stabilize your cash flow is by offering a preventive maintenance program of scheduled visits. Initial investment, $10,000–$25,000.

American Leak Detection
Box 1706
1750 East Arena, #7
Palm Springs CA 92262
(619) 320-9991 or (800) 755-6697

Mystery shopper services

This type of service monitors the level and quality of customer service and staff honesty in retail stores, restaurants, repair services, hotels, and any business that caters to consumers. These services can also be hired by firms to check out their competitors. Initial investment, $2,500–$5,000.

Property inspection services

This real estate-related service specializes in offering prospective buyers of real estate an objective evaluation of the exterior and interior of the property they are considering buying. It is especially suitable for people with a contracting or construction background. Lending institutions often require inspections, and sellers in states that have defect-disclosure laws may also request inspections to protect themselves. In some cases you will have to be certified or at least highly qualified if you are to be acceptable to lending institutions where a mortgage may depend on the results of an inspection.

This type of business is relatively flexible, and you can do the work from your home because all the physical activity is done at the house or building in question. Your cash flow will depend on how much time you devote to solicitation by simple advertising and referrals through suppliers, other contractors, banks, real estate brokers, and the like. As always in service businesses, your best advertising is a reputation from satisfied clients for dependability and quality of work. Initial investment, $5,000–$10,000.

NRI Schools
McGraw-Hill Continuing Education Center
4401 Connecticut Ave. NW
Washington DC 20008
(202) 244-1600

American Society of Home Inspectors
1725 N. Lynn St., #950
Arlington VA 22209-2022
(703) 524-2008

Property tax consulting and auditing

These services assemble and file appeals for property owners, mostly residential but possibly for businesses as well. Your fees will be a percentage of the refund. This is a specialized business, and the investment is minimal other than the advertising, promotion, and time it will take to develop a regular clientele. Also, some special knowledge and skills are required. Initial investment, $2,500–$5,000.

Résumé-checking service

This type of service confirms prospective employees' claims regarding their educational background, credit history, workers' compensation claims, driving record, and criminal record. This field could be subject to regulation because of the potential for violations of privacy. Services such as these could find a strong market among small companies that lack staffing to carry out checks on their own. Also, résumé checking may protect firms against jury awards for work-related crimes by employees. Initial investment, $2,500–$5,000.

Self-insurance services

These services organize and run self-insurance programs for consortiums of small businesses to help cut the costs of workers' compensation programs. Such services would be affected by the any national health care plan, which would probably cover workers' compensation. One disadvantage of self-insurance groups is that all members would be liable if one suffered a major loss or went out of business and left claims unpaid. Initial investment, $10,000–$25,000.

Student financial aid services

These are services that provide information about sources of financial aid for higher education; they also suggest strategies for obtaining aid. Although usually targeted to traditional college-age students, you can also try to create a niche market by appealing to other groups such as older people, retirees, immigrants, and perhaps even students from abroad who want to come to the United States to study, or U.S. students who want to study abroad. This field requires a good eye for detail as well as skills with computer financial aid software. Initial investment, $5,000–$10,000.

Telecommuting consulting services

This type of service advises and plans with companies and individuals about how to create time- and cost-efficient telecommuting structures for employees. Telecommuting can cut down on traffic congestion, wear and tear on highways, air pollution, and gasoline and energy consumption. Initial investment, $2,500–$5,000.

More Hot Prospects

- Account auditing services; initial investment, $10,000–$25,000
- Automobile insurance rate research services; initial investment, $2,500–$5,000
- Auto leasing rates research services; initial investment, $2,500–$5,000
- Barter services (match people with products and services and keep "accounts" in return for membership fees and per-transaction commissions); initial investment, $2,500–$5,000
- Cable system rate research services; initial investment, $2,500–$5,000

- Collectibles brokering (appraising and arranging for sales and purchases of collectible items of all kinds, ideally based on an area of interest); initial investment, $2,500–$5,000
- Check validation services; initial investment, $2,500–$5,000
- Commercial research services; initial investment, $2,500–$5,000
- Consumer credit rates research services; initial investment, $2,500–$5,000
- Consumer debt counseling or adjustment services; initial investment, $5,000–$10,000
- Copyright protection services; initial investment, $2,500–$5,000
- Export-related liaison consulting services; initial investment, $2,500–$5,000
- Financial brokering (matching up lenders and borrowers; requires knowledge of loan sources and how to screen clients); initial investment, $5,000–$10,000
- Inventory services; initial investment, $2,500–$5,000
- Long distance and local long distance rate research services; initial investment, $2,500–$5,000
- Medical/dental supply and equipment cost research services; initial investment, $2,500–$5,000
- Notary public services; initial investment, $2,500–$5,000
- Payroll accounting service; initial investment, $5,000–$10,000
- Quick-response consulting services (on how to create electronic data interchange services among companies to avoid over- and under-ordering); initial investment, $2,500–$5,000
- Safety-related seminars, contests, and other program to cut accident rates and workers' compensation costs in companies; initial investment, $2,500–$5,000
- Search services that specialize in finding lost owners of stock shares, bank accounts, and other financial assets to prevent escheatment (funds reverting to state); initial investment, $2,500–$5,000
- Training seminars on compliance with government laws and regulations in various industries and sectors; initial investment, $2,500–$5,000

9. PACKAGING, SHIPPING, MAILING, AND RELATED SERVICES

Packaging and shipping services will become increasingly important as urban congestion grows, specialized merchandising expands, and corporate downsizing continues. These services will be in increasing demand, particularly with the advent of interactive video, where rapid packaging and delivery of the products sold will give the sellers a strong competitive edge. Your clients can be almost any type of large or small retailer that needs to ship merchandise sold to walk-in customers or through direct mail, video, or other means.

Your big selling point is that your service does away with the customer's need for a big, expensive shipping department—the customer subcontracts that work out to you. Another selling point is that the customer pays only on a per-piece basis and is therefore likely to save a good deal in payroll. Ideally, you will carry out these services at your customers' place of business; this is preferable to having a retail-type store location. In other words, this is best performed on a commercial rather than a retail basis. Developing this type of business takes time, but localized operations do not require a large capital investment.

In addition to offering packaging services, you might do well to add an actual delivery component to your operation. However, you need not envision this aspect as a UPS-type service. Rather, look at it as a localized delivery service.

Associated Mail and Parcel Centers
10701 Montgomery Blvd.
Albuquerque NM 87111
(505) 294-6425

Paperboard Packaging Council
1101 Vermont Ave. NW, #411
Washington DC 20005
(202) 289-4100

Hot Prospects

- Courier services (local, national, international); initial investment, $5,000–$50,000

- Cross-country trucking services; initial investment, $50,000 or more

- Local deliveries of fresh-frozen seafood and other foods and products; initial investment, $10,000–$25,000
- Drop-shipping services; initial investment, $25,000–$50,000
- Errand services (there are many such, including concierge services, messenger services, firewood delivery services, and personal shopping services); initial investment, $2,500–$25,000
- Freight rate research service; initial investment, $2,500–$5,000
- Garment storage services; initial investment, $50,000 or more
- Gift wrapping services; initial investment, $2,500–$5,000
- Porter services; initial investment, $2,500–$5,000
- Shipping documents preparation service; initial investment, $5,000–$10,000
- Transportation brokerage services; initial investment, $5,000–$10,000
- Truck and van routes for laundry and dry cleaning services; initial investment, $25,000–$50,000
- Unpacking services (help the millions of busy Americans who move each year by arranging home furnishings after movers deliver; corporate-family moves can be a specialty); initial investment, $5,000–$10,000

10. RECORDS STORAGE AND RETRIEVAL SERVICES (SEE ALSO CATEGORY 6, LEGAL SUPPORT SERVICES, EARLIER IN THIS CHAPTER)

Despite the revolution in information storage and record keeping brought about by the computer age, the "paperless office" seems further away than ever—in fact, it often seems as if the deluge of paper has gotten even worse. This opens up new opportunities for records storage and retrieval services.

The most obvious areas of need are professional fields such as law and medicine, but almost any professional practice is a possible market (including accounting and veterinary services, as well as many others). If you apply your imagination, you should be able to come up with dozens of possibilities, and the need will probably expand to other non-professional businesses in the near future. Just in the legal field, for example, the need for storage of documents such as those used in tax cases or for court trials is immense.

Your principal selling points are security of storage and easy retrieval. Your initial capital investment may be somewhat greater than average, because you will need secure warehouse and storage facilities, trucks for pickup and delivery, and a staff to operate the business and provide fast response to customer needs. You will probably need computer systems for your own record keeping. Also, you should be prepared for the possibility that your customers may wish to retrieve their records and documents electronically. Initial investment, $50,000 or more.

Association of Records Managers and Administrators
4200 Somerset, #215
Prairie Village KS 66028
(913) 341-3808

Hot Prospects

- Medical records keeping and storage for hospitals, private practices, and public agencies; initial investment, $50,000 or more

11. REFERRAL SERVICES

Medical and dental care referral services are among the most common, but there is room for referral services in almost any field imaginable, from pet sitting services to appliance repair firms.

Your key to success is credibility, which in turn is based on the quality of the organizations and individuals to whom you are doing the referring. It can take a good deal of research to create your referral list.

Society of Human Resources Management
606 N. Washington
Alexandria VA 22314
(703) 548-3440

Hottest Prospect

Homesharing programs

These programs match up senior citizens with houses and younger (and not-so-young) people seeking to save money on housing. The seniors get financial help that may keep them independent, plus someone around to check up on them in case of illness or injury, while tenants cut their housing costs. This type of program can be privately funded by fees from one or both parties, but could also be carried out as a subcontracted activity for a town or city. Initial investment, $5,000–$10,000.

Another Hot Prospect

• Referral services for immigrants and refugees; initial investment, $5,000–$10,000

12. SECURITY SERVICES

If this area interests you, you may need to research several issues: legalities and licensing, relationships with local police departments, and the necessity of obtaining bonding.

Hottest Prospects

Alarm installation and maintenance services

These services, which specialize in installing burglar alarms, fire alarms, and other security devices to protect individual and business properties, are in increasing demand due to the skyrocketing crime rate. There is a substantial amount of competition, but if you can identify a niche market, you should be able to reap a good cash flow. Initial investment, $10,000–$25,000.

Entrepreneur Group
2392 Morse Ave.
Irvine CA 92714
(714) 261-2325

Private investigation services

This service is still surrounded by an aura of sleazy glamour that dates back to the "gumshoe" days of detective novels, but today's private investigator is more likely to be working on civil cases for both businesses and private clients. Other work may include investigation of fraud, or background checks on potential employees. There is a good deal of room for specialization—but you must be flexible, because you may find yourself working erratic hours. Initial investment, $2,500–$5,000.

International Security and Detective Alliance
PO Box 6303
Corpus Christi TX 78466-6303
(512) 888-6164

Security consulting services

This area can cover a wide range of activities targeted at controlling and eliminating many types of crime. Examples of specific activities might include consulting on how to redesign spaces (including redoing lighting) in office buildings and public outdoor settings to cut down on the possibility of assaults, muggings, and other crimes. Other emphases might include consulting on how to eliminate employee theft, shoplifting, and vendor fraud. Another possibility is to consult with homeowners and apartment dwellers about security devices. The field of security consulting is wide open, but it can take several years to become established. Initial investment, $5,000–$10,000.

American Society for Industrial Security
1655 N. Fort Myer, #1200
Arlington VA 22209
(703) 522-5800

More Hot Prospects

- Burglar alarm monitoring and maintenance; initial investment, $5,000–$10,000
- Credit investigation bureaus and support services; initial investment, $2,500–$5,000
- Dogs, rental of, for protective service; initial investment, $5,000–$10,000
- Drug detection services; initial investment, $25,000–$50,000
- Fingerprint service; initial investment, $10,000–$25,000
- Fire alarm monitoring and maintenance; initial investment, $5,000–$10,000
- Fire extinguisher service and maintenance; initial investment, $5,000–$10,000

- Guard, security and patrol services; initial investment, $2,500–$5,000
- Lie detection services; initial investment, $10,000–$25,000
- Metal detection operations at schools and in other settings to prevent people from bringing in firearms and other weapons; initial investment, $25,000–$50,000
- Protective services, miscellaneous; initial investment, $2,500–$5,000
- Security escort services on college campuses and from office buildings, shopping malls, and other settings, or for the elderly, the disabled, immigrants, or tourists; initial investment, $2,500–$5,000
- Self-defense seminars; initial investment, $2,500-5,000
- Services to create cooperatives for security in shopping areas by helping merchants collectively cut security costs, carry out security surveys, consult on improved lighting, and other activities; initial investment, $5,000–$10,000

13. SPECIALIZED MERCHANDISING

When thinking about business-to-business services, consider ones that will help the "big guys," both suppliers and retailers, boost sales and reduce costs by cutting their inventories, shortening their lead times, and eliminating errors. This family of businesses is especially attuned to nonlocational and nontraditional ways of selling, for example, niche selling through media advertising and direct mail.

The new technology brings with it the demand for new skills. For example, increased use of 800 and 900 numbers and infomercials will also require copywriters, designers, media producers, and so forth. From the small business standpoint, you might think about coordinating business-to-business activities rather than actually doing them yourself, perhaps working as a freelance production manager responsible for gathering together the props and arranging schedules so that the directors, actors, crew, and others involved in producing infomercials can do their work.

Hottest Prospects

Direct mail, mailing list services, and mail-order businesses and services

Direct mail and catalog sales have exploded over the past few years because they let consumers avoid traffic congestion and give them the flexibility of shopping from their living rooms—no small boon in this era of increasing "busyness."

These activities can be relatively expensive to start up, so be careful how you start out and be sure to have a plan. One way to begin is by going to work for an existing company. You'll gain valuable insights and experience. Your most important challenge is to locate an untapped market, because your chances of success increase if you can offer a specialized product or theme.

Once you've narrowed your focus, you can begin to search out products by studying trade magazines and attending trade fairs, developing a catalog, creating or renting mailing lists, and so forth. However, keep in mind that it is expensive to develop and print catalogs, rent mailing lists, and design materials that will meet the stringent requirements of the U.S. Postal Service.

These are not the cheapest small businesses to enter, but they can be among the most lucrative, and they tap directly into some of the major trends, such as congestion, changing consumer patterns, and an increasingly hectic lifestyle, that are shaping the late 1990s. Another approach might be to develop as a support service for direct marketing and direct mail operations. For example, you could create and maintain mailing lists for clients, or produce your own lists for sale or rent. In this field, as in many others, specialization can mean greater profits. Initial investment, $25,000–$50,000.

Direct Marketing Association
11 W. 42nd St.
New York NY 10036
(212) 768-7277

Mail Order Messenger
PO Box 17131
Memphis TN 38187-0131

Mail Profits
Carson Services
PO Box 4785
Lincoln NE 68504

900-number telephone services

These pay-per-call businesses provide informational, educational, and referral services over the phone to customers who pay a per-minute fee that averages between $1 and $2. There is also usually a minimum charge of $8 to $10 no matter how short the call. The 900 number may be staffed with live operators, or the caller may hear a recorded message. Beginning in the late 1980s and through the early 1990s, 900-number businesses were making substantial profits. However, high profits always breed ruinous competition, and there have been signs of this in the 900-number business. Although the range of informational services that can be provided on 900 numbers is limitless, demand and willingness to pay may not be.

If you can find a niche market for information that is not already being offered and can target that market with print media advertising such as magazines or special newspapers, you may have an opportunity for good revenue and profits. However, you would do best not to look upon 900 numbers as a long-term business; rather, you might view them as a way of getting into informational services that you can gradually adapt to other electronic media such as interactive video and computers. The easiest approach to the 900-number industry is to work through an already established service bureau that can help you get started. Initial investment, $25,000–$50,000.

Info Text Magazine
34700 Coast Highway, #309
Capistrano Beach CA 92624

The Fourth Media Journal
13402 N. Scottsdale Road
Scottsdale AZ 85254

Gift basket services

This relatively new variant on the all-occasion gift business should prosper as long as people give each other presents. It is ideally suited for a home location because space and equipment needs are minimal and scheduling can be flexible. Your start-up inventory and basic office requirements will be your biggest initial expenses. Some gift-basket operations include semi-antique items, which may allow you to charge more for your baskets but will also require more shopping time.

You might also consider offering handcrafted items in baskets by linking up with local crafts producers, but this is probably best left until your business is well established. Your principal customer base will be corporations and working women who no longer have time to shop for gifts. This business can be operated by phone or mail order or from a retail location (which would probably include sales of other gift items). You should expect to offer packaging and delivery services as well, which will involve additional coordination and expense.)

This business can be supplemental or can expand into a full-time activity. One caution: Mail order today is not inexpensive and requires the ability to focus on a particular niche market buyer, which may be difficult. Initial investment, $2,500–$5,000.

Swap meet promotion services

Swap meets are similar to flea markets but tend to focus on selling new merchandise at discounted prices. Promoters develop swap meet operations by acquiring real estate, either by purchase or by lease, doing the promoting and initial establishing of the swap meet at fairgrounds, in vacant retail or industrial buildings, in former parking garages, and at other sites such as drive-ins.

This business can require a substantial capital investment for special facilities such as restrooms and food service. Control of food service is usually essential to ensure high quality, and swap meet promoters who control the food usually have more successful operations than those who do not. A swap meet is an entertainment-oriented business, so it is best operated when it combines a flea market (used merchandise and/or antiques) with newer merchandise. There is now substantial competition, and finding a suitable location can be extremely difficult. Most markets are already well saturated with Saturday and Sunday swap meets. Initial investment, $25,000–$50,000.

Swap meet seller

Swap meets are an increasingly popular way to fight the boring repetitiveness of mall shopping. Millions of Americans are flocking to weekend swap meets and flea markets to hunt for bargains, snack, and people-watch. Antiques are the biggest sellers, with clothing and jewelry ranking close behind. Sales are highest for items that are either cheap or unusual. As a seller, you rent space on a weekend, monthly, or longer basis to sell your particular merchandise.

Most swap meet promoters want to balance the merchandise offered, so merely having something to sell doesn't mean you can go to any swap meet. If you want to set up a booth, you will probably have to have a certain kind of merchandise to fit into the promoter's desired mix. Usually sellers operate several swap meet locations simultaneously, which means that you'll need help from associates or family members. If you want to be a seller, you'll need to know where to get merchandise that you can resell at a profit. Once established, some sellers do extremely well, but on the average, swap meet sellers maximize returns only if they have multiple locations. Initial investment, $5,000–$10,000.

Telemarketing services

This type of business, which involves direct marketing by telephone on a contract basis with companies that are selling products or services, requires a significant cash investment in leasing or purchasing equipment and other fixturing. Although not location-sensitive, it does require a facility of some sort. You must also build your business through promotion, advertising, and word of mouth. Once established, this type of business can develop a significant cash flow, but relatively few do. Usually these are not long-term businesses.

Employment in this field rose from 175,000 in 1983 to 5 million by 1992 and is expected to swell by another 4.6 million by the year 2000. Rising postage costs mean marketers can reach customers by phone for about a third the cost of mail, and a 1 to 2 percent response rate is considered effective. About 80 percent of the industry (and 90 percent of the jobs) in telemarketing are geared to business rather than to private consumers, and there also tends to be fraud in the consumer end of the industry, according to *Time Magazine*.[2]

To look at this whole area from another standpoint, you might consider the opportunities presented by offering a service that would remove customers' names from direct mail and telemarketing lists! Initial investment, $25,000–$50,000.

More Hot Prospects

- Address list and mailing list compilation services; initial investment, $5,000–$10,000

- Addressing services; $5,000–$10,000

- Audience recruiting for infomercials; initial investment, $5,000–$10,000

- Consumer buying services of all kinds; initial investment, $2,500–$5,000

- Coordinating garage and lawn sales; initial investment, $2,500–$5,000

- Coordinating production of infomercials; initial investment, $25,000–$50,000

- Coupon production and distribution; initial investment, $25,000–$50,000

- Desktop publishing of marketing materials; initial investment, $25,000–$50,000

- Fax answering services that receive and store incoming faxes for subscribers, freeing up their own fax equipment; initial investment, $5,000–$10,000

- Fax "shotgun" services for delivering information about products and services to multiple machines simultaneously; initial investment, $5,000–$10,000

- Flyer distribution and production; initial investment, $10,000–$25,000

- Order-taking for mail order companies or television home-shopping firms; initial investment, $5,000–$10,000

- Search services for flea market goods; initial investment, $2,500–$5,000

14. Temporary Employment and Related Services

The consequences of massive, continuing corporate downsizing may be with us for decades. The restructurings and layoffs of the early 1990s have caused disillusionment and stress for millions of American workers—but have also created an explosion of opportunity for temporary employment and other types of personnel placement agencies.

This industry is estimated to be growing at about 10 percent a year as companies try to eliminate the skyrocketing costs of benefit packages by replacing permanent employees with temporary and contract staff who do not receive health care benefits, pensions, or vacation pay. Demand is also growing for temporary executives, also known as "flex-execs" and "contract executives," who are usually hired to oversee specific projects, such as closing down a plant or preparing a business for sale, or to fill in on a temporary basis. There may also be a market for services that specialize in finding management and higher-level staff for positions overseas, either with U.S. companies or with joint ventures in other countries.

One looming difficulty for this industry would be any national health care plan that would require employers, including temporary employment agencies, to offer health insurance benefits to any employee who works 30 or more hours a week and pro-rated benefits to part-timers. Because temporary services would have to pass these increased costs along by raising their rates, these services might become less appealing to the companies they market to. However, temporary agencies still give companies flexibility to meet fluctuations in workforce demand.

Society of Human Resources Management
606 N. Washington
Alexandria VA 22314
(703) 548-3440

National Association of Temporary Services
119 S. St. Asaph St.
Alexandria VA 22314
(703) 549-6287

National Association of Personnel Consultants
3133 Mt. Vernon Ave.
Alexandria VA 22305

National Personnel Associates
150 Fountain N
Grand Rapids MI 49503
(800) 826-4372

A Directory of Executive Temporary Placement Firms
Executive Recruiter News
Templeton Rd.
Fitzwilliam NH 03447

Hottest Prospects

Temporary employment services

Growth is expected to be especially strong for agencies that specialize in placing people with particular skills, thus saving employers from having to seek out and train new employees. Earnings can be high for the hours involved, and temporary services are almost recession-proof. However, it can be challenging to balance cash flow and to keep track of the ever-changing regulations that govern employment. Initial investment, $25,000–$50,000.

Word processing services

These services handle the overflow of typing and secretarial work for companies. Sending out such work is cost-effective compared to hiring additional staff. Although competition is intense, specialization can be a plus. Quality, quick turnaround, and pickup/delivery service can also give you a greater competitive edge. Initial investment, $25,000–$50,000.

National Association of Secretarial Services
3637 Fourth St. N, #330
St. Petersburg FL 33704
(813) 823-3546 or (800) 237-1462

More Hot Prospects

- Career transition or outplacement counseling services for employees who have been laid off; initial investment, $5,000–$10,000

- Employment services that match welfare clients and needy clients with companies (including skills training, follow-up, and counseling for job seekers); initial investment, $5,000–$10,000

- "Flexible staffing" services (specializing in placing part-time workers at various levels, including professional staff, telecommuting workers, and job-sharing positions in which two people would share what makes up a full-time slot); initial investment, $10,000–$25,000

- Labor pools; initial investment, $10,000–$25,000

- Nursing registries; initial investment, $10,000–$25,000

- Senior citizen employment services (placing them in areas of technical support, office support, and middle management); initial investment, $10,000–$25,000

- Volunteer employment services that match up volunteers with agencies and settings that need help; initial investment, $10,000–$25,000

15. MISCELLANEOUS

This final section covers a range of individual opportunities that don't fit neatly into a single category. If you've been reading along carefully, you'll start to realize that there are ideas for dozens of new entrepreneurial business ideas everywhere you look.

Hottest Prospects

Home entertainment installation services

These services are designed to help consumers by doing the custom work of installing and hooking up audio and video components and systems, and even designing special enclosures for equipment. This business may require specific construction skills as well as design aptitude.

Some ways to begin are by approaching established audio and video retail stores or by having a display at consumer electronics trade shows. As always, however, your most lucrative business will come via word of mouth from satisfied customers. As you gain a reputation, you could see a steady and reasonably high level of cash flow. However, you will have to constantly promote and advertise in order to maintain a reasonable level of business. This type of business is expected to continue expanding as two-career families decide to stay home rather than battling traffic and high admissions prices for outside entertainment. It might also expand into or be linked with installations of security and alarm systems. Initial investment, $5,000–$10,000

Entrepreneur Group
2392 Morse Ave.
Irvine CA 92714
(714) 261-2325

Import/export services

Import and export services are likely to mushroom with the opening up of the world's economies. According to the American Association of Exporters and Importers, exports grew between 10 and 15 percent a year between 1989 and 1992, while sales for small export businesses has been growing at 30 percent a year.

Your chances of success are probably greater if you start out as an exporter by approaching U.S. companies that may not have begun to explore overseas markets for their products. Federal statistics indicate that more and more manufacturing is being done by small companies, so these may be profitable clients to approach. Literally thousands of American businesses have yet to look abroad for markets for their goods and services, while the former Iron Curtain countries and newly expanding nations of Asia and in other parts of the world are eager to tap the U.S. market. However, you will need to be patient and sensitive to the cultural differences among countries. Developing this business as a distributor or manufacturer's agent has advantages in flexibility and better control of investment.

The trick is to find products that have long-term durability and can survive the gyrations of politically inspired changes in tariffs or other situations beyond individual control. And remember—this is one type of business that stands to be massively affected by the passage of the North American Free Trade Agreement (NAFTA). Initial investment, $10,000–$25,000

Entrepreneur Group
2392 Morse Ave.
Irvine CA 92714
(714) 261-2325

Language translation and interpreting services

Translation and interpreting services can only expand as international trade expands and trade barriers fall. Also, the influx of immigrants to the United States opens the doors to more use of translation services in local government offices, the courts and legal system, health care settings and hospitals, and so forth. One possibility is to act, not as a translator yourself, but as a coordinator with a stable of interpreters and translators who work for you. Government grants may be available to pay for translators' services in public-service settings.

There are possibilities for both verbal simultaneous translation or interpreting and written translations of documents of all kinds. These opportunities may also grow as international tourism picks up and more foreigners come to the United States to visit. There will also be opportunities in schools at all levels and in many other settings. Initial investment, $2,500–$5,000.

American Translators Association
1735 Jefferson Davis Highway, #903
Arlington VA 22202
(703) 412-1500

Mobile automobile inspection

More and more people are buying used cars, but they are so busy working that it's hard for them to find the time to have their choice gone over by a mechanic. These buyers may be willing to pay a premium to a mechanic who will come to the car, check it out, and give them a written report on its condition. This is a diagnostic service only and does not involve repairs. You would do well to link up with a reputable repair service or services to which you could refer buyers. This business would logically be associated with an existing automotive service center of some sort—a mechanic, a body shop, or other general automotive service business. Initial investment, $10,000–$25,000.

Travel services

The world has millions of new potential travelers—for example, people living in the former Iron Curtain countries are now much freer to travel. There is an increasing demand for travel services of all types, not just for travel agents. Some of the more interesting opportunities for single operators include personal tour development, perhaps with specialties in history or architecture or opera or battlefields. By soliciting corporations, church groups, business groups, and others, you should be able to find enough clients to create a successful business. You make all the arrangements, including developing the program, arranging transportation, accommodations, sightseeing, lectures, insurance, and so on. Initial investment, $10,000–$25,000.

More Hot Prospects of All Kinds

- Activity centers for the elderly or disabled, coupled with personalized exercise and nutrition plans and even transportation/errand services; initial investment, $25,000–$50,000

- Automobile recovery and repossession services; initial investment, $5,000–$10,000

- Bus washing; initial investment, $5,000–$10,000

- Patrolling utility lines (electric transmission, gas, pipelines); initial investment, $2,500–$5,000

- Personal affairs management (resembles errand service but is more extensive); initial investment, $2,500–$5,000

- Restaurant reservation services; initial investment, $2,500–$5,000

- Tour agencies geared to foreign travelers who are visiting the United States on visitors' visas to see family members who have immigrated; initial investment, $10,000–$25,000

- Truck washing; initial investment, $5,000–$10,000

- Vehicle title and registration errands services; initial investment, $2,500–$5,000

- Waxing and polishing vehicles at customer's location; initial investment, $2,500–$5,000

Getting Started and Staying Alive

I believe that the businesses listed above will continue to be hot prospects despite—and in fact due to—the Forces of Change discussed in chapter 3. They are particularly attractive today because businesses that can generate fast cash flow are greatly sought after by hundreds of thousands of former corporate technicians, managers, and skilled laborers who are seeking new forms of employment.

Professionals involved in business brokerage will tell you that these offer some of the best opportunities around for these reasons:

- They're relatively easy to develop and control.
- You can keep them small and highly specialized, or they can expand into large businesses with correspondingly large cash flow.
- You can perform the service personally or develop a structure in which you focus on managing and marketing the service and hire temporary or part-time employees to carry out the actual work.

I foresee great and continuing demand for dependable services in these "families" of small businesses. If you can operate yours with the same professionalism you'd bring to any traditional professional practice, a good customer base should quickly follow.

It's almost impossible to exaggerate the demand for dependable, quality, fast service in all these businesses. To be sure, there may be competition, but too many companies offer sloppy, careless, and generally undependable service. That's your real opportunity to succeed—you can be different! The niche for reliable, professional, high-quality service is wide open and always will be, and this should become your goal.

As I have emphasized, these types of businesses have a major advantage in that few of them require that you lease or buy expensive, location-sensitive office or store space. Your only location-related needs are office and storage space. There is no reason why this type of business cannot be headquartered from your home. If you need more space for storage, you can always rent (on a short-term basis) a small warehouse or garage.

Your actual services are in many instances carried out at your customers' location. Depending on your specialty, you may also need space to park trucks or other vehicles, but this kind of space is easy to find, and you can cut costs by looking for it in less expensive areas of your community. Also, if you need help, it will be easy for you to find temporary workers. You may even wish to subcontract out certain jobs.

If you make super service your byword from the day you open up shop, you will create a solid foundation for good cash flow rewards and future growth. However, you must stay on top of what's going on as you expand and begin hiring more temporary and permanent help. Remember, quality control is the secret of success in all these businesses.

ATTRACTING BUSINESS THROUGH ADVERTISING AND PROMOTION

Your best strategy for finding customers is by simple advertising in the Yellow Pages or by distributing flyers door-to-door or at shopping centers. But you should couple this with efforts to network, which should generate a few large projects. As time goes on, your satisfied customers will become your best advertisements, and you should obtain a good deal of business from word-of-mouth referrals.

Networking and developing your contacts will take patience, and you will have to pay constant attention to providing timely, professional-quality service.

The least expensive and fastest way to promote a new business is to do as much of it yourself as you can initially. This gives you "I've been there" exposure, which will be very valuable as your business grows. More important, it allows you to meet potential customers and clients personally, to determine firsthand where the potential business lies and what the real needs are. Another advantage is that your prospects will know you are really interested in them. These initial business promotions will be surveys, too. They will allow you to narrow your focus on a niche market and to explore it thoroughly.

For example, assume you've decided to go into the janitorial business. First you decide where it should be located. A study of the Yellow Pages will give you a clue as to who your possible competitors are and what they do. You think you find a possible void—you realize that service station and car wash restrooms are not generally clean or well-maintained. You come up with a series of ideas involving a periodic maintenance service, replacement equipment, supplies, security systems, decorating ideas, cost-saving programs, and so forth. Now you contact large distributors and major oil companies who serve the retail outlets. You work on selling them your service. If you're successful, you've created an agency-type client—you've not made just one sale, you've made many. Now you serve that client well! You do exactly what you said you would do, and you do it in a timely fashion. When you have a complaint, you handle it now! That's your best follow-up advertising. You'll grow by referrals from pleased customers. You'll stand out, because your competitors are not going to look anywhere near as good as you do.

HIRING MORE HELP

Many of the businesses listed in this chapter offer wide-open opportunities for referral or subcontracting services in which your business would become a center for people who want to do certain kinds of work. These people would let you know when they're available, and you would have already made contacts with potential customers in the ways described earlier. You then match up the workers with the customers. These types of operations are fee-based, and you will have to decide whom to charge. If you charge your customers, it could be difficult to collect small amounts and control your receivables, especially when dealing with individuals as opposed to established businesses. One solution would be to collect fees in advance from customers.

Another option is to charge your "employees" or subcontractors. If they are paid on a day-to-day basis, then they can return and pay you your fee. However, if you hire people as contractors, you must be sure to follow all applicable tax laws and labor regulations.

In Conclusion

Any of the businesses described in this chapter can be developed into a successful, full-time, long-term, and very profitable enterprise. Also, it will be worthwhile to talk with owners of similar established businesses and with business brokers about businesses for sale that could be improved for greater efficiency and profitability. In any event, there's nothing wrong with starting one of these businesses and letting it grow—so that someday you can be the seller of a successful entrepreneurial business.

Endnotes

1. Nan Stone, "Does Business Have Any Business in Education?" *Harvard Business Review,* March–April 1991, 46–62.
2. Elizabeth M. Brack and Julie R. Grace, "Sorry, Right Number," *Time,* 13 September 1993, 66.

CHAPTER 6

Businesses to Approach with Caution

The businesses profiled and listed in chapter 5 are opportunities that I believe offer the greatest potential today, particularly for small start-up operations. This chapter, on the other hand, describes more than 170 businesses that are much riskier, particularly for newcomers. Each of these businesses falls into one of four major categories, based in general on the key factor of location sensitivity. The categories are as follows:

1. Professional and related service businesses

These businesses almost always require specific advanced education and training as well as some form of state certification or licensing. Clients may come to the place of business, so a nonresidential location may be preferable, although not essential.

2. Service businesses that usually require more than one or two people to operate them

These businesses usually require a nonretail location where employees and contractors can meet and equipment can be stored and serviced. Because these are usually nonprofessional businesses, special education or licensing is not generally needed. However, training in the form of courses and programs at local education institutions or through seminars offered by trade associations is desirable.

3. Businesses that involve services, product sales, or a combination of services and products

These businesses may not require a specific location, but some kind of nonretail location other than the home is usually preferable.

4. Businesses that usually involve the sale or supplying of products to the public

These are highly location-sensitive businesses. Without a special location, it may be difficult to survive, not to mention succeed, in these businesses—no matter what other positive attributes the business may possess.

Businesses That Are In for Tough Sledding

The following comments and cautions apply to many of the specific businesses evaluated and discussed in this chapter. Businesses subject to the following trends and forces should be approached only with the utmost caution, if at all:

1. Businesses that may be replaced by new telecommunications technology or interactive video and cannot be converted to take advantage of these innovations

For example, independent and chain video rental stores as we know them today may become obsolete by the end of the decade as more and more movies become available through increasingly sophisticated telecommunications systems. Telephone answering services are another good example because answering machines and voice mail are more convenient and less expensive.

Before taking the plunge into any business, look around and make sure there's not something coming down the line that is going to replace it.

2. Businesses that require the use of toxic materials

Print shops, paint stores, dry cleaning, and other businesses that use solvents or potentially toxic materials are subject to very restrictive licensing. The existing equipment in a shop may not meet current code requirements, and new equipment is expensive to purchase, operate, and maintain.

3. Businesses that are facing direct competition from discount superstores

If you can develop a special niche market for your product or service, you may not have to worry about direct competition from discount superstores. But if you don't have that niche, don't fight the big guys. It's not worth it. Instead, put your energy and money into something that has a market but doesn't face such high-powered competition. Beginning a new business venture is usually tough enough—don't compound the problem unnecessarily.

Smaller retailers must offer exceptional personal service to offset the higher prices they must charge. Nevertheless, low price is a tough competitor. The big guys have not only lower fixed costs for such items as real estate but also the big advantage of quantity-purchase discounts from manufacturers. The little guy must be in a highly visible—which usually means more expensive—location, whereas the big guy can often operate from a more out-of-the-way location and much less expensive site.

And although small retailers often excel in the area of after-purchase service, customers may never get the opportunity to experience this; if their original purchase is from a superstore, they are encouraged to return there for after-purchase needs and added merchandise sales. In short, the trend away from the smaller, more expensive player is growing and appears irreversible.

Here is a list of some common, traditional businesses—most of them retail—that are under threat from discount superstores:

Groceries

Photographic equipment and supplies

Apparel of all types

Toys and games

Videos, music cassettes, and compact disks

Automotive parts

Office furnishings, equipment, and supplies

Audio books

Bedroom, bathroom, and kitchen furnishings, equipment, and supplies

Athletic and sporting goods

Hardware

Building supplies

General merchandise

Baby furnishings

Consumer electronics

Drugs and sundries

Bookstores

Nursery and garden supplies

4. Automotive services

Businesses that focus on automotive or truck fuel or repairs generally should be avoided unless you are uniquely qualified, and even then these businesses are potentially high-risk. There are a number of reasons for this. Even though profit margins can be good, there are problems. Toxics and contamination often result in expensive cleanups and lawsuits. Also, often there's difficulty in reselling these businesses because of potential contamination problems.

Gasoline stations have their share of special problems. Profit margins have declined, and major-brand franchise dealers are facing closures by their suppliers. Some major oil companies are reducing the number of outlets they serve because the real estate for many existing locations no longer represents the highest and best use of the land, or refineries are too far removed and the cost to supply is too high.

5. Restaurants

There's probably only one thing you need to know about restaurants: Whether they're small or large, restaurants have a very high failure rate. Furthermore, food services of all types are increasingly subject to expensive litigation. Alleged food poisoning seems to be particularly problematic.

Fancy, high-priced eateries have an especially hard time in weak economic times, but the fancy place is not the only one in trouble. The little donut outlet is finding its profit margin very thin these days, too. Food service, whether in the form of a fast-food outlet or a full-service restaurant, requires a significant up-front cash investment. Furthermore, restaurant owners face a full complement of special hurdles in the form of sanitary, fire, and other local, state, and federal codes. On top of everything else, it's very hard work. Restaurants are cash businesses that require constant personal attention to what's going on.

Very few people really know how to run a restaurant. It isn't as easy as you think. It's not generally recommended for the independent operator. Hooking up with a franchise may be better, but that's no free lunch either (no pun intended). Many franchisors are engaged in lawsuits with their franchisees over breach of contract, insufficient advertising, and other service support and misrepresentation regarding potential profits.

If you insist in entering the food-service business, keep it small, *small, SMALL!* Try a food cart in a shopping mall or other high-traffic location—a good hot dog is always popular. Besides, it's always nice to have a business where your customers have only one basic decision to make—with or without mustard. In keeping with the niche-market principle, a deli operation in an office building or complex can be very profitable when properly operated. You will always have a captive audience for quick breakfasts, lunches, and snacks. And if your food is especially good, you can probably generate some catering business, too.

Unless you're already very experienced with the food business and have substantial financial resources, the best advice is to go slow, think twice (and then three or four times), take a cold shower—and then see if there isn't another type of business that interests you.

YOUR CAUTION LIST OF RISKIER BUSINESSES

Note: The comments offered here for specific businesses may also hold true for other businesses that share similar characteristics but are not listed. For example, comments about the substantial investment in inventory needed for hardware stores also apply to other retail businesses that demand a wide range of relatively expensive merchandise. Also, wherever possible, we have given current information for professional or trade associations, but these are subject to change.

Advertising services

These types of businesses cover a broad range of specialized services aimed at promoting the sale and marketing of goods and services to consumers and other businesses. Advertising services can include consulting on advertising and promotion programs, developing promotional products, and creating advertising from concept to final design, as well as placing advertising in print media, radio, and television. Success in this area usually requires specialized education, training, and experience, although if you have good sales skills and talents, you might enter advertising through the client development function. However, this is a high-risk business for the small operator, and it can take a substantial amount of time for such a business to develop and mature to a reasonable cash flow level.

American Association of Advertising Agencies
666 Third Ave., 13th Floor
New York NY 10017
(212) 682-2500

Antiques and collectibles store

This specialized retail business includes several categories, among them the selective, high-quality antique specialist; the specialist in reproduction copies; the specialist in bottles or other collectibles; the generalist who will sell a mixture of junk and treasures; and the flea-market seller. You can conduct these businesses from a variety of locations—from a retail store, country home, or barn, for example. Or you might follow swap meets and flea markets, or use a combination of both permanent location and mobile selling. However, there is a great deal of competition, and true antiques are becoming harder and harder to find—they are usually found at estate sales, but supplies are limited and demand is substantial. As was mentioned in chapter 5, one way to enter this business is by selling at swap meets, initially as a weekend activity rather than full time. If you want to develop these activities into a full-time business, you'll need not only capital but also a substantial investment of patience and time before you attain enough positive cash flow to ensure a steady income.

Associated Antique Dealers of America
1798 Midlothian St.
Sarasota FL 34234
(813) 351-1148

Appraisal service

These professional services estimate the value of property or other assets such as machinery and equipment, businesses, and vehicles. Today, appraisers who wish to work in activities such as home financing that involve federal funds must be state-licensed or certified. The same is not generally true for equipment and business appraisers at present, but this may change at some point in the future. For appraisal disciplines, some form of special training and association with a professional society as a designated member should be a goal, and it is certainly preferable for building a long-term business. The appraisal profession is growing as litigation, tax laws, estate planning, and the like become more complex and the public realizes the need for expert assistance in these areas. However, getting into this profession, no matter what your specialty, requires a substantial amount of time as well as specialized education. This field can be the basis for an excellent long-term practice with excellent financial rewards—if you have the necessary educational background and can support yourself during the substantial amount of time it will take to gain recognition among clients who are willing to refer other business to you. When you are starting out, you can contract out for services such as clerical help on an as-needed basis. Clients may come to the business, so a nonresidential location may be preferable, although not always essential. As in any professional practice, there is always the risk that clients may perceive, rightly or wrongly, that they have been given bad advice; liability insurance covering malpractice or errors and omissions is therefore advisable.

Appraisal Institute
875 N. Michigan Ave., #2400
Chicago IL 60611-1980
(312) 335-4100

Art and graphics supplies store

These semi-specialized stores sell supplies and equipment for artists and graphic designers. Some stores may offer art lessons to children and adults, or workshops with artists from the surrounding community. Because this type of business involves products for sale, it is particularly location-sensitive as well as being vulnerable to competition from discount stores.

Art gallery or art dealer

These specialized retail businesses, which exhibit original or limited-edition art works such as paintings and sculptures for sale to collectors, are virtually professional businesses that require a high degree of skill and experience. They cannot be recommended for the novice. Cash flow rewards can be significant, but it takes a great deal of time to develop a reputation and clientele. Furthermore, there is a great deal of competition.

Art Dealers Association of America
575 Madison Ave.
New York NY 10022
(212) 940-8590

Artisans and crafts workers

There will always be a demand for quality, handmade products by de-signer-producers of one-of-a-kind or limited-edition handcrafted items such as ceramics, glassware and needlework to be sold at art shows, fairs, gift stores, and other locations. However, this type of business requires very special skills. Assuming that you have these skills, it is then a matter of self-promotion, which you can do primarily by making personal contact with outlets such as special distributors, gift stores, and other retailers, or through print media advertising. It is usually feast or famine for individual craft-type activities (including artists). You might do better to focus on finding a permanent outlet, such as a retail store, where you can sell your products, and you might even consider actually working in the store as a sales clerk, selling not only your own work but also general merchandise and crafts produced by others. In this way, you can gain a better understanding of what the public really wants and how better to promote your skills.

Watermark Association of Artisans
150 Highway 158 E
PO Box 397
Camden NC 27921
(919) 338-0853

Athletic supplies store (also Sporting goods stores)

This category covers a wide range of retail businesses that sell sporting goods, sports equipment, sports clothing, and other sports-related items. Also included are specialty stores that cater to one specific sport, such as golf, tennis, or swimming. Stores that specialize in fitness equipment also fall into this category. All of these businesses are facing a great deal of competition, particularly from the big discount chains.

The problem for an individual or small business operator is to find a niche in some special market, such as a resort area. It is extremely difficult to build a significant cash flow in this business, and you should count on several years before a satisfactory level is reached. This type of business is not generally recommended for a solo operator or as a start-up business unless you have substantial capital and specialized experience. It would be helpful to have experience not just with the products themselves but also in organizing hiking tours, biking tours, ski weekends, and other outings, or sponsoring junior athletic teams. The latter activities could make a significant contribution to cash flow, but again the level of competition should not be discounted.

National Sporting Goods Association
Lake Center Plaza Building
1699 Wall St.
Mount Prospect IL 60056-5780
(708) 439-4000

Auctioneer

Auctioneers are authorized to sell personal property and business assets, including cars, jewelry, business items, works of art, and other items, to prospective buyers at public auction sales. They need not always be separately licensed, although they usually are and hold some form of real estate license. Auctioneers often specialize in handling only real property, or only machinery and equipment, or only fine art, antiques, and so forth. An auctioneer may work as an individual on a contract basis or develop a business that involves warehousing goods to be auctioned in his or her own facility. Or auctions may be held at the home or business where the items are located.

This business can be relatively complex in that it requires not only considerable knowledge of the value of properties to be auctioned but also a blend of professionalism and showmanship. Once you develop some special skill and a reputation, you can go on your own. It is possible to work as a contractor without needing to have a facility where you can store the merchandise you will be auctioning. However, it can take a substantial period of time for you to develop a good reputation, which will happen as word-of-mouth advertising takes hold.

National Auctioneers Association
8880 Ballantine
Overland Park KS 66214
(913) 541-8084

Audio bookstore

In recent years, a growing number of semi-specialized stores have focused on retail sales of audiocassette tapes, particularly books on tape, educational materials, seminars, and other audio programming. There is a good demand for these products, both as rentals and for purchase, but there is also growing competition from such diverse outlets as neighborhood supermarkets as well as other specialized video and cassette tape stores. A substantial capital investment is involved, and it can take a considerable time to build up enough patronage that you can develop a satisfactory cash flow. This is a good example of a highly location-sensitive business, with all the risks that implies.

Entrepreneur Group
2392 Morse Ave.
Irvine CA 92714
(714) 261-2325

Automobile dealership, new

The retail business of selling new cars and other types of motor vehicles, which may also include automobile leasing and the sale of used cars as well, is a franchise business that requires a substantial cash investment. Automobile dealerships are a prime example of the highly location-sensitive business. If this business interests you, you should possess some knowledge of the automobile business in general. This is not recommended as a start-up business for an individual, especially if you are looking for short-term cash flow. Bear in mind also that automobile manufacturers have strict requirements regarding location, types of facilities, and financial capability when they select dealers.

National Automobile Dealers Association
8400 Westpark Dr.
McLean VA 22102
(703) 821-7000

Automobile dealership, used

Many new-car dealers also have substantial retail used-car operations; in fact, the used-car department of a new-car dealership is often the most profitable. If you are starting out, you may find it much easier to get into the used-car business than into a new car dealership franchise. Many people literally get into this business as a sideline based in their garage—they buy automobiles at auctions or from some other discount source, carry out the necessary repairs themselves, and then resell the vehicles. However, as a start-up business, this is not a dependable source of steady cash flow, and long-term longevity is also questionable. Also, as with new-car dealerships, location is critical. This type of business is often carried out in conjunction with some other auto-repair specialty such as body work, painting, frame work, tires, or mechanical work, and perhaps it makes more sense to operate that way.

National Automobile Dealers Association
8400 Westpark Dr.
McLean VA 22102
(703) 821-7000

Automobile detailing

This type of service specializes in providing quality cleaning and cos-
metic automobile maintenance, usually but not only for individual passenger cars. You should be able to rent or sublet appropriate working
space from a car wash, service station, local garage, or auto repair facility.
You might also work as a contractor for these types of businesses. Auto
detailing is simple to get into and requires relatively little in the way of
start-up costs and initial investment. However, you may come up against
zoning restrictions if you decide to open a freestanding facility rather
than subleasing space from another automotive-related business. You
need very little equipment; the main requirement is a willingness to work
hard.

As your business gains a reputation through word of mouth or simple
advertising, you can turn the actual detailing work over to employees
and spend more time marketing your service. In this way, your operation
can gradually evolve into a more formalized small business with a reasonable future. There is a relatively strong demand for this service, both
from automobile dealers who need detailing for cars to be resold and
for new cars being readied for delivery, as well as from individuals who
want their car's appearance kept up on a regular basis.

However, this is not an asset-building business; rather, it is strictly a
service activity, and you may face substantial competition. Established
detailing businesses operate at a specific location, similar to any automotive service business, but they usually connect with new-car dealerships and depend on them for a steady flow of referrals.

Paint, Body and Equipment Association
9140 Ward Pkwy.
Kansas City MO 64114
(816) 444-3500

Automobile parts store (also Tire store)

This type of retail business sells automobile and vehicle parts, equipment, and supplies and may also offer other items such as yard maintenance equipment. Gasoline service stations frequently sell parts also,

and freestanding and franchise auto parts stores are common. This is an asset-intensive business that requires large inventories and thus a substantial amount of working capital, in addition to the cost of fixtures, equipment, and so forth. These businesses are also somewhat location-specific and thus require ownership of real estate or a long-term lease to develop locational security. As a single operator, you may be able to develop a reasonable long-term business, although profit margins are usually thin, and you will probably face a great deal of competition from gasoline service stations, freestanding and franchise auto parts stores, and even discount superstores.

Paint, Body and Equipment Association
9140 Ward Pkwy.
Kansas City MO 64114
(816) 444-3500

Automobile rental agencies

These businesses specialize in renting automobiles, usually on a short-term basis, to traveling businesspeople and tourists. Some agencies specialize in supplying automobiles to dealerships and auto repair businesses when customer vehicles are being repaired. Some car rental businesses offer rent-to-own or leasing programs in which renters can buy vehicles at the end of the contract period or turn the vehicle in for a newer model. This industry is dominated by major operators such as Hertz, Avis, Budget, Thrifty, Dollar, National, and others. However, there are also scores of small independent operators who have found niche markets for themselves.

   In general, this is not the type of business that you can operate successfully as a single individual, and it can be difficult to develop satisfactory cash flow. It is somewhat location-sensitive, which means investing in real estate or a long-term lease. Profit margins can be thin even for established agencies.You will also need to put a great deal of effort into promotional activities and advertising to attract customers who may then generate referrals.

American Car Rental Association
927 15th St. NW, #1000
Washington DC 20005
(202) 789-2240

Automotive service (all types)

This category covers businesses that offer a wide range of specialized automobile maintenance services. The cash flow potential is poorest at the general mechanical repair level and improves as the business becomes more focused and specialized in such areas as lubrication, tune-ups, brake work, mufflers, auto glass, and so forth. One of the highest cash flow developers is the shop that handles painting exclusively, as distinguished from a body and paint shop. However, all automotive services are subject to problems related to environmental concerns such as soil contamination and air quality.

Automotive Service Association
PO Box 929
Bedford TX 76095-0929
(817) 283-6205

Baby store

All categories of this type of retail business, which offer a specialized range of products such as furniture, toys, clothes, and books, have good revenue potential and high margins and cash flow benefits, assuming that you are not facing too much competition. Smaller businesses in these categories always have a problem competing with the heavy discounts that the major chains can offer. These businesses are all highly location-sensitive. However, demographics today favor these kinds of businesses, and your best chances of success as an independent store operator are probably in communities where there is little or no competition and where you can focus on one product type such as children's apparel, books, furniture, and toys.

Entrepreneur Group
2392 Morse Ave.
Irvine CA 92714
(714) 261-2325

Babysitting referral services

This referral business, which specializes in referring babysitters to clients, can easily be operated by one person. You can get started by doing some simple advertising and promotion and by developing a reputation for complete dependability. Your background must be impeccable, as must that of the babysitters you send into clients' homes. This type of business has become increasingly vulnerable to lawsuits—not just because of growing societal concerns about child sexual abuse, but also because of the possibility of accidents or injuries to your babysitters' charges.

There has always been a need for this type of service, and it is growing with the number of two-breadwinner families. However, families usually find babysitters on a referral basis from among teenagers in the immediate neighborhood. This means that there is substantial competition in terms of price. If you decide to operate a formal service, your higher operating costs mean you will have to charge higher fees than the neighborhood teenagers do. This cannot be highly rated as a dependable, long-term business—rather, it is better viewed as a casual activity you can carry out on the side for supplemental income.

Private Care Association
1276 McConnell Dr., #A
Decatur GA 30033
(404) 982-9636

Bakery

Independent retail bakeries that specialize in selling such goods as breads, pastries, and cakes can be attractive and highly profitable. This is especially true if you are located in a smaller community where you can become known for offering signature specialties. It is also becoming popular to have a semi-restaurant or coffee shop operation, sometimes even with table service. In the right location, this can attract considerable added patronage. However, like all food businesses, bakeries require that you as owner pay close attention to every detail so that you become known for offering consistent quality. This means that you must be there most of the time if you are to realize maximum profit potential.

In addition, most communities impose stringent public health standards on any business that involves preparing and serving food to the public. It can be expensive and time-consuming to comply with all the applicable state and local codes and laws. Even if you are only baking pies or cheesecakes or preparing other food in your home, you may have to meet the same requirements that would apply if you had a restaurant location. For example, there may be standards regarding plumbing, double or triple sinks, dishwashers, refrigeration systems, food preparation tables, or drainage systems. Compliance can be very expensive. Nonetheless, if you are willing to work hard and can meet these requirements, the cash flow potential is very good.

Independent Bakers Association
1223 Potomac St. NW
Washington DC 20007
(202) 333-8190

Home Baking Association
2150 W. 29th Ave., #425
Denver CO 80211
(303) 455-5100

Balloon delivery services

These businesses, which deliver customized balloons for birthdays, anniversaries, retirement parties, get-well-soon greetings, and other occasions, are one example of a wide range of specialized gift and party-focused delivery businesses. The cash flow potential is only fair; also, businesses like these are highly fadlike, so you should not depend on market acceptance over the long term.

Entrepreneur Group
2392 Morse Ave.
Irvine CA 92714
(714) 261-2325

Banquet and party equipment rentals

These are service-type businesses that specialize in renting party and banquet equipment. In addition to equipment rental, party and banquet supplies are usually offered for sale. This type of business requires a substantial capital investment and usually a specific location, which means more expense for the purchase or long-term lease of real estate. It can take time to establish a reputation for quality and reliable service. However, as you become established and are able to pay for and amortize your banquet and party equipment, this can develop into a good cash generator.

American Rental Association
1900 19th St.
Moline IL 61265
(309) 764-2475

Bar (also Tavern)

These cash-type businesses, which sell alcoholic and nonalcoholic beverages and sometimes light food items, require your close attention and participation as owner if they are to realize their potential. Bars and taverns can readily gain a bad reputation if they are not carefully monitored by the owner. These businesses almost always require special licensing and are highly location-sensitive.

Entrepreneur Group
2392 Morse Ave.
Irvine CA 92714
(714) 261-2325

Barber shop (also Hair stylist)

These types of businesses provide hair specialists to cut and style clients' hair. Some salons may offer manicures, pedicures, and cosmetological services. These businesses are highly location-sensitive and are usually structured with an owner renting booths or stations to other hair and nail specialists. These businesses are not as salable as they used to be. There is a great deal of competition, and profit margins are directly related to how hard you want to work. If you wish to buy or open one of these businesses, there will be a requirement for the lease or ownership of a good location and the cost of fixturing.

National Cosmetology Association
3510 Olive St.
St. Louis MO 63103
(314) 534-7980

Beauty supply store

These types of retail business, which sell beauty aids such as facial care and hair care products as well as cosmetics, are part of a multibillion-dollar consumer market for beauty products. The dangers you would face include fad products and an immense amount of competition from other retailers, including discount superstores. The cash flow will probably be modest. These are highly location-sensitive businesses with the attendant problems of finding adequate leased or purchased space.

Beauty and Barber Supply Institute
271 US Highway 46 W, #F-209

Fairfield NJ 07004-2415
(201) 808-7444

Bed and bath store

Generally these types of businesses, which specialize in selling beds, mattresses, comforters, sheets, and related products, share many characteristics of furniture businesses. They require a high capital investment in inventory and generally face a great deal of competition as well as low profit margins. These businesses are usually location-sensitive and thus require either ownership or a long-term lease on real estate.

American Down Association
3728 Canna St.
Sacramento CA 95821
(916) 971-1135

Bed and breakfast establishments

In the last 20 years, bed and breakfasts, which offer rooms and board in private homes, have become very popular throughout the United States. In fact, there is probably no resort area—or nonresort area—that does not have an ample share. There is thus tremendous competition, and in some areas a great deal of resistance from already established hostelries as well. The major problems with this type of business are related to the close attention that you as owner must pay to its every detail. You must be cook, maid, scheduler, controller of activities—everything! In addition, the money you will receive for your services will usually be modest at best. Another problem, of course, is that this type of business requires ownership or control of real estate with a long-term lease. In short, this is not a good business if your prime concern is cash flow—it's one you must love.

American Bed and Breakfast Association
1407 Huguenot Rd.
Midlothian VA 23113-2644
(804) 379-2222

Bicycle shop

These businesses, which engage in the retail sale of bicycles and their parts and may offer bikes for rental as well, tend to be most successful when the owner directly participates in all facets of the activity. Bicycle shops do better in areas that are high in recreation demand, but today there is usually a great deal of competition, not only from other small local businesses, but also from large discount retailers.

National Bicycle Dealers Association
2240 University Dr., #130
Newport Beach CA 92660
(714) 722-6909

Boat and canoe dealer

These retail businesses, which sell new and used motorboats, canoes, and boat-related products, generally do best in recreational areas and when the owner takes a direct part in all aspects of the operation. These days there is usually a great deal of competition.

Marine Retailers Association of America
150 E. Huron St., #802
Chicago IL 60611-2912
(312) 944-5080

Boat cleaning and repair service

This type of business, which offers general maintenance as well as cleaning for boats, canoes, kayaks, and other vessels, will be seasonal depending on where you are in the United States. In warmer regions, there is often a year-round need for boat services such as bottom cleaning, which can be done while the boat is still in the water. In more severe northern climates, boats are generally hauled in for the winter, and services such as painting, varnishing, and refitting would be carried out in dry dock. One way to become established is by working as an independent contractor with boatyards that can refer clients to you for services. Given the degree of attachment boat owners have to their vessels, quality of service is your most important marketing asset.

National Association of Service Dealers
c/o National Association of Retail Dealers of America
10 E. 22nd St., #310
Lombard IL 60148
(708) 953-8950

Bookstore

Although the major chain operators increasingly dominate the bookstore scene in the United States, there is still a place for the independent bookstore, particularly in smaller communities. Your chances of success are greatest if you can create a unique atmosphere that will attract repeat patronage. Also, specialized stores, such as children's bookstores or detective-story bookstores, are immensely popular and can be very profitable in areas where there is not too much competition. Like all retail businesses, location is crucial, and running a bookstore requires a good deal of savvy. Inventory must be up-to-date and is easily damaged, which can be a problem.

American Booksellers Association
828 S. Broadway
Tarrytown NY 10591
(800) 637-0037

Bowling center

These businesses are highly capital-intensive in terms of real estate and special equipment. Modern bowling centers usually include a minimum of 32 lanes with automatic pin-setting equipment, computerized score-keeping, a pro shop, lounges for beer, wine, and mixed drinks, a coffee shop, and even a full-service restaurant. Profitability is usually related to the center being used by a large number of bowling leagues. Profit margins are fair, and competition is great in most areas.

Bowling Proprietors Association of America
PO Box 5802
Arlington TX 76005
(817) 649-5105 or (800) 343-1329

Business brokerage

Most states require licensing for this type of service business. In most cases the same license that applies to a real estate broker also applies to business brokerages. However, there are still a few states in which a formal business brokerage license may not be required. The time is probably good for developing this kind of business, and once established, this can be a good cash flow business. Like most professional services, it is a matter of developing a good reputation.

International Business Brokers Association
PO Box 704
Concord MA 01742
(508) 369-2490

Camera and photo supply store

There is a great deal of competition from the large discounters for retail sales of cameras, photo supplies, and photo processing. However, there is always a need for this service in niche markets. Developing a photo processing operation requires a substantial capital investment in equipment and can take time to establish. The near-term cash flow is minimal.

Association of Professional Color Laboratories
3000 Picture Pl.
Jackson MI 49201
(517) 788-8146

Campground

This type of business, which offers recreational facilities for a daily fee per campsite, is highly seasonal and requires a significant capital investment via ownership or leasing of land and the construction of facilities. The availability of land for sale or development is increasingly limited. Campgrounds are generally considered high-risk. Usually, this type of activity is done in association with another more stable business, for example a nearby convenience store or service station that can generate compensatory year-round income.

National Campground Owners Association
11307 Sunset Hills Rd., #137
Reston VA 22090
(703) 471-0143

Candy store

This type of retail store, which specializes in selling candies and other types of confectionery products, has the greatest chance of success in a niche market. Businesses like this do best in small communities such as resorts where there is minimal competition from other specialty stores and customers are prone to impulse purchases. To be successful, this type of business, like other specialty retail operations, requires direct participation by the owner in making candy and other activities. It would probably take a considerable period of time before the business developed enough to provide you with a satisfactory positive cash flow.

National Confectionery Salesmen's Association of America
4 Baxter Pl.
Pequannock NJ 07440
(201) 696-7806

Car wash, coin-operated

These businesses, which offer mechanical washing services for automobiles and other vehicles, can be quite successful in the right location. The main problems with coin-operated car washes, which may be drive-throughs or simply stalls equipped with the appropriate washing and rinsing equipment, are proper zoning and obtaining real estate by ownership or lease. Once you obtain a location and the equipment is in place, customers come in and wash their own vehicles. Coin-operated car washes are simple-to-operate cash businesses and can be extremely profitable in areas exposed to a relatively heavy flow of traffic. However, locations for any automotive-related service are increasingly difficult to find. Ideally, your strategy should be to open or obtain a number of such operations to ensure an adequate income so you can devote most of your time to maintaining the real estate, facilities, and equipment.

International Carwash Association
1 East 22nd St., #400
Lombard IL 60148
(708) 495-0100

Car wash, full-tunnel

This type of service specializes in automatic car washing by use of a chain-driven tunnel mechanism. Hand detailing may be offered as an option, and the facility may provide other detailing services such as waxing and polishing. Some are associated with gasoline service stations. Full-tunnel car washes require substantial investment in real estate by ownership or lease and usually ownership of the equipment, including the tunnel building. These businesses can be extremely profitable at the proper location. However, they require a great deal of labor, and you as owner must be prepared for day-to-day direct participation and control. It's beneficial to offer supplementary services such as car detailing and fuel. Location is a major problem because finding a proper site that is also properly zoned for such a business can be difficult. These businesses are often offered for sale, but relatively few are sufficiently profitable to amortize the heavy up-front costs in real estate and equipment and at the same time offer an adequate income to you as owner. It can be very tricky to buy an existing car wash or to develop a new one at an untried location.

International Carwash Association
1 East 22nd St., #400
Lombard IL 60148
(708) 495-0100

Card shop

Like all retail businesses, card shops require direct participation by the owner. You must plan on spending a substantial period of time developing a steady clientele. Other requirements include significant capital investment in your location, by either ownership or long-term lease, and in needed inventory, equipment, and fixtures. You should plan on several years before you gain a positive cash flow over and above the costs of paying for and amortizing your investment. Furthermore, there is a great deal of competition. The best location for a card shop or any other specialty shop such as a gift shop or candy store is in a small community such as a resort area. However, business in such locations may also be highly seasonal.

Greeting Card Association
1200 G St. NW, #760
Washington DC 20005
(202) 393-1778

Cellular telephone dealer

There is substantial competition from both independents and large discounters in this type of business, which specializes in selling and servicing cellular telephones and related products. If you do decide to enter it, the best way to reach your market would probably be by advertising in the Yellow Pages and other media. It will take time to develop a regular customer base, but once established you may be able to realize a good cash flow. Bear in mind that this whole industry may change in directions that are difficult to foresee, given the rapid developments in electronic telecommunications.

Entrepreneur Group
2392 Morse Ave.
Irvine CA 92714
(714) 261-2325

Check cashing service

Check cashing services have long been offered as a convenience for people who, for a variety of reasons, may not wish to use traditional banking services. Revenues come from charging a per-transaction fee. Other services such as sales of money orders, wiring money, and sending telegrams have historically been associated with these businesses, and many now offer fax and other electronic communications services. These businesses may be completely independent operations or can be based in convenience stores, liquor stores, and so on. In either case, location is crucial, and therefore a significant commitment to real estate either by long-term lease or purchase is required. Also, special security improvements may be required to protect the safety of employees and customers alike. Once it is established, this business can be relatively profitable, particularly if you can become a center for the distribution of food stamps and other specialized services. Also keep in mind that traditional freestanding check cashing operations are meeting competition from other businesses, such as drugstores and supermarkets, that are increasingly offering similar services.

Entrepreneur Group
2392 Morse Ave.
Irvine CA 92714
(714) 261-2325

Child care center

These services, which specialize in the care of infants, preschoolers, and school-age children, require special real estate facilities that must conform with local building and zoning codes as well as state and even federal regulations. Thus, you could incur substantial costs while improving either owned or leased property. This type of business is also extremely vulnerable to lawsuits, and you must take great care in hiring your employees. On the other hand, there is great demand, particularly if you can develop a reputation for dependability and safety. This is a business in which you as owner must directly participate in every phase. The cash flow potential is limited because of the heavy up-front requirements. An alternative to this is to contract out your services to already-established facilities, or to facilities that might be improved by a landlord. In this case, all you would do as a contractor is run the business, ideally with little or no up-front investment. These businesses are often run from home, but there are other places such as churches and schools that have suitable facilities but whose owners or operators do not wish to become directly involved with child care. This is where you would probably find your best opportunities as a contractor. Another option is a referral service in which you would charge clients for lists of carefully screened individuals available for babysitting and general child care; this type of business would involve somewhat less risk and much less up-front capital.

National Association of Child Care Resource and Referral Agencies
2116 Campus Dr. SE
Rochester MN 55904
(507) 287-2220

Children's apparel store (see Baby store)

Children's bookstore (see also Baby store)

There is a growing trend toward this type of specialized bookstore, and if you can find a location that is relatively free of competition—even if there are already a number of established full-line bookstores in the area—you have the potential for substantial profit. Interior design is extremely important in this kind of store, and the sales clerks must be able to communicate effectively with both parents and children. Inventory is fragile and easily damaged, which can be a problem.

American Booksellers Association
828 S. Broadway
Tarrytown NY 10591
(800) 637-0037

Children's fitness centers

As schools cut back on exercise and fitness programs, fitness centers may fill the gap. However, liability for possible injuries can be a problem.

Christmas shop

This is a retail type of business that specializes in selling Christmas trees, ornaments, house decorations, and related items. Although highly seasonal, there is a growing trend for Christmas stores to remain open year-round. Such shops emphasize Christmas decorations but also have extended lines of other decorative items such as collectibles, candles, artwork, and items related to other holidays. If this business interests you, you should try to identify a niche market where there is minimal competition. Businesses like this tend to do well in small communities such as resorts. You can maximize your chances of success by maintaining a high level of direct participation in day-to-day operations. It can take a substantial period of time to develop a steady clientele in addition to your necessary capital investment in location, either by ownership or a long-term lease, and your needed equipment and inventory.

Entrepreneur Group
2392 Morse Ave.
Irvine CA 92714
(714) 261-2325

Christmas tree lot

The major problem with this type of business, which focuses on selling Christmas trees from parking lots and similar locations, is that it's either feast or famine. What often happens is that one year there'll be a shortage of Christmas trees—so the next year everyone opens a Christmas tree lot, and no one makes any money. Then the cycle goes to the next year and next year, and so on. The bottom line is: It's hard to make money in this type of business, and of course location is critical.

Entrepreneur Group
2392 Morse Ave.
Irvine CA 92714
(714) 261-2325

Clipping service

This is a specialty service business that involves clipping media information about people or events from newspapers, magazines, and other sources. You can work as a solo operator or with a small temporary staff to clip and send information to clients. The benefit to your clients is that it's difficult for them to read everything in their particular business or profession that might affect them. It would take time to develop a reputation and gain a steady clientele in this business, but once you are established you may see a fair, if spotty, cash flow. This business is best considered a part-time activity and is not dependable for a steady income. The more viable option is to move in the direction of electronic information services, as discussed in the Information Services section of chapter 5.

Entrepreneur Group
2392 Morse Ave.
Irvine CA 92714
(714) 261-2325

Closet design services

This contracting service, which specializes in creating customized closet designs for clients, requires design and construction skills. It is best started on an individual basis using minimal advertising such as handbills, the Yellow Pages, and so forth, as well as direct solicitation, and is therefore not highly location-sensitive. As you gain a good reputation over a period of time, you could see a steady and reasonably high level of cash flow. However, you will have to constantly promote and advertise if you are to maintain a reasonable level of patronage.

National Association of Home Builders of the United States
15th & M Streets NW
Washington DC 20005
(202) 822-0200

Clothing consulting (also Image consulting)

This is a highly personalized service activity that provides advice and recommendations to individual or organizational clients on how to dress and present oneself for greatest effectiveness. Consulting for business clients might include advice on the use of uniforms to enhance a company's image, receptionists' visual image and telephone manner, advertising, stationery, interior decoration, and so forth to communicate an image of success. It is best done on a part-time basis to begin with, and you cannot expect a high cash flow level for a considerable period of time. Developing a network of clients through word-of-mouth advertising is difficult but crucial.

Association of Image Consultants International
1000 Connecticut NW, #9
Washington DC 20036
(800) 383-8831

Coffeehouse

This is a combination retail/service business that sells coffee beans and coffee accessories as well as offering coffee and other beverages and snacks; entertainment may be offered in the evenings. Coffeehouses have been very popular in recent years—so much so that cash flow and margins appear to be declining because of competition. Here, as in most retail businesses, the owner must participate directly. Also, there can be a substantial cost of improvements in addition to a long-term lease at a key location.

Specialty Coffee Association of America
One World Trade Center, #800
Long Beach CA 90831
(310) 983-8090

Community welcoming service

This business, which plans welcoming events and activities for new community residents and businesses, is a consulting activity. To be successful, you will have to obtain sponsorship from local retail and service businesses that you will then represent to new residents and firms. It is best thought of as a part-time activity. One obstacle is growing resistance to telephone and other types of solicitation. So you may find it difficult to develop the right niche or specialty to reach a large enough audience and to develop a powerful formula for attracting patronage to your sponsors.

Entrepreneur Group
2392 Morse Ave.
Irvine CA 92714
(714) 261-2325

Computer equipment store

These businesses, which specialize in selling computer equipment including software, computers, and other related merchandise, are facing cutthroat competition not only from other small computer-related retailers but also from chain discounters. They are highly location-sensitive and must be visible to the public, which means being tied to a long-term lease as well as the necessary fixturing, inventory, and equipment. The potential cash flow from this type of business is fair at best for the independent operator. There are many more promising options, as suggested in the section on Computer Services in chapter 5.

ABCD: The Microcomputer Industry Association
1515 E. Woodfield Rd., #860
Schaumburg IL 60173-5437
(708) 240-1818 or (800) 333-9532

Computer software store

Like computer equipment stores, these businesses, which sell software and related merchandise, are under increasing pressure from large chain operators and discount superstores. The comments about computer equipment stores also apply to software operations. Proceed with caution if you are thinking about entering this business as an independent operator.

ABCD: The Microcomputer Industry Association
1515 E. Woodfield Rd., #860
Schaumburg IL 60173-5437
(708) 240-1818 or (800) 333-9532

Construction contracting services, general

General contractors carry out new construction, additions, alterations, remodelling, and repairs on residential and nonresidential buildings. This business requires a number of specific construction skills as well as some design aptitude, especially if you are working on your own and not with an outside designer or subcontracted labor. Hiring a staff to help carry out services will require a considerable up-front investment, so you would do best to start out on your own and advertise using handbills and the Yellow Pages as well as direct solicitation. As you gain a word-of-mouth reputation, you could see a steady and reasonably high level of cash flow. However, you will have to constantly promote and advertise in order to maintain a reasonable level of business.

National Association of Home Builders of the United States
15th & M Streets NW
Washington DC 20005
(202) 822-0200

Consulting service

Consulting can take a myriad of specific forms. Whatever the specifics, the basic service is the same—providing specialized, professional advice to individuals or businesses for a fee. There are many areas where consulting is needed, such as management, accounting, finance, and legal and technical matters, and these needs will increase as our society becomes more complex. Becoming established as a credible and competent consultant can take a long time and also requires specialized education in most instances. Your success will depend on clients who are willing to refer other business to you. However, you will not need a special location, and when you are starting out, you can contract out for specialized activities such as clerical help as needed. The ability to sell yourself and your special skills is vital in any consulting service.

American Consultants League
1290 Palm Ave.
Sarasota FL 34236
(813) 952-9290

Convenience store (also Mini-market)

These small retail stores sell canned and dry food and sometimes simple sandwiches, snacks, and hot beverages as well as toiletries, magazines, and newspapers. This can be one of the better businesses for producing cash flow, although there is substantial competition. Location is crucial, and you must have a location that is highly accessible to automobile and vehicle traffic. You will face a significant investment in a long-term lease or acquisition of real property plus fixturing and inventory. As with all retail businesses, you as owner must directly participate in controlling the business by being involved on a day-to-day basis.

National Association of Convenience Stores
1605 King St.
Alexandria VA 22314-2792
(703) 684-3600

Cookware store

This type of specialized retail store, which sells cooking utensils, dishes, pots, pans, and other related items, faces substantial competition from discount superstores unless you can find a niche market. Businesses like these can do well in small communities such as resorts where there is minimal competition. However, such locations can also be seasonal. You will need to be involved on a direct, day-to-day basis, and it can take a substantial period of time to develop a steady clientele. You must also anticipate a substantial capital investment in location by ownership or long-term lease, needed equipment, and inventory.

International Pot and Kettle Club
c/o Hall Simons
28742 Hedgerow
Mission Viejo CA 92692
(714) 951-3005

Copy service (also Instant printing shop)

This business provides copying, duplicating, and sometimes desktop publishing and fax service to the general public. There is a great deal of competition from office-supply discount superstores, franchises, and other small operators, but there is also always a need for these services in niche markets. Copy services share many characteristics with camera and photo supply stores. They require a special location and a substantial investment in equipment, either leased or purchased. It will take you some time to develop a reputation for dependability, quality work, and quick service. You would do best to start out by soliciting business from nearby office centers. This business is probably in for some technological changes, and you should be cautious in entering the arena unless you're aware of and prepared for these changes. Cash flow from this type of business is only modest to fair, primarily because of the competition.

National Association of Printers and Lithographers
780 Palisade Ave.
Teaneck NJ 07666
(201) 342-0705 or (800) 642-6275

Printing Industries of America
100 Dangerfield Rd.
Alexandria VA 22314
(703) 519-8100

Costume rental store

These are retail services that provide costumes for all occasions. As far as the general public is concerned, this business is quite seasonal. One way to proceed is to specialize in providing costumes for theatrical productions and other entertainment businesses. This business is highly location-sensitive, but word of mouth could work favorably for the business-to-business approach.

National Costumers Association
3038 Hayes Ave.
Fremont OH 43420
(419) 334-4098

Coupon mailing service

In this business, contractors work with vendors on a fee basis, usually packaging groups of coupons from various merchants and distributing them to mailing lists obtained from telephone directories or other sources. There is substantial competition from large, well-established companies that do this, and it can be difficult to break into this field unless you create a niche market not already covered by one of the big guys. The way to start marketing yourself is to personally visit local merchants and try to sign them up for a coupon mailing effort. Service stations, car washes, hardware stores, and other small independent merchant operations might be grouped together. This business can easily be run from a relatively inexpensive space or even from your home.

Association of Coupon Processors
500 N. Michigan Ave.
Chicago IL 60611
(312) 661-1700

Crafts (see Artisans and crafts workers)

Dating service

These are highly personalized services that attempt to help individuals meet others on a social level. This is a high-risk and very competitive area. Major companies are saturating the market with direct-mail advertising. It may be possible to succeed as a solo operator in a local market, but it would take time to create a good reputation. Technological changes such as interactive video may open up new opportunities, but as of now the financial and regulatory aspects are unclear.

International Society of Introduction Services
PO Box 31408

San Francisco CA 94131
(415) 777-9769

Delicatessen

These food establishments sell assorted sandwiches, salads, and beverages. They may offer sit-down as well as takeout service. Location is crucial, so you will face a significant investment in a long-term lease or acquisition of real property plus fixturing and inventory. Compliance with all the applicable state and local public health codes can be expensive. As mentioned at the start of this chapter, restaurant operations cannot be recommended under any circumstances, but if you are determined to give it a try, look for a location near an office complex where you will have easy access to large numbers of office workers. Adding catering to your services may increase your chances of survival, but this can take some time to develop.

International Dairy-Deli-Bakery Association
PO Box 5528
313 Price Pl., #202
Madison WI 53702-0528
(608) 238-7908

Diaper service

This type of service supplies diapers and other baby linens on a pickup and delivery basis. Some services have their own laundry facilities. The market for this service should remain steady and even perhaps improve as concerns grow about saving trees and the clogging of landfills with disposable diapers. The difficulty in establishing this type of business is to find a niche market that is not already served. One good way to start would be to conduct an aggressive mail campaign that focuses on the advantages of reusable diapers and is targeted at couples of childbearing age. Also, you will have to constantly look for new markets. This business will require a nonretail location where laundry can be done and vehicles can be stored and maintained.

National Association of Diaper Services
2017 Walnut St.
Philadelphia PA 19103
(215) 569-3650 or (800) 462-NADS

Donut shop

These types of retail stores, which specialize in offering donuts and may serve coffee and other beverages, are extremely location-sensitive, with all the associated risks. Like bakeries, these businesses will usually be subject to licensing and sanitation laws because food is served; meeting hygiene codes can be costly.

Independent Bakers Association
1223 Potomac St. NW
Washington DC 20007
(202) 333-8190

Dressmaking service (also Sewing service and Tailoring service)

This service offers custom-made women's and men's garments and alterations. You can work out of your home or in space provided by a clothier. If you are working on your own, it can take time to develop a word-of-mouth reputation. It's probably better to start out doing alteration work with an established clothier and then gradually develop clients who will commission you for custom work. You can also look for piecework from large garment manufacturers, but this type of activity pays very little and must be done to stringent deadlines.

American Apparel Contractors Association
PO Box 720693
Atlanta GA 30358
(404) 843-3171

Drugstore (also Pharmacy)

Drugstores often operate without a pharmacy, although a pharmacy contributes substantially to the profit of the business. Pharmacies do have some liability risk. This needs to be considered, and insurance must be obtained to the extent possible. Drugstores are highly location-sensitive, and pharmacies are facing increasing price competition from discounters.

National Association of Retail Druggists
205 Dangerfield Rd.
Alexandria VA 22314
(703) 683-8200 or (800) 544-7447

Dry cleaning (also Laundry service)

These businesses come in two different forms. They can be operated as agencies for a commercial laundry and dry cleaner that has a plant, in which case you as agent are merely the receiving station for clothing to be cleaned. You turn it over to the plant, where the cleaning actually takes place. In the other form, you would have an on-premise plant and do all the work there. Environmental restrictions at the local, state, and federal levels are making these businesses much more expensive to operate, which is reflected in the high cost of dry cleaning today. The trick with this business is to try to keep prices below the competition—and there is plenty of it—while still making a profit.

International Fabricare Institute
12251 Tech Rd.
Silver Spring MD 20904
(301) 622-1900 or (800) 638-2627

Electronics store

Like computer stores, electronics stores, which sell a variety of home entertainment systems, household appliances, and other related merchandise, are asset-intensive, location-sensitive, and under increasing pressure from large chain operators. They should be eyed with great caution because of these vulnerabilities.

American Electronics Association
5201 Great America Pkwy., #520
Santa Clara CA 95054
(408) 987-4200

Engineering, geological, soils, environmental specialists and consultants (see Consulting service)

Equipment rental service (see Banquet and party equipment rentals)

Espresso stand (also Food cart)

These mobile carts, which sell foods and beverages on sidewalks and in shopping malls, can be extremely profitable ventures and have the advantage of not locking you into what might turn out to be a poor location. If business is slow at one location, you can always move to another. The initial capital investment is relatively modest and operation is simple. These businesses are high cash generators with good profit margins, and you can charge more for your products than standard stores can, with a much lower overhead. Again, excess profits breed competition, and there is a great deal of competition—just look around at the types of mobile food and drink carts in shopping malls and other locations where people congregate. That does not mean there isn't room for more specialists, and it is an opportunity to get into business fairly simply. The best strategy is probably to develop a chain of such operations in some area. However, if you create a chain or a number of carts, there will come a time when you will need a headquarters for food preparation and administrative activities.

Event planning services

This is a specialized service that provides advice on planning events of all types such as fund-raisers, banquets, and so forth. Like seminar services, this is a relatively complex consulting business that can be operated from home on behalf of companies or individual clients who lack the time or specialized knowledge to set up events themselves. Event planning may involve not just finding a location but also advertising, mailings, displays, and overall program coordination, including lighting, music, staging, room arrangement, meals, timing, and follow-up.

Executive recruiting services

This service is similar to employment services, except that it is tailored to mid- and upper-level management recruiting. Remuneration is usually done on a fee basis paid by the company, not the potential employee. Executive recruiting requires a stable of steady clients so that you can develop a good rapport over time. Eventually, this business can be a good cash flow developer, but it does take time—at least three to five years, if not more. Location is important. Your location must be attractively furnished and equipped. Your objective is to bring in potentially high-salaried individuals, so your first job is to sell them on your being a real professional.

Society of Human Resources Management
606 N. Washington
Alexandria VA 22314
(703) 548-3440

Fabric store

This type of business, which sells fabrics and sewing supplies, is asset-intensive in the form of inventory and thus requires a substantial amount of working capital in addition to the cost of fixtures and equipment. This business is highly location-sensitive, so you would need ownership or a long-term lease of property. You may develop a reasonable business, but profit margins are usually thin, and there is a great deal of competition. This business also does best with direct owner participation.

American Home Sewing and Craft Association
1375 Broadway
New York NY 10018
(212) 302-2150

Family fun center

These recreational centers, which provide large water sports, miniature golf, and other amusements for the entire family, require a substantial up-front capital investment. Location is crucial, so you would need to make a substantial investment in real estate or a long-term lease. Once you establish yourself in a location and target a particular niche market—the neighborhood market, children's market, or high school market—you can see a substantial cash flow. However, today there is a great deal of competition, and cash flow potential is therefore diminished unless you can establish yourself in an area where it is virtually impossible for other competitors to come in.

Fast-food outlet

These are usually referred to as takeouts—retail services that sell prepared food and drinks for consumption on or off the premises, often with drive-up windows where customers can purchase food without leaving their vehicles. It takes both skill and luck to find a suitable location. The next problem is to find an area not already saturated with major fast-food chains. Another problem—as if the location requirements were not enough—is that everyone thinks they can run a restaurant, but not many can. The risks in this type of business, run on an independent basis, are very high.

International Franchise Association
1350 New York Ave. NW

Washington DC 20005
(202) 628-8000

Financial advisor

This consulting business can involve a wide range of specialized financial activities including budget planning, business plans, financial research, venture capital, working capital loans, advice on loans and investments, and so forth. It can take several years to develop your reputation for professionalism and results. You can start this business from home, but eventually you should consider locating in an office complex where clients can feel comfortable in the surroundings. Your home may not offer the professional image you wish to project unless it is a place where potential clients would themselves like to come and work. If you don't have that kind of home, an office is the best option. This business can be done part-time, but only during the initial start-up period. To be successful, you should plan on devoting full time to it. You must also have the patience and the financial resources to wait out the flow of clients and adequate cash flow. Special licensing may or may not be required, but related education is certainly preferable. Membership with certification as a designated specialist such as a CFA (certified financial analyst) in a recognized professional organization is also extremely helpful.

Fitness center

There's a great deal of competition in this type of business, which offers exercise equipment and classes, and it can require a substantial capital investment. Also, zoning and other ordinances may restrict locations. The better-established fitness centers have done extremely well, with significant cash flows. However, getting to the point of a positive cash flow today would be difficult in most communities and would most likely take a considerable amount of time to develop.

Association of Physical Fitness Centers
600 Jefferson St., #203
Rockville MD 20852
(301) 424-7744

Flower shop

This type of retail business specializes in the sale of cut flowers and artistic flower arrangements. It is virtually mandatory that you be able to offer rapid delivery of flowers and arrangements in your market area. Also, you should be associated with FTD or an equivalent national and international delivery system so you can offer delivery outside your immediate area. Like other retail businesses, direct owner participation on a day-to-day basis will increase your chances of success. It can take a substantial period of time to develop a steady clientele, and you will need to make a substantial capital investment in location by ownership or long-term lease, as well as in the necessary equipment. Furthermore, there is a great deal of competition, and profit margins are very thin. As always in retail operations, it's helpful to identify a niche market where you can operate with minimal competition.

Society of American Florists
1601 Duke St.
Alexandria VA 22314
(800) 336-4743

Food and party catering services

This type of service, which provides catered food for parties and other events in homes and offices, can be run from home and is almost entirely dependent on word of mouth for the establishment of a reputation. You will wish to carve out a niche for yourself in terms offering unique, highly individualized foods or presentations. It can take a long time to become established, but once your satisfied clients recommend you to others, the business may become reasonably profitable. You must plan on direct involvement throughout every phase of a particular service to ensure consistent high quality and to control costs and cash flow.

Banister and Associates
c/o National Off-Premises Caterers Association
500801 Pine Creek Dr.
Westerville OH 43081-4899
(614) 895-1355

Food cart (see Espresso stand)

Food catering truck (also Lunch wagon)

This "lunch wagon" business provides breakfast, lunch, and snack foods and beverages to construction sites, offices, complexes, parks, and other locations. This business requires a location where the food is prepared, packaged and so forth, as well as where trucks can be stored and serviced. Although a storefront location is not necessary, you will need a significant amount of real estate on a long-term lease or ownership and a significant capital investment. Gaining clientele may be a problem if there are established catering trucks in the area.

Freelance photography (see Photography, freelance)

Freelance writer (see Writer, freelance)

Frozen yogurt shop (see also Ice cream shop)

Frozen yogurt shops are a current fad, and this presents a danger for new entrants. Although these shops have become very popular, cash flow and margins appear to be declining because of competition. Here, as in most retail businesses, the owner must participate directly. Also, there can be a substantial cost of improvements in addition to a long-term lease at a key location.

National Dairy Council
6300 N. River Rd.
Rosemont IL 60018
(708) 803-2000

Fruit and vegetable shop or kiosk (also Produce shop)

These retail businesses specialize in selling fresh fruits and vegetables, usually in a commercial storefront. As for all location-sensitive retail businesses, owner participation on a day-to-day basis will increase your chances of success. It can take a substantial period of time to develop a steady clientele, and you will need to make a substantial capital investment in location by ownership or long-term lease, as well as investment in the needed equipment. Furthermore, there is a great deal of competition, and profit margins are very thin. As always in retail operations, it's helpful if you can identify or create a niche market where you can operate with minimal competition.

U.S. Fresh Fruit and Vegetable Association
727 N. Washington St.
Alexandria VA 22314
(703) 836-3410

Furnishings and furniture, home, new

These businesses, which sell household furniture and accessories, cannot do well without a street location that can attract pedestrian and vehicle traffic and thus require a long-term lease or ownership. You will also need to make a substantial investment in inventory. On top of all this, the furnishings business is usually thin-margined at the retail level, and many of these businesses ultimately fail. When they do sell, it is difficult to sell them for goodwill unless they are well-established and unusual. Competition from large-scale discounters and franchisors is also a problem unless you can develop a niche market.

National Home Furnishings Association
PO Box 2396
High Point NC 27261
(919) 883-1650

Furnishings and furniture, office, new (also Office furnishings and furniture store, new)

This type of retail business, which specializes in selling office furniture and related supplies, requires a highly visible street location and thus a long-term lease or purchase of real estate as well as a substantial investment in inventory. Profit margins are usually thin; many of these businesses ultimately fail; and it can be difficult to sell them for goodwill. There is also substantial discounter competition.

National Office Products Association
301 N. Fairfax St.
Alexandria VA 22314
(703) 549-9040

Furnishings and furniture, office, used (also Office furnishings and furniture store, used)

These businesses, which specialize in used office furniture obtained at liquidation prices and resold at a discount, may have certain advantages over the new retail office business because deep discounts can be given. However, location, with its substantial investment in real estate or a long-term lease, is still a factor. You must also take into account your investment in inventory and extensive advertising. Businesses of this kind take considerable time to develop into positive cash flow on top of the significant up-front investment required.

Furniture rental store (also Rental furniture store)

This type of business, which leases and rents home furniture and accessories on a limited-term or option-to-buy basis, requires a substantial capital investment and also usually requires a specific location, which means more expense for the purchase or long-term lease of real estate. It can take time to develop a good reputation, and competition is intense. Once established, which might take two or three years, it can become a good cash generator after you pay for and amortize the furnishings purchased for rental or lease.

Furniture Rental Association of America
Blendonview Office Park
5008 Pine Creek Dr.
Westerville OH 43081-4899
(614) 895-1273

Furniture store, unfinished

This type of business offers an interesting way to compete with large discounters by offering furniture pieces and sometimes home cabinetry that can be finished by customers. This type of business appeals to customers in two ways: Prices are lower for unfinished furniture, and customers can finish the furniture to suit their own taste. However, it is not without competition, and it also requires a location that can attract pedestrian or vehicle traffic. Thus, you will have to invest in a location, either by ownership or long-term lease, and in a significant inventory. The cash flow potential from this type of business once it flies is usually significantly higher than for other retail home and office furnishing businesses.

National Hardwood Lumber Association
PO Box 34518
Memphis TN 38184-0518
(901) 377-1818

Futon stores

This retail business, which sells futon beds and related furniture items and accessories, is somewhat faddish. Although futons have become very popular in recent years because they provide inexpensive, space-saving, multifunctional bedding for college students and single career people, the cash flow and profit margins appear to be declining because of competition. This business is asset-intensive in the form of inventory and thus requires a substantial amount of working capital in addition to the cost of fixtures, equipment, and so forth. Also, this is a highly location-sensitive operation that requires ownership of real estate or a long-term lease to develop locational security. You would do well to fight the competition by identifying a niche market, but market acceptance over the long term is questionable.

Futon Association International
PO Box 6548
Chico CA 95927-6548
(916) 534-7833

Garden supply store (also Nurseries and Tree and plant store)

These businesses, which sell trees, shrubs, plants, seeds, bulbs, fertilizers, and other gardening supplies, are location-sensitive, and there is substantial competition. They require special knowledge, and you might have to wait several years before seeing a satisfactory cash flow level. Cash flow may also be influenced by weather and climatic conditions. A substantial cash investment will be required to acquire or lease the needed real estate, inventory, and related equipment.

American Association of Nurserymen
1250 I St. NW, #500
Washington DC 20005
(202) 789-2900

Gasoline service station

Gasoline service stations, which used to offer oil and tire checks, towing services, and automobile maintenance service, are gradually disappearing and being replaced by gas-only outlets, self-service outlets, and gas-only outlets with convenience stores. The best way to enter this business is through a major-brand franchisor. Generally, gas-with-convenience-store operations generate much more cash flow than fuel-only operations. Location is crucial.

American Petroleum Institute
1220 L St. NW
Washington DC 20005
(202) 682-8000

Gift shop (see also Souvenir and novelty store)

Like card shops, gift shops, which sell gift items in addition to cards, wrapping paper, and novelties, are highly location-sensitive and require direct participation by the owner. It can take a good period of time to develop a steady clientele, and you will have to make a substantial capital investment in location by ownership or long-term lease and the needed equipment. Furthermore, there is a great deal of competition, not the least of which is coming from superstore discounters. The best location for this type of specialty shop is probably in a small community such as a resort area where customers will be especially prone to impulse purchases. However, the usual downside of such locations is seasonality.

Gift Association of America
612 W. Broad St.
Bethlehem PA 18018
(215) 861-9445

Graphic design

This is a consulting business that can be done at home by an individual or can be extended to a special location with additional staff. Specialized education is required, and gaining an established reputation as competent, careful, and prompt can take a long time. Your success will depend on clients who are willing to refer other business to you. You can contract out for support services if needed.

American Center for Design
233 E. Ontario, #500
Chicago IL 60611
(312) 787-2018

Hair stylist (see Barber shop)

Hardware store

This type of retail store, which sells building and major construction supplies (but usually not lumber), hardware, tools, garden equipment, household appliances, decorative items, cookware, and gifts, is facing severe competition from the large discounters. These stores are highly location-sensitive and asset-intensive in the form of inventory. However, your chances of success may be greater if you can offer services and expertise that compensate for your necessarily higher prices.

National Retail Hardware Association
5822 W. 74th St.
Indianapolis IN 46278
(317) 290-0338 or (800) 772-4424

Health food store (also Vitamin store)

These stores, which specialize in selling organic foods and nutritional supplements such as vitamins and minerals, are subject to all the drawbacks of any retail operation. They are location-sensitive and will require a substantial investment in real estate, either owned or leased. You will need to invest in substantial inventory, and your presence will be necessary on a day-to-day basis. It could take some time before you see a positive cash flow, and you may also see increasing competition from discounters as well as supermarkets and pharmacies that are starting to offer these types of products.

Organic Foods Production Association of North America
PO Box 1078
Greenfield MA 01301
(507) 452-6332

Home appliance repair service

These businesses offer repair and maintenance services for home appliances such as refrigerators, stoves, and so forth. They can be operated out of your home (assuming there is no conflict with applicable zoning laws) or in a nonretail location. There is a considerable demand for this type of business and, if operated properly, it could be a real moneymaker.

National Association of Service Dealers
c/o National Association of Retail Dealers of America
10 E. 22nd St., #310
Lombard IL 60148
(708) 953-8950

Home contractor specialist (see also Construction contracting services, general)

This type of business, which focuses on residential additions, alterations, and repairs, requires special skills. It is usually best to work out of your home, although you may wish to lease or rent some property where you can store supplies and vehicles as well as carry out carpentry or other fabrication work. You could do small fabricating jobs at home, but you might come into conflict with zoning ordinances. This is almost certain to happen if your business grows. Cash flow growth can be rapid but erratic. The trick is to develop a strong enough referral network and customer base through simple advertising in the Yellow Pages, door-to-door flyers, and contacts with lumber yards and other hardware suppliers. Naturally, the best advertising of all is quality work and dependability in meeting deadlines. If you can offer both on a consistent basis, you may get more business than you can possibly handle.

National Association of Home Builders of the United States
15th & M Sts. NW
Washington DC 20005
(202) 822-0200

Home furnishings and furniture store, new (see Furnishings and furniture, home, new)

Hot dog stand or cart (see Espresso stand)

House painting

This is a contracting business that offers house painting, not including interior decorating services, and requires a certain amount of skill and expertise. You can work out of your home and store supplies and equipment in your garage, if zoning ordinances permit. The key to success is to develop referrals and a customer base through simple advertising in the Yellow Pages, door-to-door flyers, and contacts with lumber yards and related businesses. Your best advertising is quality work and dependability.

National Association of Home Builders of the United States
15th & M Sts. NW
Washington DC 20005
(202) 822-0200

Ice cream shop (see also Frozen yogurt shop)

One danger with these types of businesses is that they can become too plentiful. In many instances, these businesses, like yogurt shops, were very popular when they first came onto the scene. However, there was soon a great deal of competition, demonstrating once again that excess profits—and many of them were extremely profitable—breed ruinous competition. So be careful with regard to competitors. Try to get a location that lacks competitors but attracts a significant concentration of people, such as a shopping mall or resort area where you can depend on a steady flow of clientele. The trick is to avoid becoming cluttered by starting to add things like hot dogs and pizza and so forth. The simpler you keep your business and the more focused it is on your particular product, the more successful you will be in the long term.

International Ice Cream Association
888 16th St. NW
Washington DC 20006
(202) 296-4250

Image consulting (see Clothing consulting)

Instant printing shop (see Copy service)

Insurance agent

This type of business, which provides sales and advice on various types of insurance policies, can be a good long-term choice, particularly if you sell life insurance, annuities, and other special products where there can be a buildup of ongoing income. People are generally reluctant to change insurance agents and often keep annuities and life insurance for substantial periods of time. The casualty end of this business can also be good, although you will probably see a more rapid turnover of clients. Before you get involved, be sure to investigate the legislation that affects this business. Furthermore, this type of business is extremely competitive and requires a good deal of patience as well as, of course, a high degree of selling skill.

National Association of Health Underwriters
1000 Connecticut Ave. NW, #1111
Washington DC 20036
(202) 223-5533

Interior design and decorating

Although there is always a need for interior design skills, this type of business can certainly be affected by downturns in real estate such as those experienced in the early 1990s. However, the future might be excellent—if you have the staying power. These services can be carried out for homes or offices as an independent consulting service or in association with a furniture or other interior decorating store. Although licensing is not required, it is preferable to have specialized education, unique skills and, if possible, membership in a relevant professional society such as an architectural interior design group. Advertising is done through the Yellow Pages and referrals from architects, contractors, building owners and managers, and, most importantly, satisfied customers. The income generated by successful interior design businesses can be excellent, but it takes considerable time to get to that level, as it does for most professional practices.

National Association of Home Builders of the United States
15th & M Sts. NW
Washington DC 20005
(202) 822-0200

Jewelry store

This type of store, which sells various types of jewelry, precious metals, and precious stones in settings, is subject to all the negatives of any retail operation. It is location-sensitive and will require a substantial investment in real estate, either owned or leased. You will need to invest in substantial inventory, and your presence will be necessary on a day-to-day basis. It could take some time before you see a positive cash flow, and there is extensive competition. In general, this is a high-risk business and cannot be recommended unless you are particularly skilled or interested in it.

American Gem Society
5901 W. Third St.
Los Angeles CA 90036
(213) 936-4367

Juice shop or kiosk

These businesses sell blended fresh fruit and vegetable juices. As is true for all location-sensitive retail businesses, owner participation on a day-to-day basis will increase your chances of success. It can take a substantial period of time to develop a steady clientele. You will need to make a capital investment in your location by ownership or long-term lease, as well as in the needed equipment. Furthermore, competition is intense, and profit margins are thin. You can increase your chances of success by identifying or creating a niche market where you can operate with minimal competition.

Landscape architect

This professional service specializes in planning, designing, and overseeing the development of land improvements, especially landscaping. Although not always required, it is helpful to have specialized education as well as experience and to be a member of a recognized architectural or landscape professional organization. Becoming established as credible and competent can take some time, and your success will depend on clients who are willing to refer other business to you. In most cases, you will not need a special location, and when you are starting out, you can contract out for specialized activities such as clerical help as needed.

American Society of Landscape Architects
4401 Connecticut NW, Fifth Floor
Washington DC 20008
(202) 686-2752

Laundromat

These businesses, which offer coin-operated washers and dryers, are relatively easy to operate—in fact, many are operated without an employee on the premises. However, many communities are now charging a substantial up-front sewer connection fee, and this, coupled with the cost of rapidly depreciating equipment, means that you need a very good location to develop a cash flow that will not only amortize out your initial investment but also provide an income. Usually the best strategy is to have more than one location. This type of business is not recommended if you are just starting out in business for the first time unless you are already very skilled in location selection and have the capital necessary to get started.

Coin Laundry Association
1315 Butterfield Rd., #212
Downers Grove IL 60515
(708) 963-5547

Laundry service (see Dry cleaning)

Lingerie shop

This type of retail specialty store, which sells intimate apparel and other accessories, is subject to the caveats of any location-sensitive business. Competition and the considerable investment required for a lease or purchase in a good location, plus your inventory and fixturing costs, make this a difficult business to enter. It is also very competitive, with only fair cash flow at best.

Intimate Fashion News
309 Fifth Ave.
New York NY 10016
(212) 679-6677

Liquor store

These retail stores sell alcoholic beverages as well as cigarettes, foods, snacks, and nonalcoholic beverages. This business can generate substantial cash flow, but it is location-sensitive and usually you must obtain a special liquor license. Liquor stores are highly vulnerable to crime, so security and safety are major concerns.

National Association of Beverage Retailers
5101 River Rd., #108
Bethesda MD 20816
(301) 656-1494

Luggage and leather shop

These retail stores, which sell luggage, leather goods, and related items, are highly location-sensitive and are vulnerable to competition from discount superstores. You will face a considerable investment for the lease or purchase of real estate in a good location, plus your inventory and fixturing costs, making this a difficult business to enter and one that offers only fair cash flow at best.

American Luggage Dealers Association
610 Anacapa St., #G
Santa Barbara CA 93101
(805) 966-6909

Lunch wagon (see Food catering truck)

Mail-order novelties

This business, which sells by sending promotional flyers and magazines to prospective customers, can be operated from home or a retail location. Business is obtained through advertising in the business Yellow Pages or direct contacts with business owners, or at swap meets, fairs, and craft shows. Cash flow is only fair.

Direct Marketing Association
11 W. 42nd St.
New York NY 10036
(212) 768-7277

Manufacturer's agent

These agents may represent a single manufacturer or many companies. Usually, agents concentrate on a particular type of product. You do not directly buy products or merchandise but rather represent the manufacturer as its sales representative. The NAFTA and the GATT trade agreements could provide new and expanded opportunities for manufacturers' agents offering products from the United States for sale in other countries and vice versa. This business requires a substantial amount of time to develop into one that will generate a meaningful cash flow. It is best started by someone who already has well-established contacts with a manufacturer. This is a very competitive business, although the cash investment is minimal. You will need a reserve so you can meet your own needs during the start-up time, as well as funds for advertising, telephone service, and a small office. Long-term cash flow can be excellent, but the risk is high.

Manufacturers' Agents National Association
23016 Mill Creek Rd.
Laguna Hills CA 92653
(714) 859-4040

Marine repair service (see Boat cleaning and repair service)

Meat market

This retail business sells fresh, frozen, and cured meats, including fish, beef, and poultry, usually in a commercial storefront. As for all location-sensitive retail businesses, owner participation on a day-to-day basis will increase your chances of success. It can take a substantial period of time to develop a steady clientele. You will have to make a capital investment in location by ownership or long-term lease, as well as the needed equipment and supplies. Furthermore, there is a great deal of competition, and cash flow is only fair. It's helpful to identify or create a niche market where you can operate with minimal competition.

American Hereford Association
PO Box 014059
1501 Wyandotte
Kansas City MO 64101
(816) 842-3757

Medical equipment rental

With the growing attention to national health care, this type of service, which provides medical equipment to hospitals, health care facilities, and patients, will be increasingly in demand. Already, businesses specializing in this activity seem to be very profitable. This business is location-sensitive and ideally should be based near hospitals or other medical centers. It requires a substantial investment in equipment in addition to a long-term lease or purchase of real estate. It also requires some specialized knowledge. Cash flow over time may be fair, but it could take quite a long time to reach an acceptable level.

Health Industry Distributors Association
225 Reinekers La., #650
Alexandria VA 22314
(703) 549-4432

Men's clothing and accessories store

These types of specialty retail stores, which sell men's apparel and accessories, are highly location-sensitive and require direct participation by the owner. It takes a substantial period of time to develop a steady clientele. It will probably take a significant amount of time to begin seeing a positive cash flow over and above paying for and amortizing your investment. Furthermore, there is a great deal of competition, not the least of which is coming from superstore discounters.

Menswear Retailers of America
2011 "I" St. NW, #300
Washington DC 20006
(202) 347-1932

Milk outlet

These retail operations sell milk and other dairy products. As for all location-sensitive retail businesses, direct owner participation increases your chances of success. It can take a substantial period of time to develop a steady clientele and to amortize your capital investment in location by ownership or long-term lease, and the needed equipment. Furthermore, competition is intense, and profit margins are thin. You can increase your chances of success by identifying or creating a niche market where you can operate with minimal competition.

National Dairy Council
6300 N. River Rd.
Rosemont IL 60018
(708) 803-2000

Mini-market (see Convenience store)

Mobile lunch wagon (see Food catering truck)

Mortuary

This business, which offers funeral arrangements, burials, cremations, and related services, requires a special location and facilities and thus a substantial up-front investment. If you can find a good location, particularly in an ethnic area where there is little or no competition, the business could be a good cash flow generator. However, dealing with ethnic groups as a specialty also requires special knowledge of and sensitivity to the customs of that particular group. It also may require the ability to speak a foreign language or to hire staff who can.

National Funeral Directors Association
PO Box 27641
Milwaukee WI 53227
(414) 541-2500

Motorcycle shop

This type of business usually also engages in maintenance and repair as well as sales of motorcycles and related products. It can be cyclical (no pun intended!), is location-sensitive, and requires a significant up-front investment in facilities and perhaps in the cost of a franchise. Your inventory may be on consignment or on a flooring basis, similar to the cars in a new-car dealership. If you start out as a new dealer, it may take a long time to build the business to a satisfactory level of cash flow. Obtaining a good franchise is not an easy task.

Motorcycle Industry Council
2 Jenner St., #150
Irvine CA 92718
(714) 727-4211

Moving and storage service

This type of service provides assistance in moving and storing individual and business furnishings and belongings. You will require a nonretail location for garaging of vehicles and related equipment. Advertising is usually done through the Yellow Pages. This business requires a substantial up-front investment. Some form of bonding, insurance and licensing may also be required.

National Moving and Storage Association
11150 Main St., #402
Fairfax VA 22030-5066
(703) 934-9111

Music and video store (see also Videocassette rental store)

These retail stores rent prerecorded videocassettes and laser discs as well as selling music tapes and compact discs. Video stores are in abundant supply. Not only is there the threat of immediate competition from already well-established stores, but possible changes resulting from the introduction of fiber optics will make many video stores obsolete. A great deal of study should be done before you invest any money in this type of business.

Entrepreneur Group
2392 Morse Ave.
Irvine CA 92714
(714) 261-2325

Musical instrument store

These specialty retail stores, which sell musical instruments, sheet music, and supplies, may offer lessons and instrument rentals as well. This business is location-sensitive, and your presence as owner is more important than usual because this tends to be a family-oriented operation. It takes a substantial period of time to develop a steady clientele. You will also need to make a capital investment in location by ownership or long-term lease, as well as investing in the needed inventory. Furthermore, there may be a good deal of competition from other independent operators, but not much from discounters. You may be able to obtain business by establishing relationships with schools or private music teachers in your area.

National Association of Music Merchants
5140 Avenida Encinas
Carlsbad CA 92008
(619) 438-8001

Nail salon

This service, which specializes in nail care and sometimes the sale of nail products, is highly competitive but also in growing demand. However, you need to watch the potential fad aspects of this type of activity. Like barber and hair styling services, it's usually very personalized. You can develop a reasonable cash flow, but this is not a strong business for resale.

National Cosmetology Association
3510 Olive St.
St. Louis MO 63103
(314) 534-7980

Nanny placement

This type of business, which specializes in supplying nannies to clients seeking qualified, reliable child care, can easily be operated by one person. The family pays a fee to the agency when a nanny is placed. There has always been a need for this type of service, and nannies are highly sought-after by affluent two-career families. You can get started by doing some simple advertising and promotion and by developing a reputation for complete dependability. However, your background must be impeccable, as must that of the nannies you introduce into clients' homes. You will need to be able to match your nannies' personalities with the proper families. You'll also need to know how to carry out background checks on prospective nannies and how to deal with insurance issues. Plus, there is always the possibility that emergencies could result in accidents or injuries, followed by expensive lawsuits.

American Council of Nanny Schools
Delta College
University Center MI 48710
(517) 686-9417

Private Care Association
1276 McConnell Dr., #A
Decatur GA 30033
(404) 982-9636

Newsletter publishing

This business, which publishes newsletters for other organizations, is extremely competitive, and finding a niche is extremely difficult unless you already have some association with an established group that needs some form of regular communication and is willing to pay for it. These businesses are most successful when you are able to work for a number of organizations that all need newsletters. Cash flow potential is minimal, and the business would probably take a great deal of time to develop. This activity is best done on a freelance basis as a subsidiary to other activities such as editorial, computer design, or résumé services, and so forth.

Newsletter Publishers Association
1401 Wilson Blvd., #207
Arlington VA 22209
(703) 527-2333 or (800) 356-9302

Newspaper and magazine home delivery

In this type of service, which takes care of delivering or mailing newspapers and magazines to home addresses, you probably need to associate yourself with several publications. Otherwise it will be difficult to generate enough cash flow, even for a very small staff. Competition is substantial.

Newspaper Association of America
11600 Sunrise Valley Dr.
Reston VA 22091
(703) 648-1000

Newspaper and magazine store or kiosk

This type of retail business, which sells a wide variety of newspapers and magazines, is highly location-sensitive. However, the right location may generate a substantial cash flow. You will have to create arrangements with distributors, who will deliver publications to your location and take away unsold products. Your profit will come from a small margin for each periodical you sell. You can try to develop a niche market by stocking specialized publications, but it may take a long time for customers to find their way to your newsstand.

Newspaper Association of America
11600 Sunrise Valley Dr.
Reston VA 22091
(703) 648-1000

Nurseries (see Garden supply store)

Office furnishings and furniture store, new (see Furnishings and furniture, office, new)

Office furnishings and furniture store, used (see Furnishings and furniture, office, used)

Office supplies broker

In this business, you operate as a wholesale specialist who solicits by brochure, telephone, and general advertising to provide office supplies

---

146   Businesses to Approach with Caution

at a discount. You must be careful to avoid gaining a reputation for operating some kind of "scam." You can operate from home or a non-retail location, particularly if other employees, such as telephone solicitors, packagers, and those filling orders, are involved. However, many of the latter services may be done on a contract basis.

National Office Products Association
301 N. Fairfax St.
Alexandria VA 22314
(703) 549-9040

Office supplies store (also Stationery store)

This type of business differs from the brokering described above in that it is retail and thus vulnerable to the location-sensitive factors that apply to most retail operations. It can take a substantial period of time to develop a steady clientele, and you will need to make a capital investment in location by ownership or long-term lease, as well as investing in the needed equipment. Furthermore, competition is intense, and profit margins are thin. You can increase your chances of success by identifying or creating a niche market where you can operate with minimal competition.

National Office Products Association
301 N. Fairfax St.
Alexandria VA 22314
(703) 549-9040

One-hour photo laboratories

This type of business offers speedy photo developing and printing services. There is a great deal of competition from other businesses that offer similar services—drugstores, supermarkets, discount superstores, franchises, and other camera stores. This business requires a special location and a substantial investment in equipment, either leased or purchased. It will take you some time to develop a reputation for dependability, skill, and quick service. Cash flow from this type of business is modest to fair, primarily because of the substantial competition.

Association of Professional Color Laboratories
3000 Picture Pl.
Jackson MI 49201
(517) 788-8146

Pager service

This business, which offers pager equipment rental and services, is already very competitive, but demand is growing. It requires obtaining the right franchise. A capital investment would include an up-front franchise fee as well as some equipment and initial advertising and promotion to develop a flow of clientele and thus cash flow. Pager equipment is becoming more sophisticated and will probably involve two-way systems in the near future.

Parking lot striping and maintenance

This business involves providing striping, restriping, and maintenance on a contract basis with large independent parking lot operations or lots that serve commercial retail and office centers, hospitals, or other institutions. It requires special equipment, such as sweepers and line painters, and a facility where you can store and maintain equipment and supplies. The capital investment is substantial, and there is considerable competition. However, like any contracting service, there is room for an operation that is dependable and offers a good price. One complication is that many communities have codes that govern the storage, mixing, and use of paints and related products. This business may not be particularly easy to enter for these reasons, but once entered it can be quite profitable, especially in areas where there is limited competition.

National Parking Association
1112 16th St. NW, #300
Washington DC 20036
(202) 296-4336

Party equipment rentals (see Banquet and party equipment rentals)

Party goods store

This type of retail store, which sells party favors and gift novelties, is highly location-sensitive and requires direct owner participation for maximum success. It can take a substantial period of time to develop a steady clientele, and you will need to make a capital investment in location by ownership or long-term lease, as well as investing in the needed equipment. Furthermore, there is a great deal of competition, not the least of which is coming from superstore discounters.

Entrepreneur Group
2392 Morse Ave.
Irvine CA 92714
(714) 261-2325

Pawn shop

These businesses are a combination of loan broker and retail outlet. Valuables such as guns, jewelry, radios, televisions, and almost any other type of personal property are held as collateral for small loans. In recent years, pawn shops have moved out of the seedier areas of cities and towns and are now found in some of the best areas. Running this type of business requires expertise, especially the ability to accurately assess the value of a wide variety of personal property. However, the rewards can be great. Property left in pawn beyond the specified time, usually 30 to 60 days, is brought out of pawn and sold as used merchandise at retail or near-retail prices. The difference between the money loaned on the property and the money it will bring when sold can be much greater than the normal profit margin in a regular retail store. Pawn shops are vulnerable to theft, so safety and security are a major concern.

Personal shopping service

This type of personal service caters to individuals, often career people but also sometimes shut-ins and invalids, who need someone to do their shopping and other errands for them. Services can range from grocery shopping to wardrobe consulting. This activity is best thought of as a part-time, strictly one-person business because it would be very difficult to develop a significant cash flow, and a good word-of-mouth reputation could take a long time to develop.

Pest control service

These contracting services exterminate insects, rodents, and other pests through the use of chemical and nonchemical methods. Special licensing is usually required, and communities may have codes that govern use of and exposure to the chemicals used. In addition, this type of business requires special skills, expertise, and equipment, and there is a great deal of competition. You can work out of your home and store supplies and equipment in your garage, if zoning ordinances permit. The key to success is to develop referrals and a customer base through simple advertising in the Yellow Pages, door-to-door flyers, and contacts with contractors and related businesses. Your best advertising is quality work and dependability.

National Pest Control Association
8100 Oak St.
Dunn Loring VA 22027
(703) 573-8330

Pet hotel and grooming service (see also Pet sitting)

This type of specialized service offers temporary room and board as well as grooming for pets. It may be associated with a veterinary practice but can be run independently. Because animals are involved, special licensing and zoning codes may apply. A related business is a mobile pet grooming service, in which you travel to pet owners' homes to carry out grooming services. These businesses require a substantial capital investment in a facility or vehicle, and they are not easy to place today because of zoning ordinances and other restrictions. Once established, however, a good cash flow could be developed.

Entrepreneur Group
2392 Morse Ave.
Irvine CA 92714
(714) 261-2325

Pet shop

This type of retail store, which sells pet animals and pet-related items, is highly location-sensitive and requires direct owner participation for maximum success. It can take a substantial period of time to develop a steady clientele, not to mention the capital investment in your location by ownership or long-term lease, needed equipment, and inventory. There is also great deal of competition.

Entrepreneur Group
2392 Morse Ave.
Irvine Ca 92714
(714) 261-2325

Pet sitting (see also Pet hotel and grooming service)

This service, which provides pet care while owners are out of town, is a very individualized business, and getting a cash flow from this activity alone would be difficult. If you're going to build this business with a staff, where income can be generated from many clients, it might be satisfactory, but then you would need a special facility to house the animals. If you are doing pet sitting in individual homes, the number of clients you can take is limited. But even if you are working on your own, you could handle a number of requests by just dropping in and checking on the animal, doing the feeding and so forth in the clients' homes. This form of business is not easy in that you are going to people's homes while they are gone, which can lead to potential liability. Generally this type of business is not highly recommended.

Entrepreneur Group
2392 Morse Ave.
Irvine CA 92714
(714) 261-2325

Pharmacy (see Drugstore)

Photography, freelance

In this type of service, you carry out individual photography work on assignment from clients, usually advertising agencies. You could also do art photography for sale to retail galleries. There is a great deal of competition, and becoming established usually requires years of reputation building before you can gain a modicum of success based on referrals from established clients.

Professional Photographers of America
1090 Executive Way
Des Plaines IL 60018
(708) 299-8161

Physical fitness center (see Fitness center)

Pinball and video game arcades

These recreational centers, which offer coin-operated pinball and video games for entertainment, are highly location-sensitive as well as faddish. This business can take two forms. One is to be the owner or master leaseholder of spaces devoted to video games. Finding a good location for this type of business is difficult, and there is immense competition not only from other arcades but also from arcades placed in odd corners of retail stores, convenience stores, and other settings. The risk is extremely high. The other form is to own or lease video games and place them in various locations. Again, there is a great deal of competition, but perhaps less risk than in being an arcade promoter.

Entrepreneur Group
2392 Morse Ave.
Irvine CA 92714
(714) 261-2325

Pizzeria (see Restaurant)

Plant store pizzeria (see Restaurant)

Plant store (see Garden supply store)

Plumbing, heating, and air-conditioning services

This contracting service specializes in the installation and repair of plumbing, heating, and air-conditioning equipment and systems. You will need some special training and probably a state license. You would do best to start out on your own and advertise using handbills and the Yellow Pages as well as direct solicitation. As you gain a word-of-mouth reputation, you may see a steady and reasonably high level of cash flow as well as a certain amount of repeat business. It may be possible to develop niche markets by specializing in retrofitting schools, hospitals, and other types of public buildings to meet changing codes.

National Association of Plumbing/Heating/Cooling Contractors
PO Box 6808
Falls Church VA 22040
(703) 359-0826

Printing shop, instant (see Copy service)

Private mailbox service

This retail operation, which offers private mailboxes as well as postal, shipping, fax, and sometimes photocopying services, is location-sensitive. The capital investment is primarily in fixtures and equipment as well as the cost of owning or leasing real estate. There is a great deal of competition, so cash flow could be minimal unless you find an especially strong location with good vehicle and pedestrian traffic and ample parking. This type of business is best associated with other services such as secretarial or clerical work so that people are encouraged to come to you for a variety of reasons.

Association of Mail and Parcel Centers
10701 Montgomery Blvd. NE
Albuquerque NM 87111
(505) 294-6425

Produce shop (see Fruit and vegetable shop or kiosk)

Promotional services

This type of business covers a wide range of activities including the distribution of promotional and advertising materials such as flyers and coupons door-to-door or through the mail. A retail location is not necessary, but this is best thought of as a part-time activity in which you must contract with a number of clients to distribute their materials. This is not a business that is likely to build long-term value.

Entrepreneur Group
2392 Morse Ave.
Irvine CA 92714
(714) 261-2325

Quick oil change and lubrication services (see Automotive service)

Real estate brokerage

In this type of service business, you are licensed as a real estate broker and authorized to represent buyers and sellers of real estate. As we know from the experience of the past few years, real estate is highly cyclical and vulnerable to macroeconomic trends. It can be a good cash flow business under the right circumstances. Your success will depend on word-of-mouth recommendations by satisfied clients.

National Association of Real Estate Brokers
PO Box 5683
Washington DC 20041
(202) 785-4477

Recreational vehicle rental service

These rental services provide recreational vehicles such as motor homes and boats for a limited time. They are location-sensitive and require a substantial initial capital investment for real estate and vehicles. Cash flow is fair but will take time to develop. You will also need to put a great deal of effort into promotional activities and advertising to attract customers who may then become a steady network of referrals.

Recreation Vehicle Dealers Association of North America
3251 Old Lee Hwy., #500
Fairfax VA 22030
(703) 591-7130

Recycling consultant or broker

This type of business specializes in consulting on recycling and brokering the reuse of recycled items such as paper, bottles, newsprint, aluminum cans, and plastics. It is often combined with a recycling center. If this is the case, you will need a real estate location that is properly zoned or has a conditional use permit.

However, you can do consulting, particularly for businesses, without actually owning a recycling center. In this case, you would make contact with centers where recyclable goods would be sent. This activity does not necessarily require state certification, but you should check this point in your local area. This business does require substantial specialized knowledge about the materials you will be handling as well as considerable knowledge of relevant local, state, and federal codes and regulations. This is a good business for an individual or small group if you want to work on a fee basis to create recycling facilities. There will be an increasing need for this type of business; it is competitive, but there is currently plenty of room for more entrants.

Rental furniture store (see Furniture rental store)

Restaurant

Restaurants can take an almost infinite variety of forms ranging from coffee shops to full dinner houses to ethnic specialty restaurants. Everyone thinks they can run a restaurant, but very few people actually can. A major problem in this business is not only being able to manage one properly, but also finding a good location. There is enormous competition, and even established restaurant chains often blow it when it comes to location selection. Because restaurants are a major item of discretionary spending, they are highly vulnerable to downturns in the economy. In addition to location, restaurant owners must also deal with health and sanitation laws and staffing. Restaurants are expensive to create and you must plan to spend most of your waking hours on the scene if you expect to survive. They are also vulnerable to lawsuits and robbery.

Résumé-writing service

This is a personal consulting service operation that offers specialized knowledge and advising along with actual assistance in creating résumés for people seeking jobs. It is best run as a subservice of a secretarial operation. There is a great deal of competition, and gaining a reputation strong enough to generate referrals will take a substantial amount of time.

Entrepreneur Group
2392 Morse Ave.
Irvine CA 92714
(714) 261-2325

Second-hand store (also Thrift store)

These are privately operated businesses that sell used clothing, furniture, and personal items. Sometimes these stores are run by nonprofit associations as a fund-raising activity, but there are also many private thrift stores that are run for profit. These businesses are somewhat location-sensitive, but a secondary location with relatively low rent is usually satisfactory because customers do not expect fancy facilities. As a private operator, you would see a great deal of competition from stores operated by nonprofit organizations. However, independent operators can find a niche, and for a particularly skillful operator, the cash flow can be good.

Secretarial services

These services provide all forms of secretarial services to individuals or companies for a fee. There is a good demand for a wide variety of secretarial services, and if you have the needed personal skills as well as word-processing equipment and knowledge, you will find yourself in demand. The risk is that there is already considerable established competition, so working your way into the market will take time. If you can draw on specialized skills, such as technical vocabularies, you may be able to develop a niche that will speed up the process of becoming established.

Society of Human Resources Management
606 N. Washington
Alexandria VA 22314
(703) 548-3440

Self storage or mini-warehouse

These rental services provide storage space for household and business possessions and records. This is a very expensive business to enter, and there is a great deal of competition. A specific location is crucial. Well-established locations do develop a significant cash flow, but much of that is likely to go toward your real estate investment.

Self Storage Association
4147 Crossgate Dr.
Cincinnati OH 45236
(513) 984-6468

Seminar service

This is a relatively complex activity, but it can be operated as a one-person, home-based business. It essentially involves consulting and providing services for companies or individual clients who wish to promote products or services through seminars. This business fills a need because many companies lack the time or specialized knowledge to set up their own seminar programs. You may be involved not just in finding a location but also in developing advertising, handout materials, and displays; co-ordinating the overall program, including lighting, music, staging, room arrangement, coffee breaks, lunches, and program timing; and carrying out after-program follow-up contacts, program evaluations, and so forth. This business requires a wide range of skills, and it may take some time to develop a word-of-mouth reputation and a positive cash flow.

Entrepreneur Group
2392 Morse Ave.
Irvine CA 92714
(714) 261-2325

Service station (see Gasoline service station)

Sewing service (see Dressmaking service)

Sewing service contractor

This is a specialized business in which you contract to pick up piece items that have been cut by a clothing manufacturer, do the finishing work, and then return them within a specified time. Pay is usually on a per-piece basis. There can be substantial cash flow involved. However, there is a great deal of competition and not a great deal of loyalty by major manufacturers to their contractors. The U.S. garment industry is undergoing vast changes because so much manufacturing is shifting to developing nations that can offer significantly lower labor costs. Should you set up a domestic operation, price and ability to deliver on time are all-important. You will need to make a significant investment in equipment and to lease or buy a reasonably convenient location. Once established, you may be able to develop a significant cash flow. Labor laws must be adhered to with great care.

American Apparel Contractors Association
PO Box 720693
Atlanta GA 30358
(404) 843-3171

Shoe repair and shoeshine service

There is a good demand for this type of craft service, which focuses on repairing and cleaning footwear and usually includes sales of shoe care products. This business requires special skills and training. It is location-sensitive, and there can be a significant investment in equipment and a lease for real estate. Once established, the cash flow can be quite good as satisfied customers bring you repeat business and tell others about you.

Shoe Service Institute of America
5024-R Campbell Blvd.
Baltimore MD 21236
(410) 931-8100

Shoe store

This type of retail business, which specializes in footwear for men, women, and children, is extremely location-sensitive and vulnerable to increasing cutthroat competition from discounters and other independent operators who may heighten their appeal by targeting niche markets. Direct owner participation will heighten your chances for success, but it can take a substantial period of time to develop a steady clientele, not to mention the capital investment in your location by ownership or long-term lease, needed equipment, and inventory.

National Shoe Retailers Association
9861 Broken Land Pkwy., #255
Columbia MD 21046-1151
(410) 381-8282

Sign creation and painting

This is a contracting business that specializes in the design and painting or carving of signs for personal and business uses. It requires special skills, and cash flow can be fairly irregular, similar to that experienced by any artist, craftsperson, or contractor. If you are to grow, you will need to develop a substantial clientele through long-term advertising and word-of-mouth referrals based on reputation and association with contractors in related businesses.

Sock store

This is a specialized retail operation that focuses on sales of socks and other hosiery items. It is highly location-sensitive, which means a substantial investment in the lease or purchase of real estate, and there is great competition from discounters. Cash flow will probably be hard to develop over the long term. Because it can be so hard to carve out a marketing niche, this business is not highly recommended.

Entrepreneur Group
2392 Morse Ave.
Irvine CA 92714
(714) 261-2325

Souvenir and novelty store (see also Gift shop)

Souvenir and Novelty Trade Association
7000 Terminal Square, #210
Upper Darby PA 19082
(215) 734-2420

Sporting goods store (see Athletic supplies store)

Stationery store (see Office supplies store)

Suntanning salon

This is a location-sensitive business that provides tanning beds for people who wish to tan without the sun. Income usually comes from short- and long-term memberships. Competition is intense and special equipment is required. Cash flow in most start-up operations would be minimal, and it would take a substantial period of time to develop to a satisfactory level. Also, given increasing concerns about the dangers of tanning, such as the promotion of skin cancers and premature aging, the future for this type of business may be cloudy.

Entrepreneur Group
2392 Morse Ave.
Irvine CA 92714
(714) 261-2325

Survey researcher

This is a consulting service in which you would contract to organizations or advertising agencies to design, carry out, and analyze public opinion polls, marketing research studies, and similar projects. The operation of this business requires special education and the development of a word-of-mouth reputation for competence, accuracy, and prompt delivery of contracted services.

Council of American Survey Research Organizations
3 Upper Devon Belle Terre
Port Jefferson NY 11777
(516) 928-6954

Tailoring service (see Dressmaking service)

Talent agency

This service provides personal managers for artists in the entertainment industry. These agents negotiate terms with employers and maintain contacts with their representatives. This kind of business will take a substantial time to develop and faces stiff competition.

National Conference of Personal Managers
210 E. 51st St.
New York NY 10022
(212) 421-2670

Tavern (see Bar)

Tee shirt and novelty shop

These retail operations sell custom-decorated and manufacturer-decorated tee shirts and other novelties. This is a highly location-sensitive business, which means a substantial investment in owned or leased real estate, and it is notably faddish. The best location for this type of shop is probably in a small community such as a resort area where customers will be especially prone to impulse purchases. However, such markets are usually seasonal.

Entrepreneur Group
2392 Morse Ave.
Irvine CA 92714
(714) 261-2325

Telemarketing service

This service specializes in direct marketing by telephone, with work performed on a contract basis for companies that wish to sell their products or services. Although not location-sensitive in the sense that retail businesses are, you will need to make a significant cash investment in leasing or purchasing equipment and other fixturing. You will have to build the business through promotion, advertising, and word of mouth. Once established, you may be able to develop a significant cash flow, but relatively few do. Usually these are not long-term businesses.

Telephone answering service

The traditional forms of this service, in which employees answer calls and take messages when subscribing individuals or businesses are unavailable, are quickly becoming obsolete because of the growing use of voice mail and other electronic receiving services offered by telephone companies or set up in homes and businesses. However, there is still a need for some personal service in some industries (medical practices are one example). Also, users of highly structured voice mail services are feeling some backlash from customers, so we may see a return to more personalized answering services. This service is probably best tied to clerical, computer, and other specialized office services.

Association of Telemessaging Services International
1150 S. Washington St., #150
Alexandria VA 22314
(703) 684-0016

Testing laboratory

These businesses conduct tests of metals, water, chemicals, and other items. They require special equipment and training as well as a substantial capital investment. Once established, you could see significant cash flow, but there is considerable competition.

Thrift store (See Second-hand store)

Tire store (see Automobile parts store)

Tobacco shop

This is a retail activity that specializes in selling cigars, cigarettes, tobacco, and other products for smokers. It is highly location-sensitive, which means a substantial investment in the lease or purchase of real estate, and there is great competition. Cash flow will probably be hard to develop over a long term. Because it can be so hard to carve out a marketing niche, this business is not highly recommended.

Tobacco Merchants Association of the United States
PO Box 8019
Princeton NJ 08543-8019
(609) 275-4900

Tour guide, trip packaging, and travel organizing service

These services are often associated with travel agencies, but there are frequently guides who tour with the travelers. Although Americans are working hard and long, they also like to travel—especially to places where they can explore their interests. Organizing and operating tours, especially ones with a special focus, can be a lucrative and enjoyable small business. Once you find your niche, you can start marketing your tours to like-minded travelers.

American Society of Travel Agencies
1101 King St.
Alexandria VA 22314
(703) 739-2782

National Tour Association
PO Box 3071
Lexington KY 40596
(606) 253-1036

Towing service

This service, which specializes in towing vehicles that have broken down or are illegally parked, is usually offered in association with service stations and other car repair locations. Because special tow trucks are required, you will have to invest in equipment. Cash flow can be good if you develop the right connections, for example, with a police department. On the other hand, this type of business can require a substantial amount of real estate where towed and impounded cars can be stored, although this can be in a properly zoned secondary area. You will face a great deal of competition from established contractors.

American Petroleum Institute
1220 L St. NW
Washington DC 20005
(202) 682-8000

Toy store (see also Baby Store)

Toy Manufacturers Of America
200 Fifth Ave., #740

New York NY 10010
(212) 675-1141

Trash pickup service

This type of service operates on an independently contracted basis to collect waste and trash materials from residences and businesses on a scheduled or as-needed basis. It can be a relatively lucrative business. However, there are problems: You can face substantial dumping fees imposed by local government, and there are often restrictions on the types of items that can be placed in dumps or landfills. Special licensing or permits may be required, and you would have to invest in trucks, either purchased or leased. Even the equipment used for hauling trash to dumps may need to comply with local ordinances. There is a growing need for this type of service.

National Solid Wastes Management Association
1730 Rhode Island Ave. NW, #1000
Washington DC 20036
(202) 659-4613

Travel agency

This type of service provides travel information, tours, hotel accommodations, car rentals, and transportation for individuals and business-people. It is somewhat location-sensitive, and there is substantial well-established competition in most communities. Cash flow can be fair; only in rare instances is it excellent.

American Society of Travel Agents
1101 King St.
Alexandria VA 22314
(703) 739-2782

Tree and plant store (see Garden supply store)

Trophy and awards store

This is a specialty retail operation that sells trophies and awards, often personalized by engraving. It is highly location-sensitive, which means a substantial investment in the lease or purchase of real estate, and there is great competition. Cash flow will probably be hard to develop over the long term.

Souvenir and Novelty Trade Association
7000 Terminal Square, #210
Upper Darby PA 19082
(215) 734-2420

Unfinished furniture store (see Furniture store, unfinished)

Used office furnishings store (see Furnishings and furniture, office, used)

Used video and music cassette store

This type of business, which resells used video and music cassettes and compact discs at heavily discounted prices, is similar to video and music cassette stores that sell new products. There is already substantial competition, and many franchise retail stores are starting to get into used equipment to compete with the independent used-product stores. This type of business could be affected by the same factors that are going to affect new video and music cassette stores. Also, there is substantial investment required, and cash flow might take time to develop. If you can find an area where there is no competition, cash flow may build more quickly.

Vending machine route

This service business supplies and stocks leased or owned vending machines in office complexes, retail stores, and other locations. Products can include popcorn, candy, beverages, light meals, and so forth. Vending machine distributors buy products from various sources at wholesale prices and resell them in the machines at a premium. This business can develop into a good part-time or even full-time activity—the problem is to get enough locations where you can place and service the machines. There is substantial competition, but if you can find enough locations, this can provide good supplemental income. You can operate from home or from a nonsensitive industrial location where you can store your vehicles and supplies.

National Automatic Merchandising Association
20 N. Wacker Dr.
Chicago IL 60606
(213) 346-0370

Veterinary practice

This professional service for the care of animals requires a doctor of veterinary medicine degree. It may be a difficult business to get into because of zoning codes and the substantial investment needed for your plant, equipment, and trained staff. However, more and more Americans have pets, and a qualified practitioner can realize a good cash flow.

American Veterinary Medical Association
1931 N. Meacham Rd., #100
Schaumburg IL 60173
(800) 248-2862

Videocassette rental store (see also Music and video store)

These retail stores provide customers with prerecorded videotapes and laserdiscs of movies and music for a limited time. Stores may also rent out videocassette recorders and video cameras. This type of business may be in for rough sledding, depending on the success of fiber optics and other new telecommunications advances that will allow virtually any movie to be selected from the viewer's home or office.

Entrepreneur Group
2392 Morse Ave.
Irvine CA 92714
(714) 261-2325

Videotaping service

This type of service specializes in making video recordings of events such as weddings, music videos, and so forth. A substantial start-up investment is required, and this business will definitely be affected by advances in electronic communications, many of which cannot be predicted ahead of time. There is already much competition. An existing business of this nature can generate good cash flow, at least for the time being. However, there is the hazard of an uncertain future. To start a business of this nature today would be highly risky.

Vitamin store (see Health food store)

Wedding planner

This type of personal service provides start-to-finish planning for weddings based on clients' desires, needs, and budget. You take on responsibility for making contact with all the individuals and businesses needed to carry out a wedding, everything from cakes to gowns to photographers to good locations. Your business will come mainly from word-of-mouth referrals and, to a lesser extent, from advertising in the Yellow Pages and other places. Cash flow can be reasonable, and you can work out of your home; a specific location is not essential.

Association of Bridal Consultants
200 Chestnutland Rd.
New Milford CT 06776-2521
(203) 355-0464

Wedding shop

This type of retail store sells wedding-related merchandise such as bridal gowns, veils, and wedding invitations. Wedding-planning services may also be offered. This is a highly location-sensitive business, which means a substantial investment in the lease or purchase of real estate, and there is great competition. Cash flow will probably be hard to develop over a long term.

National Bridal Service
3122 W. Cary St.
Richmond VA 23221
(804) 355-6945

Window display service

This is a contracting service that assists retailers with creative window displays. You might work with an advertising agency on concepts that you would then execute. Business will come through referrals, so it will take some time to develop.

Women's clothing and accessories store

These specialized retail stores sell women's clothing as well as purses, hats, belts, and other items. They are highly location-sensitive, which means a substantial investment in the lease or purchase of real estate, and competition is fierce. Cash flow will probably be hard to develop over a long term. Because it can be so hard to carve out a marketing niche, these businesses are highly risky.

National Fashion Accessories Association
330 Fifth Ave., #205
New York NY 10001
(212) 947-3424

Writer, freelance

This type of independent writing service can cover a wide range of specific projects, with fees paid on a per-project basis. You can also market your own proposals for small- or large-scale projects to newspapers, magazines, film, television, and book publishers. Freelance writers can specialize in nonfiction or fiction, and the financial arrangements and rights situations can become quite complex. This is a precarious business. It can be difficult to break into and requires constant attention to generate new business.

National Writers Union
873 Broadway, #203
New York NY 10003-1209
(212) 254-0279

CHAPTER 7

If You Decide to Buy

If, after careful study and consideration, you decide you'd rather buy a business than start one up, I believe the best and safest way to proceed is by working with an experienced broker. Their input can be like gold—this chapter shows you how to mine it. I also discuss things to look for if you decide to buy an ongoing business, whether through a broker or on your own, and I add some notes on the pluses and minuses of one of today's major business trends—franchising.

Brokers can muster strong arguments for buying existing businesses, especially particular kinds of businesses, rather than starting one from scratch. Jeff Jones, a principal at Certified Business Brokers (CBB) in Houston, outlined some of the reasons:

- Statistics show that buying an existing business reduces the risk of failure.
- Existing businesses can produce immediate cash flow.
- Permits and licenses may already be in place, thus avoiding delays.
- Existing businesses have established customers, vendors, credit, and trained employees.
- Sellers can offer training and financing.

Why Go to a Broker?

Asking this question is like asking, "Why hire a real estate agent to sell your house? Why not do it yourself and save the commission?" The answer, to put it simply, is that brokers and other intermediaries are professionals who are out there in the small-business trenches every day. They're the ones who are looking at "the whites of their eyes." They know where the action is, and where it isn't. Or, as Jeff Jones puts it, brokers are "the supermarket of businesses for sale."

It's the brokers' business to put themselves in the best position to know what kinds of opportunities are available, and their professional advice can help you avoid the pitfalls and possible risks involved in taking on an existing enterprise.

"Once a buyer has been qualified as to interest and financial ability, brokers can provide a wealth of information on various businesses that can save prospective buyers months and years of research time and costs," Jones says.

"You have to keep in mind that brokers basically represent sellers," says Thomas L. West, former executive director of the International Business Brokers Association (IBBA). "There's an increasing trend for brokers to represent buyers, but that's a problem because brokers are entitled to a fee or commission.

"When dealing with a seller, the commission is included somehow in the sale price, but the fee has a different feel to it from the buyer's perspective because it will come out of the money he or she has set aside for their investment. So it feels different, and buyers can be reluctant to pay a broker to work for them."

How to Find a Broker

Now you know why you should look for a broker. How do you actually find one? One way to is check out real estate companies, because many real estate agents see business brokering as a natural byproduct of their business. About 20 states require that business brokers be licensed just as real estate agents are.

According to Thomas West, the best place to start looking is the obvious one: the newspaper classifieds. "When people get serious about buying a small business, the first place they probably look is at the business opportunities listings in their newspaper classifieds," he says. "Most of these are actually placed by brokers, although a few ads may come from private owners or owners of franchises."

San Diego-based appraiser Jack Sanders, who also publishes the annual BIZCOMPS reports on asking and selling prices of small businesses nationwide, agrees that reading the paper is the best way to educate yourself about the businesses that interest you. "You can do your own market search, but this takes a sophisticated buyer," he warns.

CBB's Jeff Jones cited the following resources for finding out about businesses that might be for sale:

- Suppliers
- Trade associations
- Competitors
- Advertisements in trade journals in addition to newspaper ads

Suppose you see a "Business for Sale" classified ad that seems to just leap off the page and speak to you. You call the number listed, and it turns out to be the broker who is handling the sale. What should you be looking for? Here are two important guidelines:

- Does he or she have experience in the self-employment and small business scene in the region that interests you? This applies whether you're looking for a business in the area where you now live or are thinking of relocating.
- Do you feel comfortable with him or her? Can you talk candidly about your goals, expectations, financial resources and obligations, and any other factor that is playing a role in your plans?

You should be able to trust your broker the way you trust your doctor, lawyer, or pastor. Like many other professionals, brokers are best sought out via word of mouth.

As you've been thinking about the small-business opportunities that might be best for you, you may already have spoken with people in the field you're considering entering. Get in touch with them again and ask them about brokers in your area. Ask your friends if they know someone you might consult. You might even do the obvious and look in the phone book. If you're thinking of relocating, go to the library and look at the phone book for the area that interests you.

Also, as you go about your daily rounds of errands, talk to your dry cleaner, the owner of your local bakery, the manager of your video-rental store. Ask them how they bought their business, who helped them, and what their experience was like. In other words, do your homework.

It's also a good idea to find out if there's a business brokers' association in your state. Get a list of the members in your area or the region that interests you. You should also get copies of its newsletters and publications, because these will tell you what things look like from the brokers' perspective. These materials often contain information about what brokers like to have happen when potential clients come to them.

Finally, CBB's Jeff Jones says his firm gets a lot of referrals from accountants and attorneys as well as from satisfied clients.

How to Be a Good Client

KEEP AN OPEN MIND

But no matter how you find your broker, you need to keep an open mind if you're to get the most out of your relationship with him or her. You need to be willing to explore. Again, you might think that having an open mind is second nature, but brokers we spoke with often commented that potential clients have too often ruled out certain kinds of small businesses even before they walk into the broker's office. Buyers who do that have closed their minds to possible opportunities.

One broker says early retirees often get cold feet when it comes to making the decision to buy a business. "They're used to their paychecks, and putting a big sum of money down on a business scares them," he says. "They'll research a business for six months to two years but then not buy one and end up taking a job that's the same as the one they had before."

In his view, the most promising opportunities are to be found in service-oriented areas such as landscaping, house cleaning, window washing, and janitorial work. However, he adds that such businesses "don't appeal to retired executives because they aren't glitzy, and [buyers] feel they project a poor image."

Another broker says that too many buyers "are looking for and will pay more for a business situation that has shorter hours, fewer days, a safe location, and also if there is an image with the business." He says corporate executives who have been laid off or golden-parachuted out of their corporations are so used to having secretaries take notes for them, get them coffee, and offer general assistance that they want to maintain that prestige in their life and are willing to pay more for this factor as an "intangible."

One broker in Louisiana says he always tries to match people up with a business that suits their personality. "Most people don't know what they want to do," he says. "They just want to buy a steady stream of money. A lot of people don't have the right personality for certain businesses or couldn't handle the expertise needed for certain businesses."

However, another broker commented that the worst people to turn to for advice on buying a small business are "your attorney, your CPA, and your banker." Rather, he says, you should go out and "talk to someone who already owns the same type of business. That's where you'll find out the truth about things." He adds, "When people are searching for self-employment, they think they know what they want, but after they research it and talk to a broker, they find out that they really don't want that particular business. So they find something together that fits their skills, financial situation, etc."

A Wisconsin broker comments, "When people come to me, they don't know what they want, but they definitely know that they don't want restaurants or bars. New buyers will usually ask for 'a little manufacturing company,' but they really don't know what that means."

Another Wisconsin-based broker says, "People want something that's a business-to-business type company or service. Their attorneys tell them to stay away from retail and anything that deals with the general public. They usually want an easy business, something simple and relocatable like mail-order or catalog businesses."

One Midwest-based broker prefers that clients have an accurate idea of how much money they have for a down payment and what they're going to live on. "A lot of early-buyout people seem to think they can go in and buy a business and maintain their lifestyle," he says. "They just don't realize what it takes." He adds that potential buyers are too often "not interested in the content of what they're doing, only the money—but this is a big problem because if they're making money and not happy they'll be discontented."

And Jack Sanders says, "If buyers call because they're interested in a specific type of business, I catalog the information and call them when something comes on the market. But "buyers should also prepare themselves on how to sell a broker on their seriousness," he adds. "We jealously guard our time because it's the only asset we have. For example, you should show willingness to come to our office." Brokers are generally reluctant to go out to meet with a potential buyer because of the time factor, he explains.

Jeff Jones likes to see potential buyers bring a résumé and financial statement to the initial meeting, although buyers are reluctant to provide these upfront. "We have to try to zero in on what they have access to" in terms of resources and skills as quickly as possible, he explains.

BE REALISTIC

One Midwest broker says potential buyers often feel disillusioned and disappointed after being shocked into reality by their first meeting with a broker. "I try to help them out and work with them," he says. "I have guides and publications that I give to people to help them along."

He says he will try to find a business whose owner will carry back one-third to one-half of the financing. "A carryback keeps the seller around, which can heighten the chances of success," he adds. But even under the best of circumstances, the new owner may "come in and, because of his or her unfamiliarity with the business, it may go through a slight downturn, even if the owner sticks around," he warns.

This broker says the chances of finding a seller who will carry back some of the financing are greater if the buyer puts together "as accurate a personal résumé as possible—the true facts."

If You Decide to Go It Alone

Although IBBA's Tom West believes that working with a broker can speed the search for a small business, he also says that potential buyers can search for businesses themselves. This might be especially useful if you're looking for a very specialized type of business. West recommends two ways to proceed:

- You can get in touch with American Business Information (ABI) in Omaha, Nebraska, (5711 S. 86th Circle, PO Box 27347, Omaha NE 68127; 402/593-4593). Supply them with the U.S. Government Standard Industrial Classification code (the book listing these codes is available in any public library), postal zipcodes of locations that interest you, and the annual range of sales amounts you're seeking. ABI will supply you with a list of companies that meet your criteria, along with the presidents' name. You can then write to the company president directly and begin exploring the possibility of a purchase.
- You can also go to your local Dun & Bradstreet office and place inquiries for the same kinds of information. Both Dun & Bradstreet and ABI may also be able to carry out these researches for you by computer as well.

A Buyer's Checklist

If you're considering buying a business, and whether you work with a broker or go it alone, here is a checklist of features and factors that will give you some idea of whether a particular business is a relatively good risk or one to avoid.

APPEARANCE OF FACILITIES

What is the ambience or atmosphere of the business? Does the atmosphere generate patronage? Does the appearance fit the surrounding area? What is the condition of the store or office, the fixtures, the equipment? Is the merchandise clean and well displayed? In short, are the facilities competitive?

The facilities do not need to be fancy or in an expensive neighborhood, but they should be inviting. If they look shabby, that is how the customer will see you and the way you do business. A facility should reflect success.

CASH FLOW TRENDS

Although the most recent year's cash flow is usually the best indicator of current business level, be sure to review several recent years of financial information.

COMPETITION

Competition has always been an important consideration, and in today's cutthroat environment it is more crucial than ever, particularly if you're looking at an independent retail business. As we've mentioned, discount superstores are forcing smaller operators out of business or forcing them to make major changes in their product lines, pricing, and ways of operating. But even these defensive tactics often prove to be futile. The mere announcement that a major discounter is planning to enter a market area can kill the value and salability of a small business, particularly in smaller communities. Also, keep in mind that some businesses, particularly those that offer products and services consumers "shop" for, perform better when there is competition nearby. Automobile dealerships in an auto row, or shoe stores in a shopping mall, are good examples.

COMPETITIVENESS

If you are considering buying a business, it isn't enough to look outward, at the competition. You must also decide whether the business is itself competitive. Are active steps being taken to ensure that pricing, appearance, service, product quality, employee training and compensation, and other such elements, are competitive? Businesses can, and do, become obsolete. They require almost constant "dusting-off" to remain competitive. In today's fast-moving and competitive economy, merely having an established location or a favorable reputation may not be enough. It's how the location and reputation are used that makes the difference between profit and loss.

CONDITION OF INVENTORY

Is the inventory clean and up-to-date? The condition of the inventory has a significant influence on how much a business is worth. Even a salvage yard can be kept neat, and it pays off in the ability to charge higher prices. It also makes inventory easier to maintain and improves customers' impressions of the operation. If the merchandise appears outdated or soiled, or if it includes too many slow-moving items, this reflects negatively on the overall condition of the business. Inventory is usually included with the sale of the business, but it is priced separately when the transaction is closed. The total is then added to the price previously agreed upon for the other business assets, such as furnishings, fixtures, equipment, leasehold improvements, lease, intangibles, and goodwill.

COVENANT NOT TO COMPETE

Many businesses are not salable unless the seller is willing to give a covenant not to compete. Such covenants can raise legal issues that differ from state to state and should be investigated. Before deciding to buy, consider whether a noncompetition covenant is an important issue, and determine what basic conditions you require in such a covenant.

EASE OR DIFFICULTY OF ENTRY

Not all businesses are equally difficult or easy to start. The relative ease or difficulty of entering a particular industry has an impact on the value of a small business in that industry. When you think about buying a business, you should weigh carefully the relative benefits and disadvantages of buying an existing business compared to starting a brand-new one.

An existing business may have the only suitable location; or it may be grandfathered in some manner, such as its ability to continue using certain kinds of machinery or equipment; or it may have a permit or license that is desirable but no longer available to new entries in the market area. Or the costs of starting a particular business from scratch may be prohibitive. On the other hand, it might be possible to attract patronage to a new venture by such simple means as offering discount pricing.

The relative costs and difficulty of starting a new operation are directly related to how much of a premium you should consider paying for the goodwill or intangibles of an established business. Do not consider paying an inflated price just for the privilege of becoming the proud owner of a business that cannot possibly provide a reasonable return on your investment.

INDUSTRY CONDITION AND OUTLOOK

A particular industry may exhibit different trends and thus a different outlook from the general economy. The overall economy may be performing well or poorly, but that does not always mean that a specific industry will follow suit.

LEASE TERMS

As has been emphasized throughout this book, location is crucial. If the business you are considering is location-sensitive, you should be guaranteed that it will be able to remain at the same location, ideally because the business owns the property or because there is a written lease. In most instances, five years of assured tenancy is minimal, and there should be an option to extend the lease for an additional five years at a stated rent. Some businesses are difficult to sell if they have a lease of fewer than 10 or 15 years remaining, and a lease that provides for renewal options but does not specify rental terms is of little or no value. If the business is operating on a month-to-month tenancy at a location, think long and hard before buying, even if revenue, cash flow, and other factors are favorable.

LONGEVITY

As a general rule, the longer the business has been established, the greater its value. A reputation for honesty, fair prices, service, quality of product, and so forth only grows stronger over time. However, many businesses become obsolete and thus less valuable over time. Such businesses have often failed to evolve with changing markets and customer needs. Declines in value may also be due to conditions, such as changes in traffic patterns or neighborhood demographics, that are beyond a business's control.

OWNERSHIP OF PREMISES

Ownership of the premises occupied by the business can be an important attribute because it assures security of location. However, be sure to keep the value of the property separate from the value of the business. This is usually accomplished by adjusting the income statement to add a market rent, if rental expense has not already been included. Also, the seller may not want to sell the business and the real estate together. It is common for a seller to sell only the business and to offer a lease for the property. The terms of such a lease could damage the value of the business. For example, a five-year lease with no option to renew at a set rental rate would normally detract from value, particularly for highly location-sensitive businesses.

PARKING

Almost all businesses today must be accessible to automobile traffic. Safe, adequate parking is a must. If customers can't get to the business because they can't find parking, it isn't much of a business.

PRODUCT QUALITY

The quality of the product or service is always an important ingredient in establishing repeat business. Does the business have a reputation for consistent product or service quality?

RECORD KEEPING

Sloppy record keeping is a reflection of a sloppy business operation. With so many government regulations today, no business can afford poor record keeping. Every business needs careful, complete records on customer follow-up, sales programs, and other aspects of the business on a current, real-time basis.

Repeat Patronage

A business with well-established repeat patronage will tend to be more valuable than one that depends on transient customers. However, if the relationship between customers and the business owner is very close, it may be difficult to transfer patronage to a new owner. You should also consider how up-to-date the customer list is. Most such lists become at least 25 percent obsolete after one year and are virtually worthless after 18 months. A business that focuses on its customers by keeping in touch with them helps keep customers focused on its products and services.

Reputation

What is the business's reputation with the public, established suppliers, bankers, and others? Does the business depend on the unique personal skills, abilities, personality, or reputation of the owner? Are there managers other than the owner who will remain and help sustain the business's reputation during the transition to new ownership?

Return on Investment and Return of Investment

Consider the business's ability to provide a fair return of and on your investment. Return of investment refers to recovering the original amount you have invested, usually through profits, while return on investment refers to your profit on your investment over and above the return of that investment. If you're like most prudent investors, you'll be seeking a full return of the capital you have invested within three years, and usually less, plus a competitive return on that capital. In addition, the business should generate enough cash flow to compensate you for labor and to provide for growth capital.

Revenue Trends

Take a close look at the business's recent revenue trends. What is the most realistic outlook for the near future? It is important to note that even if a business shows increasing revenue during the previous year or two, this does not necessarily mean that the same trends will continue.

Most business revenues tend to be cyclical in nature: increasing for short periods, leveling for a time, and then increasing again or declining. When analyzing revenue trends, also look into the ability of the business to cope with revenue increases given the limits of its store area, equipment, and parking, as well as the availability of additional patronage from its market area. During inflationary periods, a business that shows increasing revenue in terms of dollars may not be increasing in terms of its customer base, and the increase in dollar revenue may actually be due only to price increases. Any business that shows a leveling of revenue is a business in decline.

SIGNAGE

Is the business doing everything possible to make it easy for people to find it? Big, visible signs are not always practical, but at the very least, customers should be able to find the street address. It never fails to amaze me how many businesses can't seem to be bothered to post a clearly visible street address! Bear in mind that improving inadequate signage will cost money.

SPECIAL PERMITS AND LICENSES

Some businesses require special operating licenses or permits. For example, in most states a privately operated liquor store cannot be in business without a liquor license. In many areas, some businesses, such as auto wrecking or salvage yards, cannot operate without a conditional-use permit. You must research whether any such licenses and permits would be transferable to you as the new owner.

STAFF AND MANAGEMENT

Very often, the only thing potential customers ever "see" about a business is the telephone reception—so the person who answers the phones *becomes* the business. Telephone reception must be prompt, efficient, and friendly. How hard is it to get through to the boss? For the most effective telephone public relations, everyone, including the boss, should be accessible. If customers don't like to call a business, most likely they'll never tell anyone. They'll just call somewhere else.

Does the business operate on the principle that the customer is always right? Do staff workers and managers have the authority to satisfy customer complaints and problems on the spot, without having to wait for a rubber stamp from upstairs? That's how a business makes friends. The good word gets around, and so does the bad word (sometimes followed by a subpoena). Are staff and management kept informed and made to feel a genuine part of the business's success? Do they participate financially with some form of regular review and bonus program? Are there formalized and consistent policies and procedures for holidays, vacation, sick leave, and so on?

TERMS OF SALE

There is substantial information available that shows that the terms of sale of a small business have a significant impact on the price. Typical terms are a 30 to 50 percent cash down payment with a note at a competitive rate of interest payable at least quarterly in not more than 20 installments. Discounts should be given for cash sales or sales with significantly fewer than 20 quarterly installments. Conversely, you should expect to pay a premium if you offer less up-front cash and longer terms.

Franchising—Some Cautionary Words

If you're at all considering creating or buying a small business, you're probably wondering why I haven't talked about franchising. My overall opinion about franchising can be expressed in two words: *Be careful!* If I were to repeat what many franchisees have told me about their experiences, these pages would turn blue!

WHAT IS A FRANCHISE?

The *Boston Business Journal* recently offered this simple definition: "Franchising . . . typically involves a franchisor selling his or her trade name and business system to a franchisee who pays a royalty and often an initial fee for the right to do business under the name and system."[1]

There's no need for you to look for a franchise if you want to get into any of the businesses described in chapter 5. However, there can be advantages to associating yourself with a reputable franchisor under certain conditions. For example, if you can find a franchise for the type of business that interests you, and if the initial investment would be about the same as what you'd need for your own start-up, give it a close look.

Also, you can benefit from the franchisor's training programs, economies of scale in advertising and promotion, and merchandising tips.

One major advantage of dealing with reputable and successful franchises is that the franchisors will carefully evaluate your basic qualifications and chances of success to determine if their operation seems to be the right business for you long before they sell you a franchise.

According to the *Boston Business Journal*, there are more than 540,000 franchised units in the United States, and a new franchise opens every 6.5 minutes during each business day. Costs range from a low of $6,500 to $14,000 for a commercial cleaning service to between $500,000 and $700,000 for a well-known video rental store chain.[2]

Because franchise operations try to maximize success by giving you a cookbook formula, you may be able to realize a profit faster than if you try to start the same type of business entirely on your own. However, as has often been said about sex, anticipation can be better than the realization. And, be aware that a franchise is no guarantee that you'll do better than you would have on your own. According to Robert Barkoff, chairman of the American Bar Association's committee on franchising, one-third of all franchisees in a typical chain do well, one-third break even, and the rest lose money.[3] However, estimates of the success of franchises vary wildly. John Hayes, author of *Franchising: The Inside Story*, claims that 93 percent of franchise businesses continue year after year, while 50 percent of nonfranchise businesses fail within their first year.[4]

Another factor to consider is community resistance to franchise operations. According to *Nation's Restaurant News*, restaurant chains have been finding it harder to move into small suburban communities due to increasing red tape and zoning restrictions. These communities fear that franchise restaurants will hurt local businesses, create traffic congestion, generate trash, become gathering places for alcohol and drug abuse, and violate local aesthetics because of their architecture.[5]

How to Maximize Your Chances of Franchise Success

If you still feel that franchising is the way you might want to go, here is a four-step approach recommended by Ann Dugan, assistant director of the Small Business Development Center at the University of Pittsburgh:

1. Gather information.

It's important to gather as much market information as possible before buying a franchise. Looking through business magazines is helpful.

2. Research and analyze the franchises that interest you.

This means testing the products first-hand and researching other chains—especially ones that are struggling. See if you can see what the problems are and come up with possible solutions. Also be sure to research any litigation that has affected those franchises that interest you.

3. Do a self-evaluation.

Evaluate your personality, interests, and style and consider how these mesh with the franchises that interest you. Evaluate your skills and see how you can expand your talents in the business you choose.

4. Make a decision.

Ask yourself these questions: Do you have sufficient funds to invest in the business? Do you enjoy it? Does it fit your personal style?

Dugan also recommends that prospective buyers attend at least one seminar on small business management and running a franchise before making a decision.[6]

MY ADVICE?

The basic thing to keep in mind if you're considering a franchise is the old maxim: *There are no free lunches.* Or, to put it another way: *If it sounds too good to be true, it probably is.* These may be clichés, but clichés become clichés because they are true.

Endnotes

1. Catherine Walthers, "Franchise Owners Can Create Their Own Jobs," *Boston Business Journal,* 23 April 1993, sec. 1, p. 18.
2. Ibid.
3. Meg Whittemore, "The Franchise Search: Steps to Becoming a Franchisee," *Nation's Business,* April 1993, p. 49.
4. Cited in Catherine Walthers, "Franchise Owners Can Create Their Own Jobs," *Boston Business Journal,* 23 April, 1993, sec. 1, p. 18.
5. Milford Prewitt, "Local Zoning Laws Thwart Chains' Expansion Drives; Operators Blast Stubborn Communities for Unfair 'Victimization,' " *Nation's Restaurant News,* 24 May, 1993, p. 1.
6. Whittemore, "The Franchise Search," p. 49.

CHAPTER 8

Relocation Possibilities

To help you decide which small business is best for you, we did a telephone survey of business brokers all over the United States, speaking with them about the current small-business climate in their area. This "snapshot" of business conditions is of course subject to change, but many of the brokers offered useful information and observations (sometimes quoted directly here) about general economic, demographic, and business trends that you should take into account if you are considering moving to another geographical area and going into business there—or even if you want to get a sense for what is going on in your present area.

Population Growth Trends

None of us can predict the future. If we could, you wouldn't need to be reading this book, and we would all have made our fortunes a long time ago. Nevertheless, our government spends millions of dollars a year trying to predict trends for us, so we may as well take advantage of all that effort and use it in our own planning.

One of the things the government does relatively well is predict population growth trends, and where population goes, business tends to follow. This is why we are beginning this chapter by listing all 50 states in the order of expected population growth as of the year 2000, according to the U.S. Bureau of the Census. If you're looking for new opportunities, population growth alone may not give you all the answers you need, but it should definitely be taken into consideration.

POPULATION GROWTH PROJECTIONS FOR YEAR 2000

1.	Wyoming	+28%		North Dakota	+9%
2.	Hawaii	+24%		Virginia	+9%
3.	Utah	+21%	15.	Kansas	+7%
4.	New Mexico	+20%		Maine	+7%
5.	Alaska	+19%		South Dakota	+7%
6.	Idaho	+19%	16.	Delaware	+6%
7.	Colorado	+17%		Maryland	+6%
	Texas	+17%		Missouri	+6%
8.	Louisiana	+15%		Vermont	+6%
	Oklahoma	+15%	17.	Kentucky	+5%
9.	Washington	+14%		Nebraska	+5%
10.	Arizona	+13%		New Jersey	+5%
	Georgia	+13%		West Virginia	+5%
	New Hampshire	+13%	18.	Connecticut	+4%
	Oregon	+13%		Illinois	+4%
11.	Montana	+12%		Minnesota	+4%
	South Carolina	+12%	19.	Indiana	+3%
12.	Alabama	+11%		Wisconsin	+3%
	Arkansas	+11%	20.	Iowa	+1%
	California	+11%		Rhode Island	+1%
	Florida	+11%	21.	Michigan	0
	Mississippi	+11%		Ohio	0
	Nevada	+11%		Pennsylvania	0
13.	Tennessee	+10%	22.	Massachusetts	−2%
	National Average	**+9%**		New York	−2%
14.	North Carolina	+9%	23.	District of Columbia	−3%

Sales, Demand, Financing, and General Conditions: A National Survey

ALABAMA

Birmingham

Recent sales Service-oriented businesses (auto parts, machine, heating/air conditioning shops, dry cleaners, grocery); fast-food operations, both franchises and mom-and-pop restaurants

Demand   Information not available

Financing   Information not available

General comments   An area of steady growth that attracts new residents because of its relaxed pace and laid-back lifestyle; brief, mild winters and good climate; formerly a steel-manufacturing area, now perhaps the most important center for medical research in the South; home to several colleges and universities; new industrial parks and subdivisions; high-speed railway is being built between Birmingham and Atlanta; many big businesses have moved to Atlanta

Mobile

Recent sales   Fast-food franchises, manufacturing (sheet-metal, industrial chemicals, water-pump), accounting practices

Demand   Franchises and small manufacturing

Financing   Information not available

General comments   "Boomtown" atmosphere on the Gulf Coast (good climate, beaches) with strong population growth and relatively low cost of living; recent additions include Super Wal-Mart, four hotels, outlet shopping mall, and regional antique center; attracts young people as well as retirees from the North and corporate refugees who can buy both a small business and a home with equity gained from sales of houses in more expensive regions of the country

ALASKA

Anchorage

Recent sales   Kite and toy store, restaurant, telecommunications firm

Demand   Service-oriented businesses

Financing   Seller; banks involved with larger transactions

General comments   Population now increasing after downturn in late 1980s due to changes in oil market; Costco, Pace, Kmarts, Wal-Mart now in area

ARIZONA

Flagstaff

Recent sales   Restaurant, liquor store, apartment complex

Demand   Manufacturing and distribution

Financing   Bank loans if buyer has prior good credit, good down payment, ability to pay back loan; otherwise, seller

General comments   Regional population growing by an estimated 5 percent a year, attracted by quality of life, availability of national parks and recreation; residents of nearby Navajo reservation shop in city; need for leisure activities (movie theaters, bowling alleys, video game arcades, etc.) targeted to 16,000 area college students; also a shortage of affordable single-family and apartment housing

Phoenix/Scottsdale

Recent sales   Retail and service (truck stop, upscale restaurant, convenience store/car wash, computer software company, jewelry-case manufacturer)

Demand   Information not available

Financing   Seller; SBA

General comments   Estimated 50,000 new residents moved to the area in 1992–93

Tucson

Recent sales   Unspecified light manufacturing, distribution business, CPA firm, gas station, professional maintenance company

Demand   No specific trend; buyers seeking something that will bring in a certain level of income; overall need for more small businesses in general to keep up with population growth

Financing   Seller

General comments   Growing population attracted by climate, laid-back lifestyle, arts activities based at University of Arizona; demand for small businesses currently outstrips supply; Hughes Aircraft has consolidated in area; national firms moving to region; new resorts being built

ARKANSAS

Little Rock

Recent sales   CPA firm, small retail shop, small company that manufactures an automatic fishing reel, retail tee shirt silk-screen business, convenience store

Demand   Corporate pink-slip employees know only how much they have to spend (usually $50,000 to $75,000), not what business to buy

Financing   Almost all seller-financed; state law forbids banks to charge more than 5 percent over treasury discount rate for loans, which deters banks from helping small businesses

General comments   Strong recreation area with lakes and fishing appeals to retirees and younger people drawn by new industry; state "right-to-work" laws (union membership is optional rather than compulsory) are popular with industry; small retailers (hardware stores, retail shops) have been hard-hit by club-type discounters and superstores; big businesses have been downsizing

Fort Smith

Recent sales   Janitorial business, restaurant

Demand   Buyers rarely know exactly what they want

Financing   Seller; occasionally SBA

General comments   Population growth has been spurred by quality of life in the Ozarks region

CALIFORNIA

Fresno

Recent sales   Video arcade/game room, video rental stores, grape harvesting business, beauty salon, restaurant, 26-truck ice cream route, "good-size" computer store, boat manufacturer

Demand   Already "one too many" of every type of business; "golden parachuters" seek franchises, but also tend not to be risk-takers

Financing   Principally seller; some banks will loan up to 50 percent for larger deals, but there must be a large inventory for collateral and buyer must be experienced

General comments   Area of rapid population growth with large influx of Asians; low cost of living is an attraction, as is (inaccurate) perception that crime rates are low

Orange County

Recent sales   Manufacturing (trophies and awards, clothing), self-storage business, medical gas and oxygen distribution, Subway sandwich businesses, print shop

Demand   No demand for retail or food-related businesses

Financing   Seller-financed; bank loans only in the form of home equity loans that can be used as borrower desires; no loans with new businesses as collateral

General comments   New residents still attracted by California lifestyle, but may be disappointed by shortage of white-collar jobs

Redding

Recent sales   Bakery, fast-food (not franchise), RV and mobile-home park, some licensed retail; businesses (such as contracting businesses) are harder to sell because buyer must apply for new license

Demand   Buyers seeking route-type and service-oriented businesses, also distributorships; also demand for convenience stores, gas stations, food businesses; need for businesses that would create jobs

Financing   Seller; bank loans available only if SBA-guaranteed

General comments   Popular area for retirees, who spend a good deal on services and health care; thus, a good area for health-related businesses and services; however, overall population decline due to cutbacks in logging because of environmental concerns; economy is down; people who have been laid off from logging seeking businesses to buy so they don't have to move

Riverside

Recent sales   Liquor store, bar, restaurant

Demand   Information not available

Financing   Seller; SBA very difficult to work with

General comments   Weak economy, closure of military bases, high workers' compensation payments, other antibusiness state policies and mandates have resulted in small businesses moving out of state; sales of businesses have been slow over past year; overbuilt shopping centers having trouble retaining prosperous business

San Diego

Recent sales   Dry cleaners, gas station, flower shop, auto painting franchise, mailbox service, packaging service, liquor store

Demand   Supply currently exceeds demand; certain immigrant groups tend to seek particular kinds of businesses ("Asians, dry cleaners;

Iraqis, liquor stores; Persians, gas stations") that require less English; English-speaking immigrants from India will seek businesses in high-tech that require more negotiating skills

Financing   Mostly seller-financed; only one bank offering SBA loans

General comments   Heavy influx of immigrants, especially from Asia, attracted by weather and environment; however, military population has declined in recent years

San Francisco/Sacramento

Recent sales   Service-oriented (gas stations, commercial janitorial businesses, restaurants), distributorships (garden tools), some manufacturing; no high technology

Demand   First-time buyers at first seek the same businesses they have seen friends get into but ultimately decide based on whether they can live on the bottom-line cash flow; "people are not trying out new businesses"

Financing   Seller-financed principally; some small or partial bank loans

General comments   Lower living costs and relaxed lifestyle attract newcomers

COLORADO

Colorado Springs

Recent sales   "All over the map": motels, restaurants, dry cleaners, convenience stores, retail

Demand   Information not available

Financing   Information not available

General comments   "Tremendous" population growth due to quality of life, economic situation, strong job growth

Denver/Boulder

Recent sales   High-end restaurant (purchased by three former executives as a partnership), "simple businesses" (dry cleaning and liquor stores)

Demand   Light manufacturing, distribution, convenience stores with good inventories, accounting practices; little demand overall for restaurant and retail businesses; "any profitable business that produces a strong cash flow"

Financing   Information not available

General comments   Large influx of new residents from both the east and west coasts who are attracted by Rocky Mountain lifestyle; "good small-business climate and strong entrepreneurial spirit"; healthy business climate, with active market in business sales/purchase; primary clients have been "golden parachute" males with $300,000 to $400,000 in severance pay; large corporations have been buying midrange businesses ($1 million and up); however, one estimate is that "40 percent of small businesses in area are not making money"

CONNECTICUT

Recent sales   Slow to moderate, "spotty" market; wholesale/retail book operation, wholesale hardware distributor

Demand   Manufacturing   and   distribution;   theme   businesses (restaurants)

Financing   Information not available

General comments   State economy has declined due to federal defense cutbacks and job cuts, with eastern sections hit hardest; southeast region is most industrialized, while northwest region is less industrialized

DELAWARE

Wilmington

Recent sales   Restaurant, dry cleaners, food businesses, convenience store, gas stations

Demand   Laid-off corporate and professional workers seeking business-to-business companies; foreign buyers seeking traditional businesses such as gas stations, convenience stores, dry cleaners

Financing   Banks are interested in making loans and have even been willing to finance goodwill but require large down payment

General comments   Stable population linked to downsizing of DuPont; downtown redevelopment plan includes new convention center, entertainment center, purchase of professional baseball team, and plans to add soccer and basketball teams

DISTRICT OF COLUMBIA (SEE WASHINGTON, D.C.)

FLORIDA

Boca Raton

Recent sales   Auto repair shop, advertising business, title insurance company, furniture manufacturer, large chiropractic clinic, awning manufacturer, printing company

Demand   More manufacturing and production-oriented businesses

Financing   Seller

General comments   New residents moving from northern and northeastern states, also from Miami to escape hurricanes; area's pluses include climate, lifestyle, and low cost of living compared to northern states; new housing is spurring demand for small businesses in general

Clearwater

Recent sales   Direct mailing service, guard service, janitorial and floor cleaning service for large companies

Demand   Manufacturing and distribution

Financing   Information not available

General comments   Population growth spurred by influx of retirees attracted by good climate

Fort Myers

Recent sales   Quick-printing shops, travel agencies, tee shirt silk-screening business

Demand   Information not available

Financing   Seller-financed

General comments   One of the nation's fastest-growing areas; mild climate, water, beaches, nonmetropolitan area

Jacksonville

Recent sales   Information not available

Demand   Distribution

Financing   Information not available

General comments   Big population growth

Miami

Recent sales   Gas station, dry cleaners, hotel, manufacturing (plastics, metal), men's hosiery distribution company

Demand   Demand for new small businesses especially strong in late 1993 in wake of severe damage from hurricane

Financing   Mostly seller; some third-party money available

General comments   Population growth fueled by climate, lifestyle, and international ambience; predictions of upturn in Caribbean tourism if Castro regime falls in Cuba

Orlando

Recent sales   Manufacturing (aluminum lawn furniture and desk manufacturers, sheet-metal job shop), truck-parts distributor, accounting service franchise, fast-food operation, bar and grill, commercial irrigation company, convenience stores, dry cleaners

Demand   Manufacturing and distribution

Financing   Information not available

General comments   New residents attracted by lifestyle, strong economy, and climate

Tallahassee

Recent sales   Dry cleaners, laundromats, convenience store, distributorships (swimming-pool supplies, paper), video stores, yogurt shops, appliance repair, marble manufacturing, lock and key shop, pizza parlor, cleaning service

Demand   Service-oriented businesses

Financing   Seller; some home-equity bank loans

General comments   State capital, 40 miles from Gulf beaches, site of several universities; climate offers seasonal changes that attract new residents; strong economy; supply of businesses for sale was outstripping demand in late 1993

GEORGIA

Albany

Recent sales   Niche furniture, apparel; no recent distributorships

Demand   Light manufacturing and distribution

Financing   Almost all seller-financed

General comments   Rural area of small towns with slow population growth

Atlanta

Recent sales   Franchises (apartment landscaping, corporate entertainment, maid service), manufacturing (metal and wood), window-and-door manufacturing/distribution firm, beauty shops and college, time-management consulting firm, real estate magazine, auto repair shops; convenience stores, liquor store

Demand   Demand exceeds supply; manufacturing and distribution are asked for, but not available; little demand for food service and retail; however, "too many people want a get-rich-quick business"; good turn-over with service businesses that do not require a lot of skills

Financing   Seller-financed; SBA if real estate is involved; some from venture capital

General comments   In Top 10 for population growth nationally in the past five years, with new residents drawn by mild climate and good recreational sites; regional headquarters for many large companies that contract with small businesses; import/export businesses are popular

Augusta

Recent sales   Ice cream parlor, liquor store, self-serve car wash, food distributor, video rental store

Demand   Simple retail, such as convenience stores

Financing   Almost entirely seller; occasional SBA

General comments   Increasing population attracted by climate, low cost of living, recreation (golf, lakes rivers, proximity to both mountains and beaches); new manufacturing in area; Savannah River nuclear plant, a major employer, is being cleaned up

HAWAII

Honolulu

Recent sales   Restaurants, flower manufacturing, sandwich shop franchise, one-hour photo lab, beauty shop, yogurt shop

Demand   Restaurants and retail

Financing   Cash; seller sometimes to rarely; almost no banks

General comments   Population growth has slowed, as has building of resort hotels; people are drawn by beauty, climate, and lifestyle but deterred by highest cost of living in the nation coupled with lowest salaries; "30 to 40 percent of Hawaii is restaurants"; little manufacturing presence; another Waikiki-type resort city is scheduled to be built over the next 10 to 20 years in an area called Koolima; each island has different problems; cost of office space and other factors make starting a business in Oahu very expensive

IDAHO

Boise

Recent sales   Retail (pet store, beauty shop, cookie shop, building materials center, bakery), door manufacturer, fishery/smokehouse, convenience store, restaurants, vending company

Demand   Most people "want to buy a job; they have money and want something that will interest them"

Financing   Mostly seller-financed; "a lot of help from SBA"

General comments   Heavy population growth as Californians and Easterners are attracted by lifestyle and low cost of living; demand for jobs has outstripped supply

ILLINOIS

Chicago

Recent sales   Retail outlets, fast-food operations, computer distributor, fast-food products distributor

Demand   Service-oriented businesses

Financing   "Always" seller-financed; no bank loans on service-oriented businesses

General comments   Some population growth; jobs available

Moline

Recent sales   Restaurant, bar, convenience store, copper and brass fittings manufacturer/distributor

Demand   A business that is a "moneymaker, respectable, and has good terms"

Financing   SBA dealing with banks with a collateral pledge; next is seller-financed; also some "gifting" by wealthy friends of buyers

General comments   Recent diversification has aided in recovery from job losses with John Deere Co. several years ago; industry has increased; new trend is for residents to buy 40 to 100 acres of land and build, commuting about 30 minutes to work

Springfield

Recent sales   Information not available

Demand   Laid-off and downsized corporate executives typically start out seeking franchises but do not realize the risks and up-front costs

Financing   Information not available

General comments   Much out-migration to Southeast

INDIANA

Indianapolis

Recent sales   Wood and metal manufacturing

Demand   "Buyers (many of them former corporate executives) usually have $100,000 to $150,000 in liquidity that they want to stretch by five times that"

Financing   Seller-financed; bank

General comments   Growing community, with more industry moving in and a revitalized downtown; United Airlines has an expanding aircraft rebuilding facility in the region

IOWA

Des Moines

Recent sales   Plumbing company, dry cleaners, laundromat, machinery and industrial sewing machine companies, restaurant, daycare center

Demand   "Half the people know what they want and half don't"

Financing   Very little seller financing; 99 percent by banks along with SBA loans

General comments   New residents are attracted to school system

KANSAS

Kansas City

Recent sales   Information not available

Demand   Veterinary/groomer/pet store operation, brewery/restaurant; buyers are looking for an income

Financing   Banks are involved in about 70 percent of larger transactions; only about 30 percent are completely seller-financed

General comments   Area of steady growth supported by good lifestyle, mild climate, "good values"

Wichita

Recent sales   Kitchen cabinet company, distribution (hardware and specialty products, aircraft parts), Caterpillar engine rebuilder, bicycle shop, dry cleaners, print-and-frame retail shop

Financing   Smaller deals usually seller-financed; larger deals may be one-third down payment, one-third seller-financed, one-third bank-financed

General comments   Slow population growth, with new residents attracted by quality of life; "pro-business climate" (right-to-work laws, low labor and workers' compensation costs, low taxes, and less stringent environmental protection laws) has attracted business relocations, especially from California

KENTUCKY

Louisville

Recent sales   Electric manufacturing, concrete-related, heavy-manufacturing, tool-and-die companies, Baskin-Robbins ice cream franchises, florist, nightclub with restaurant, pet shops, hydraulic scaffolding business, coffee shop, computer education school, vending route, paper and gift shop, janitorial business, meat wholesaler, pizza shop, childcare centers, maid service, nut shop franchise, pub, tavern, gourmet ice cream stores, coin-operated laundries

Demand   Light manufacturing, "but when asked for examples, (buyers) draw a blank. It seems to be a buzzword"

Financing   Seller-financed or bank and seller combined; in general, "banks are becoming less and less involved"

General comments   Population in the area has remained relatively unchanged

LOUISIANA

Baton Rouge

Recent sales   Dry cleaners, convenience store, service station, monogram/silk screening shop, mailbox-service franchise, hubcap business, yogurt shop, daycare centers, industrial supplies

Demand   High demand/scarce supply of convenience stores (especially sought by Vietnamese immigrants)

Financing   Seller-financed; banks will lend with strong collateral such as a home loan

General comments   Some migration, with notable influx of Palestinians, Pakistanis, and Asians; former residents also returning to their roots; economic situation improving and diversifying after late 1980s oil crunch; "old country courtesy" lifestyle

New Orleans

Recent sales   Tourism, hospitality, service-oriented (grocery, delicatessen)

Demand   Need for "money managers" to service small businesses; many Asian newcomers buy grocery stores, put in kitchen, and create grocery/delis; however, "most people don't know what they want—they just want to buy a steady stream of money"

Financing   Seller-financed; banks advertise that they will finance, but in fact do not; SBA can be intrusive

General comments   Population said to be growing (despite drop shown in census) due to slower pace than Dallas and Houston plus reputation as "party town"; recent influx of Southeast Asians; lack of industry attracts escapees from more industrialized regions

MAINE

Bangor

Recent sales   Information not available

Demand   Heavy demand among older, educated managers looking to "buy a job" after being laid off, or who fear being laid off, are unhappy at their present company, or foresee no more advancement

Financing   Information not available

General comments   Area of slow population growth; business strength derived in part from Canadians who buy in Bangor to escape high taxes in their own country

MARYLAND

Baltimore

Recent sales   Information not available

Demand   "Walk-in buyers" don't know what they want, but know how much money they have to spend and how much annual return they need to live on

Financing   Mostly seller-financed (75 percent to 85 percent); for strong businesses, seller demands 50 percent down payment and will carry 50 percent; for weaker businesses, cash deal; some financing through bank home-equity loans

General comments   Population growth perceived as stable despite decline shown in census figures

MASSACHUSETTS

Boston

Recent sales   Bars, convenience stores, "any distribution"

Demand   Businesses in $50,000 to $100,000 range; manufacturing operations that have a small niche market; business-to-business service, travel, commercial cleaning, noninventory, nonpersonnel businesses; nothing in retail or with high inventory

Financing   Information not available

General comments   Restricted growth limited by tax situation, despite appeal of top-ranked universities, historical importance, and European ambience; new residents drawn mainly from New York area; video store, motel, and print store "booms" seen as having ended

Springfield

Recent sales   Information not available

Demand   Manufacturing and distribution, especially computer-related or high-tech; buyers seek salary, debt service, money to replace equipment, and return

Financing   Information not available

General comments   Slow population growth

MICHIGAN

Grand Rapids

Recent sales   Service-oriented (cleaning services, linen-supply services, tool-and-die company)

Demand   "The full spectrum"

Financing   Majority seller-financed

General comments   Region has seen sustained growth over past decade due to good labor market, strong economy, and good quality of life

Royal Oak

Recent sales   Information not available

Demand   Laid-off or pensioned-off buyers from corporate backgrounds or the auto industry seek small businesses that require little skill

Financing   Almost always seller

General comments   Metropolitan Detroit is losing population due to high crime rate and recession in the auto industry, but region continues to experience slow, steady growth

MINNESOTA

Minneapolis

Recent sales   Information not available

Demand   Light manufacturing and distribution; but overall demand slow

Financing   Information not available

General comments   Despite growth shown in census figures, popular perception is that severe winters deter in-migration; stable economy; area is headquarters to several large corporations (3M, General Mills)

MISSISSIPPI

Jackson

Recent sales   Food brokerage firm bought out by larger firm

Demand   Computer- and telecommunications-related; business machine sales and services; legal and legislative support services

Financing   Mostly seller-financed; neither SBA nor banks active with start-ups; state has one-year-old minority capital fund and upcoming venture capital fund

General comments   Jackson is the state capital and thus is not typical of the entire state, which still ranks 50th in nation in terms of per capita income; however, the economy is booming and unemployment is down due to the recent establishment of casino gambling on riverboats, which has boosted tourism and construction

MISSOURI

Columbia

Recent sales   Large travel agency, CPA firm, consulting firm (state and county government), fast-food franchise, convenience store, office-supply store

Demand   "Population is growing so rapidly that more volume of present businesses is needed to keep up with growth"

Financing   Some seller financing; bank loan policies very "aggressive"; SBA very active

General comments   Perceived as area of substantial population growth with strong economy (less than 3 percent unemployment), good recreational facilities, proximity to state capital, large proportion of professionals; Columbia was named second-best place to live by *Money Magazine;* another strong pocket of growth is Branson, a center for country-music industry (studios, performance halls); however, small towns and rural areas to north suffered in recent recession

St. Louis

Recent sales   Auto-parts store, machine shop, entertainment facilities, gift shops, farming-supply (equipment, feed, and grain)

Demand   Light manufacturing and distribution; moderate population growth creates need for "more of the same" of all small business types

Financing   Mostly seller; some banks

General comments   Moderate population growth spurred by lifestyle, relatively low crime rate, stable economy

Montana

Billings

Recent sales   Dry cleaners, franchise fast food, restaurants, casinos (poker gambling is legal, but law requires liquor license, food and bar license)

Demand   Information not available

Financing   Banks, SBA, venture capital and loans from corporations

General comments   Population influx, mainly from California and New York, attracted by low crime rate and better quality of life (*Cosmopolitan* cited it as a top place to find eligible cowboys); recent opening of Wal-Mart has hurt small retailers

Missoula

Recent sales   Supermarkets, wholesale office supply, trucking freight company, health club, manufacturer of printing devices that also does printing

Demand   Light manufacturing and distribution

Financing   Seller-financed; SBA, but will loan only on hard assets

General comments   Definite population growth, with people attracted to the region's recreational possibilities and lifestyle amenities

Nebraska

Omaha

Recent sales   Lawn service and sprinkler-installation companies, lumberyard building center

Demand   Information not available

Financing Mostly seller; some SBA; some banks are primary SBA lenders

General comments Stable economy, some population growth, low cost of living; recent growth of large shopping malls and strip malls

NEVADA

Las Vegas

Recent sales Franchises (hamburger chains, ice cream, submarine sandwiches)

Demand Service-oriented; manufacturing and distribution; displaced executives decide to buy jobs when disappointed with pay scales

Financing Information not available

General comments Many new residents each month (4,000 to 5,000), attracted by Las Vegas's "vitality," good economy and hope of finding jobs in $50,000 to $60,000 range; however, most offer much lower pay

Reno

Recent sales Day care, video store, pizza operation, fast-food, license-plate frame manufacturer, fire extinguisher and first-aid distributor

Demand Business-to-business operations and those where customers come to the business rather than the reverse; buyers do not want bars, restaurants, sales businesses, or those that cater to the public

Financing Seller-financing; occasional SBA

General comments New residents, especially from California, attracted by lower taxes, quality of life, and small-town atmosphere; plans for 2,000-room hotel/casino/theme park, which is expected to generate more tourism; new Lockheed facility also under construction

NEW HAMPSHIRE

Manchester

Recent sales   Information not available

Demand   Displaced manufacturers are seeking light manufacturing and distribution

Financing   Seller

General comments   Stable population, but manufacturing has been lost because of recession; Wal-Mart openings will hurt mom-and-pop stores in area

NEW JERSEY

Fair Lawn

Recent sales   No specifics available, but decline in mom-and-pop stores

Demand   Franchises

Financing   Information not available

General comments   Many empty stores in area

Freehold

Recent sales   Liquor store, restaurant, automotive shop

Demand   Information not available

Financing   Seller-financed only

General comments   Growing population; area is bedroom community for New York City

Matawan

Recent sales   Information not available

Demand   Light manufacturing and small distribution businesses; no interest in restaurants or retail businesses

Financing   Information not available

General comments   None available

NEW MEXICO

Albuquerque

Recent sales   Franchise auto-body shop, midscale jewelry manufacturing company, restaurants, retail stores, large janitorial business

Demand   Service-oriented, then manufacturing, then retail

Financing   Seller; occasional SBA bank loans

General comments   Population is growing; housing market is strong; Intel computer chip manufacturing facility located in area

Santa Fe

Recent sales   Information not available

Demand   Small manufacturing, retail businesses, service-oriented (printing, auto repair, dry cleaners); automated car wash

Financing   Information not available

General comments   Area of steady population growth, with new residents from East Coast (also California) drawn by region's beauty and lifestyle; real estate values remain strong

NEW YORK

Buffalo

Recent sales   Information not available

Demand   Light manufacturing and professional businesses being sought by early retirees and buyers desiring to leave corporate life

Financing   Information not available

General comments   Growing population attracted by clean water, good climate, recreation around Niagara Falls, Lake Ontario, and Lake Erie, and low cost of living compared to New York City; factories being replaced by high-tech businesses

Lake Placid

Recent sales   Information not available

Demand   Mainly hospitality- and tourist-oriented

Financing   Information not available

General comments   Population growing again after recent slow-down; new residents attracted by rural lifestyle, recreation

Long Island

Recent sales   Information not available

Demand   No specific trends; "all types of general business"

Financing   Information not available

General comments   Population is decreasing due to negative tax situation

New York City

Recent sales   Restaurants, small retail (greeting card, stationery stores), sandwich shops, food franchises

Demand   People who want manufacturing find out there's not enough income in it

Financing   Seller; "SBA doesn't give money for small businesses"; some brokerages may offer financing but at high interest rates

General comments   Sales have been declining over the past several years because population has been moving out of the city; landlords have become more flexible and are now willing to renew and for longer time periods, but some want cost-of-living and other increases built in; many former garment industry workers who have lost jobs are buying small businesses; immigrants are more likely to open their own shop using money from relatives than to buy existing ones; best current bet in New York is bagel stores, with hot dog stands and similar small food businesses good profit makers

Scarsdale

Recent sales   Light manufacturing and distribution

Demand   Highly educated former corporate executives seeking light manufacturing and distribution, also general franchises (mailbox services, fast food)

Financing   Information not available

General comments   State residents tend to move within state rather than outside, except for retirement or financial problems; area attracts residents who want to be near the New York cultural/financial hub

Syracuse

Recent sales   Cruise-ship line, precision metal machine shop, dry cleaning operation, bar, tavern, restaurant, funeral home, camera shop, convenience store, manufacturing (key rings, furniture)

Demand   Cash-type businesses and manufacturing; buyers are "searching for a change" from corporate career to self-employment or from one type of small business to another

Financing   Mostly seller-financed; occasional small or partial loans from banks; SBA seldom

General comments   Population declining, linked to poor economy, high taxes, severe winters, relocation of manufacturers; however, some in-migration from other parts of state, Massachusetts, and Oklahoma; good family area; proximity to Lake Ontario recreation

NORTH CAROLINA

Charlotte

Recent sales   Information not available

Demand   "Executive parachute" buyers looking for light manufacturing (low- and high-tech), distribution (for buyers with background in marketing or sales); demand for restaurants and retail stores has declined

Financing   Information not available

General comments   Perceived influx of new small-business purchasers attracted by good business climate (light manufacturing, distribution centers, trucking, fabrication), presence of three of nation's largest banks

Raleigh

Recent sales   Convenience stores, dry cleaners, grocery stores

Demand   Small technical, light manufacturing, and computer-related businesses and stores, business-to-business; some buyers are middle managers who have been laid off

Financing   Information not available

General comments   Growing population from all over nation, attracted by presence of research-and-development, pharmaceutical, and other corporations; however, there have been some recent layoffs

NORTH DAKOTA

Bismarck

Recent sales   Service-oriented: audio company with retail electronics, residential care home for elderly, combination car wash/laundry

Financing   Strong bank financing to qualified buyers with personal guarantees and SBA-backed loans

General comments   Bismarck (state capital, also regional medical center), Grand Forks, and Minot relatively strong economically, but state population has declined; smaller towns have been hard-hit by recession

OHIO

Cincinnati

Recent sales   Dry cleaners, bakeries, wholesalers (office supplies, medical supplies), retail, metal-working shops

Demand   Service-oriented and manufacturing (but latter is often out of buyer's price range)

Financing   Mostly seller-financed (90 percent); occasional bank involvement if there is real estate and cash flow; 30 percent discounts possible on asking price if buyer has cash

General comments   Stable economy, population growth; important employers include General Electric and U.S. Air Force

Cleveland

Recent sales Delicatessen and convenience store chains, often bought by immigrants from Middle East

Demand Information not available

Financing Seller-financed "always"

General comments Population is decreasing as older residents die or retire and move to Florida

OKLAHOMA

Oklahoma City

Recent sales Mailbox business, liquor store, nightclub, mall popcorn shop, fast-photo business, math/reading tutoring center franchise

Demand Demand currently outstripping supply

Financing Almost all seller-financed (20 to 40 percent down)

General comments "Slow but steady growth" historically affected by trends in energy industry (growth in early 1980s, followed by exodus due to energy crisis and bank failures, has been picking up again); new residents coming from California and the Midwest

Tulsa

Recent sales Restaurant, donut shop, manufacturing (charcoal cookers, fishing lures, oil industry pumps), bicycle shop, picture framer, equipment rental, beverage store, auto-window tinting

Demand Information not available

Financing Mostly seller-financed; recent trend to more bank financing after lack of involvement in late 1980s; SBA involvement is very rare

General comments Population growth in area, with more jobs available

OREGON

Bend

Recent sales Graphics businesses, fast-photo service, mall retail store, sign shop, auto-repair business

Demand Light manufacturing and service-oriented businesses with $30,000–$50,000 a year in net profits

Financing Information not available

General comments Rapidly growing population, mainly from California, attracted by lifestyle and region's natural beauty; however, recent slowdown due to recession's impact in California

Eugene

Recent sales Information not available

Demand Service-oriented (automotive, restaurants, home-improvement outlets, car washes, grocery stores)

Financing Information not available

General comments Population growth spurred by influx of retirees and corporate employees, who do not buy businesses; main attraction is small-city lifestyle and area's natural beauty; not the place to go to make "big money" in small business

Portland

Recent sales Convenience store, grocery, dry cleaner, taverns, bars

Demand Service-oriented

Financing   Almost 100 percent seller-financed; no banks or SBA

General comments   Strong population growth spurred by area life-style, natural beauty, and good business climate; area was experiencing a video poker craze in early 1990s

PENNSYLVANIA

Lancaster

Recent sales   Information not available

Demand   Light manufacturing and distribution; nontechnical businesses or those with many assets (machinery); little demand for service-oriented areas, which are seen as "too much risk"

Financing   Information not available

General comments   No perceived population growth; stable

Pittsburgh

Recent sales   Manufacturing (metal vending, machine tool, plastics) and distribution (wholesale tires, industrial oils and lubricants, snack foods, vending machines); some retail

Demand   Light manufacturing and distribution

Financing   Information not available

General comments   Population exodus in mid-1980s has now stabilized, perhaps with some revitalization; area is known for university presence and computer corporations

SOUTH CAROLINA

Hilton Head Island

Recent sales Information not available

Demand Light manufacturing and distribution are in demand, but supply is scarce; best opportunities are in service-oriented areas (landscaping, house cleaning, window washing, janitorial), which offer very little risk and initial outlay coupled with flexibility and good growth; mom-and-pop businesses (groceries, restaurants, food, and retail) are being bought by large chains or replaced by franchises; property management very popular

Financing Information not available

General comments Area's recreational facilities attract early retirees (aged 40 to 55) who start out thinking they want a small business but often end up taking jobs again

SOUTH DAKOTA

Rapid City

Recent sales Software company, ice manufacturing company, travel agency, steam cleaning business, new and used appliance store

Demand Service-oriented businesses

Financing Primarily SBA

General comments Population is growing, but area is "anti-development"

Sioux Falls

Recent sales Restaurant, laundromat, antique store, motel

Demand Light manufacturing, but little is for sale

Financing   Seller; occasional SBA help

General comments   Area has been listed among Top 10 places to live in the United States; good business climate is attracting new industries (computers, meat packing); credit card companies moving there due to relatively few restrictions; unemployment was 2 percent in late 1993

TENNESSEE

Knoxville

Recent sales   Injection molding

Demand   New markets and small-business spinoffs may be generated by recent growth of automotive industry (Nissan, Saturn, Toyota plants) in region

Financing   Almost all seller-financed; little bank financing

General comments   Slow, steady growth with lower unemployment rate than national average; good climate and lifestyle; some influx of Cambodian, Korean, and Laotian immigrants

Memphis

Recent sales   Distributorships, franchises

Demand   No specific trends; small businesses in general

Financing   Seller; some bank help

General comments   Growth area with downtown at estimated 98 percent business occupancy; new residents attracted by lifestyle and climate

Nashville

Recent sales   Dry cleaners, laundromats, convenience stores, restaurant, mail/packaging center, neighborhood market, cocktail lounge, boat-propeller repair, trophy/awards manufacturer, temporary secretarial service, small advertising firm, coupon advertising business

Demand   "Something that makes money"

Financing   Mostly seller-financed (70 percent, with 30 to 60 percent down payment); combined bank and seller financing; some cash sales

General comments   Rapidly growing population due to attractions of mild climate, recreational facilities, status as nation's country-music capital, proximity to other major cities (New York, Chicago, Pittsburgh), and hospitable ambience; also, strong employment picture due to presence of big industry (farming, car manufacturing)

TEXAS

Amarillo

Recent sales   House cleaning and check-cashing businesses, dry cleaning plants, wedding chapel

Demand   Service-oriented businesses with "as few employees as possible"

Financing   Little seller-financed; mostly SBA; some unsecured bank loans

General comments   Slow influx of new residents, fueled by presence of one prison with new high-security facility being built and providing new jobs; also the site of a large medical complex, which attracts physicians and patients; little manufacturing in area

Austin/San Antonio

Recent sales   Photo-engraving shop, printing business, restaurants, video store, manufacturing (security systems, plastic ejection molding), daycare business, news publication business

Demand   "Any business that's making money"; hard to sell businesses that are too specialized or too technical, or where owner is too much a part of the success

Financing   Almost all seller-financed; banks will loan for working capital only; some SBA-guaranteed loans

General comments   Growing population attracted to area's lifestyle and strong economy

Fort Worth

Recent sales   Secretarial service, car lubrication center, rope distributor, long-established family bakery, hot-pad and oven-mitt manufacturer

Demand   Supply presently outstrips demand due to depressed local economy; laid-off workers seldom have enough cash to buy

Financing   Mostly seller-financed (90 percent with buyers asking 30 to 35 percent cash down payment); some SBA assistance and guarantees

General comments   Area has suffered from closure of two military bases and downsizing of several large industries, causing extensive layoffs; residents have been moving to other parts of Texas, back to original home states, or to "any area where they can use their skills"

Houston

Recent sales   Accounting practice, flooring company, sign company, printing shop, women's clothing store, wholesale flower company, retail florist, office supply company, bicycle parts distribution company, manufacturing (canvas)

Demand   Businesses that have short hours, safe location, "image" (especially important for former corporate executives)

Financing   Mostly seller-financed, but SBA "a good source": seller will finance 50 to 70 percent if buyer has SBA guarantee

General comments   Companies and new residents moving to area from both "Rustbelt" and "Sunbelt" regions of U.S.; attractions include lifestyle, relatively low cost of living, and diversified economy no longer totally dependent on oil and gas industry

Odessa

Recent sales   Beauty shop, liquor store, ice cream shop, laundry, dry cleaner, trucking companies, seal-manufacturing company

Demand   Demand is slow; area presently slightly depressed

Financing   Almost all seller-financed; businesses with gross annual sales of $5 million and up will attract investors and venture capitalists; almost no SBA loans available

General comments   Population stable; an oil-field area that has been hard-hit by overall poor economy in state

UTAH

Salt Lake City

Recent sales   Manufacturing (awnings), distribution (computer software), "traditional small businesses (convenience stores, copy shops, mailbox businesses, dental lab) also moving well"

Demand   Light manufacturing ("usually requires a larger down payment") and distribution

Financing   Information not available

General comments   Population growth fueled by region's natural beauty, strong economy, recreation facilities

VERMONT

Brattleboro

Recent sales   Manufacturing (wood products, wooden models, parts for nuclear industry), wholesale distribution (food, chemicals, tires)

Demand   Light manufacturing and wholesale distribution

Financing   Information not available

General comments   Slow population growth; new residents attracted by rural New England atmosphere; middle- and upper-management workers seeking "lifestyle change, clean air, and profitable businesses" throughout New England

VIRGINIA

Richmond

Recent sales   Barber shop, beauty salon, camera store, photo-processing lab, gas stations/convenience stores, machine repair parts distributor

Demand   Gas station/convenience stores; liquor stores; consumer, service-oriented operations; supply of fast-food and automotive operations currently outstrips demand

Financing   Seller-financed; occasional SBA; recently, more bank financing; occasional venture-capital financing

General comments   Slow, steady growth, with population erosion in northern part of state as federal government shrinks; construction and real estate markets slow due to overbuilding in Washington, D.C., area; new residents may simply be moving closer to other family members in area

WASHINGTON

Seattle/Bellevue

Recent sales   Information not available

Demand   Manufacturing and distribution, no specifics given; "all buyers care about is price, usually under $500,000"; possibly some high-end restaurants

Financing   Information not available

General comments   Population influx spurred by region's beauty and economy that is generally stronger than in rest of U.S.

Spokane

Recent sales   Traffic consulting

Demand   "Whole gamut"; manufacturing, service-oriented businesses, restaurants; demand for print shops has declined

Financing   Information not available

General comments   Strong influx of new residents from southern California, Oregon, western Washington, and northern Idaho drawn by quality of life, recreation, and strong economy relative to rest of U.S.

WASHINGTON, D.C. (DISTRICT OF COLUMBIA)

Recent sales   Liquor store, dry cleaners, beer/wine shop, fast-food store, franchise convenience store, food takeout business, supermarket

Demand   Retail, manufacturing, some service-oriented

Financing   Sellers who carry paper secured by business's inventory

General comments   Slow but steady growth; some emigration because of high-crime image portrayed in media, but others attracted to nation's capital; a need for small strip shopping centers

WEST VIRGINIA

Charleston

Recent sales   Chimney-cleaning firm, wholesale distributor of baseball and football cards, manufacturing (aluminum windows, storm windows, and marquees)

Demand   Foreseen upsurge in tourism may create demand for related businesses (hotels, restaurants, gas stations)

Financing   Mostly seller-financed; area has active venture-capital market, but usually seller must finance part of transaction to make deal work; bank loans hard to get

General comments   Population declining due to depressed economy, lack of jobs

WISCONSIN

Green Bay

Recent sales   Service-oriented (temporary employment agency, child care, house and office cleaning, carpet cleaning, janitorial)

Demand   Small manufacturing companies; buyers do not want restaurants or bars

Financing   Mostly seller-financed (90 percent); bank involvement only if business is "rock solid" or if buyer has home equity loan

General comments   "Recession-proof" area of high population growth, with appeal of water recreation, professional football; major industries include paper mills, insurance companies, medical facilities

Madison

Recent sales   Manufacturing/distribution (metal fasteners, cutting tools, textbook publishing), catering, coupon and advertising firm

Demand   Business-to-business company or service; "easy, simple, relocatable" (mail order, catalogs)

Financing   Sellers will adjust price for all-cash deals; bank financing available only if there are assets for collateral

General comments   Population growth, with new residents attracted by quality of life, relative lack of crowding, lower cost of living

WYOMING

Casper

Recent sales   Car wash, manufacturing (tourist products, retail), communications company, answering/paging service

Demand   High-technology and "new-type" industries

Financing   Seller; home equity loans from banks

General comments   Noticeable population growth in western section of state spurred by slow-paced lifestyle, mountains, low cost of living; state has introduced new health care system

CHAPTER 9

Before You Make Your Decision

We've almost come to the end of this guide to your best entrepreneurial business choices. Before we say goodbye and you begin the serious task of deciding what opportunity is best for you, I'd like you to think about some important questions and to consider a few major dos and don'ts about any business you may enter, whether you buy it or create it.

First of all, here are the major questions you should be asking yourself before you proceed further:

1. Should I start a new business or buy an existing one?
2. How much money will either choice require?
3. What skills should I have?
4. Do I need to know how to sell?
5. Assuming I have a choice, should I be in a large metropolitan area or a small town?

You already know my view about the basic trends affecting traditional small businesses today. Here it is in one sentence: In general, the independent retailer is disappearing, except in isolated areas.

The big chain discounters, superstores, and established franchise operations are taking the place of the independent mom-and-pop retailers. Franchise food operations are increasingly dominant, taking the greater share of revenue. Franchise and chain operators are buying up the better-located independent small businesses. The larger operators are at the moment the only ones that can effectively meet the expensive challenges of regulations and taxes and the uncertainties of health care reform, the economy, and so forth. We're going to see more homogeneity in the goods offered for sale. However, the pendulum will swing. Consumers will tire of this sameness and will seek independent creativity.

Thus we see two forms of opportunity: First, the Forces of Change will themselves create new self-employment and small-business opportunities; second, the growing dominance of the omnipotent mass retailers will create opportunities when consumers begin seeking relief from sameness. Now let's turn back to the questions listed above.

1. Should I start a new business or buy an existing one?

The best choice is to start your own, but you'll need to be very selective. Be sure to choose something that has a high probability of surviving and succeeding. For example, you might feel that it's beneath your dignity to become a janitor, particularly if you've been a vice president or CEO or manager of marketing or something else in corporate America. You might prefer to see yourself going into manufacturing or distribution, but I've already argued that there's too much competition in those areas. I'd say, "Don't look at janitorial as being low-life or something you don't want to touch—rather, it's an area where you can make a heck of a lot more money than in some other areas, and with a lot less risk."

Start-up time is faster, and you don't necessarily have to be the one who goes out and does the actual work. And suppose you lack computer skills or consulting skills. Think about going into janitorial, or into temporary help, or into referral services where you can use your management skills and bring in temporary employees to actually perform the services. Build the business up gradually. Start out with minimal advertising and supplies; you make the contacts and telephone calls yourself. You set up the system and get started, but you don't hire people until you actually have a job or a contract to perform cleaning restrooms in all Mobil service stations in Oshkosh or whatever. Then you bring in the people and put them on your payroll. You'll probably see some cash flow relatively quickly. And you haven't put $150,000 to $500,000 into a franchise business that you may not understand and may not succeed in.

2. How much money will either choice require?

This will vary greatly, as you saw in chapter 5. It's probably unrealistic to think you can get into any self-employment business for less than $2,500, which would cover the bare basics for a venture that requires little or no equipment. Start-up costs for equipment-intensive efforts could be as high as $50,000 before you even talk to your first customers.

Also, if you estimate that costs should be a given amount, triple it and you'll probably be closer to a realistic figure. Even the least risky business will require capital if you want to get your message out to potential customers, and you're going to have to sustain yourself until enough customers begin to respond to your calls and networking. Just using the telephone can be relatively expensive. Mailing programs don't receive massive response. Experience shows that the response to a good, high-quality mailing list might be 1 to 2 percent. If you receive more than a 2 percent response, you're a great exception to the rule. Plus, you can anticipate that mailers are going to run 30 cents to a dollar, minimum, for quantities of 5,000 to 50,000 units, and postage is 19 cents minimum.

If you plan to start with telephone solicitation, you should plan on a minimum of 15 to 20 calls per day. And that may not be possible, because some of those calls are going to result in the need for personal visits. If you can make three or four effective visits per day, you're in the genius category. Most days aren't going to result in any effective calls. You may have just two or three effective calls a week at best. By effective calls, we mean that people at least get back to you and seriously consider ordering services from you. But then it may be a month or two, or longer, before they make a decision. It's rare that clients or customers meet you for the first time and order from you immediately.

Thus, under the best of circumstances you should plan on at least three months of your own personal requirements for cash plus your office setup, computer, desk, chair, file cabinet, other minimal equipment, telephone costs of $200 to $400 per month, plus initial installation of the telephone, which might be $100 to $200. Add to these another $500 for printing stationery and business cards plus design costs for a good logo that will catch the attention of potential customers. If you want to follow up on your calls with a brochure or mailer, plan on a minimum of $1,000 to $3,000.

Remember, the cash that comes into the cash drawer isn't yours; it belongs first to the business, to your employees, your vendors, the tax man—then, if there's anything left over, there might be some small return on your investment. And lastly, there's the possibility of a small pittance for yourself, for at least the first 12 to 18 months.

3. What skills and knowledge should I have?

No matter what business you choose, you'll never know enough. But you must know enough that people will have confidence in you and you can develop a reputation for skill and quality. You have to know enough to be able to sell yourself and to perform at an acceptable level. *Your clients are the judges who determine what is acceptable.*

If they don't come back, or if they're complaining, you know you're not doing acceptable work. It's that simple.

4. Do I need to know how to sell?

The type of business you go into may be dictated in part by skills you already possess. If you have no unusual or unique skills, you will have to go into a type of business that doesn't require special skills—other than selling. The one essential skill you must have is the ability to sell yourself as well as your product or service.

This is the most important question you need to answer, and the way you answer it is in terms of what happens when you go out and try to sell yourself and your service. How responsive are people? Do they open their doors to you? Taking a sales course may be helpful, but it's not a panacea. Some people just plain can't sell. They have the wrong personality, or the wrong telephone approach, or the wrong voice, or the wrong appearance, or the wrong something that does not promote confidence.

You need to know something about yourself, particularly with regard to how other people react to you. It's not a matter of being a genius—lots of geniuses can't sell. However, if you've chosen to be self-employed or to go into a small business, you had better be able to sell, because it's the main attribute required for success.

5. Assuming I have a choice, should I be in a large metropolitan area or a small town?

Clearly the trend is for people to move out of large metropolitan areas and to begin or buy businesses in small communities. There is something romantic today about being in a rural area, away from the madding (and maddening!) crowd. Also, modern electronics and telecommunications make it possible to locate many businesses in smaller communities where contact with clients can be made everywhere.

However, there is no magic in being in a small town versus a large metropolitan area. Metropolitan areas provide the advantage of a much larger customer base for many types of businesses. Certainly location-sensitive businesses such as retail or food depend on volume, and the more people there are, the more opportunities you have to serve them.

If you are contemplating consulting or some form of research or other service that can be performed or headquartered anywhere, this widens your options. If you prefer to live in a small community, you could well be just as successful there as in the heart of downtown. But you must consider carefully the kind of business you're going to be in, where yur customer base is, and how your customers will reach you.

If you do decide to "think small" in a big city, consider looking for a community with small-town characteristics—that is, a location with a sense of cohesiveness or uniqueness. This could even be a residential-commercial village in a large metropolitan area. This is a good strategy because it's easier for potential patrons to identify your business if you're in a small community. You will have a chance to get to know the locals, and people will have a chance to get to know you.

Some Basic Small Business Dos and Don'ts

If I can give you one basic rule for success in small business, it is this: *Whatever you do, keep it small, keep it simple, and keep it specialized.* Don't try to cover the waterfront with every conceivable related product on the theory that if customers come to you for one thing, maybe they'll buy something else while they're there.

We've all seen the little fast-food operation that opens up with a few simple but good food items—hot dogs, lemonade, and a few other closely related items. It starts out looking reasonably clean and attractive. Within a month, the windows are covered with hand-lettered signs hawking pizza, fruit salad, dipped ice cream bars, yogurt, and so on. That business has lost its focus. It's a turnoff to lots of potential customers who can no longer identify—or were never given the opportunity to identify—that establishment as the best place in town to get a hot dog.

In the long run, the focused specialist will still be there and has a much better shot at being successful and probably wealthier. To be sure, your specialty operation may experience slower growth initially, and you will have to be patient, but the chances of survival are better. You'll have a much better chance of building your identity, which is to be the business or professional that potential patronage in your small market area think of first, or at least always include in their list of potential sources. If you offer a limited, specialized line of products or services, you can focus your attention on being better than anyone else. You can build slowly, get your feet on the ground, and develop a solid foundation for the future. Also, your business's value and marketability for resale down the line should be far greater.

If you specialize, you'll no doubt miss some potential sales, but the cost of those sales would be high. If your business lacks focus, you'll be creating a fuzzy identity. You'll be thought of as just being there, but nobody will have a clear idea of what you do best. So you'll end up way down at the end of the list—if you even get on it at all.

Create a niche.   Try to find a niche market for a product or service where competition is limited. If you're successful, others will inevitably follow, but if you're the first kid on the block and maintain your focus and identity, you'll always retain a substantial share of the market. You will have an advantage that will be difficult to overcome. That's why you focus on specialization and identity right from the beginning.

Stay flexible.   Stay in tune with the demands of the market—your customers—for your specialty. These will change, and you will have to make changes, too. Being focused on a relatively narrow specialty does not mean being blind to changing ideas and customer needs.

Be realistic about your expectations.   If you set unrealistic goals, you'll only get discouraged. Your enthusiasm will be sapped, and this could result in a failed business. List your objectives, such as sales and profits, and the time you estimate will be needed to reach them. Then talk things over with trusted advisors—and think those projections through again, and again. Then cut them in half. You'll usually be closer to reality.

Be patient.   We all enjoy the sweet smell of success, but it rarely comes quickly. Real success in business usually takes much longer than we think it should. Building a solid foundation gradually will pay off in the long run. Don't be easily discouraged just because the first month, or even the tenth month, is not yet profitable.

Let your dream grow slowly.   It's easy to dream of building an empire from a humble start in your garage. We've all heard the stories. But there are few who actually go beyond that humble start successfully. Why? Because many choose the wrong business. In some cases it's probably the right business, but the owner tried to make it grow too fast. In either case the result can be the same—failure.

Keeping your new venture small will allow you to determine whether you've selected the right business before you make too much of a financial commitment. You need to let the business marinate for a while. Let yourself get used to it. Things will rarely happen the way you expect. You'll be asking yourself more than once, "What the hell am I doing here?" That's the moment you should realize that either you've gone into the wrong business or you've simply lost your focus. That's also the moment to get your focus back—and when you do, your chances of success will increase immeasurably.

Do your homework.   If you're interested in a business that you know little or nothing about, go to work for someone else in the same activity. Take an extension course at your local college or university. Talk with experts in the field. Read current trade journals and business magazines and newspapers to find out what's happening. Attend seminars. In short, learn all you can before getting into it.

Build for the long term.   If you're going to put your time and hard-earned money into a small business, you might as well decide to build for the long term. Have a long-term plan for any business you buy or start. This will help you develop a mental attitude strong enough to get you through the early setbacks, bad news, mistakes, and false starts you're bound to encounter. Patience, patience, patience!

Steer clear of long-term financial commitments.   Avoid getting into long-term loans, leases, and other commitments until you're established and have learned how to operate your small business. Think about the long term, but make only short-term commitments to start. This is a crucial way to cut your risks.

If you're buying, don't buy goodwill.   If you've decided to buy an established business, be very careful how much you pay for goodwill. In fact, your best bet is not to pay anything for it if possible. Goodwill is transitory. Even if you have a covenant not to compete with the seller, that's no assurance that you'll be able to retain the goodwill. When you buy an existing business, your main accomplishment may unfortunately be to give the existing patronage an excuse to go elsewhere.

If you buy, don't overpay.   Look and talk to experts before you leap! Too often buyers are so anxious to get started that they find themselves with a business that's not worth anywhere near what they paid. If you must buy, buy with lots of contingencies and don't pay cash up-front. Drive the car around the block first. If the seller's not willing to work with you (assuming your concerns and requests are reasonable), that business is not worth your time. There are lots of businesses for sale. Better yet, start one of your own.

Remember, not all businesses are salable.   If you start a small business with the idea that some day you might sell it, be aware that not all businesses are salable. There are millions of small businesses in the United States, but only about 1 in 20 is salable, based on information from business brokers about the number of businesses listed for sale compared to the number that actually sell. Actually, most businesses are never listed—they are just liquidated and disappear from the scene.

This is not to say that nonsalable businesses are not profitable. On the contrary, many small business operations are quite profitable—for their owners. But, as I said earlier, many businesses rely on the special skills or unique circumstances related to the owner-founder, and these can seldom be passed along to outsiders who have not been involved in it over a long period of time.

Related to the foregoing point, if you choose to enter a business that may not eventually be salable as a going concern, at least consider developing one that you could someday turn over to your children or to a valued employee. In this way, you may at least be able to enjoy some retirement benefits for your years of effort.

Go it alone.   If at all possible, make your business a one-person operation. Don't be too hasty about getting a partner, silent, active, or whatever. (Based on my observations, there is no such thing as a "silent" partner, although there are lots of "inactive" ones!) If you absolutely must have assistance, get it in a way that lets you retain control. You'd be surprised how a minority interest (even one as small as 5 percent) can be interpreted as though it's a full equal partnership by its holder.

To be sure, there's something euphoric in that off-guard moment when you say to a friend, neighbor, or business associate, "Let's open a donut shop—I found this fabulous location!" But you've just opened your mouth when you should have kept it locked shut. Going into business with a friend is a great way to end that friendship. I realize there are exceptions, but I've been asked too often to appraise small businesses that were being destroyed because of a bitter disagreement between former friends. These battles usually end with both sides dissatisfied and the business in a shambles.

Get advice from people you trust.   As your planning proceeds, be sure to talk with advisors you trust and who are knowledgeable about business in general or about your particular idea. You must be prudent—don't give your pet idea away to someone who isn't trustworthy. That goes without saying. But there's nothing to prevent you from obtaining advice. At least listen—then go home and think!

Consider consulting the SBA, bankers, accountants, lawyers, business brokers, or even appraisers. Try to find someone who has a recognized certification with an organization that enforces a code of ethics. You can always call your state's licensing departments or trade association headquarters to locate the right person.

Trust your intuition.   The best advice you can get will come from your own intuition. Well-meaning friends and family members may make suggestions about what you should do—we all have opinions, but much of the time we should keep them to ourselves. You should certainly be willing to listen to advice from knowledgeable persons. Consider it carefully—but then listen to yourself. Learning to listen to your own intuition is not easy, but it's well worth the effort.

Finally, and most important, let go.   Don't push yourself into some business just for the sake of being in it. Let your ideas unfold gradually. There is no such thing as "the last chance." Your "last chance" might turn out to be something you'll end up wishing you had never heard of.

Let go, and let things happen.   If you have an idea in mind, let it marinate for a while. The best course of action for you will unfold if only you're willing to listen to your own intuition. If you don't have a clear sense of direction and aren't sure what to do, do nothing. You may not know why immediately, but sooner or later you'll find out. Letting things happen naturally usually results in the best outcome.

What we need most of the time is a little more patience. A friend of mine used to say that chasing after something is only an expression of our sense of limitation. It's a little like running to catch a bus that's pulling away from the bus stop—even though there's another one coming along right behind it.

APPENDIX A

Small Business Development Centers

Note: The Small Business Administration has a toll-free phone number, (800) 8-ASK-SBA (800 827-5722), that will refer callers to their nearest area SBA office.

Alabama

John Sandefur
State Director
Alabama SBDC
University of Alabama
1717 11th Ave., #419
Birmingham AL 35294
Tel: (205) 934-7260
Fax: (205) 934-7645

Alaska

Jan Fredericks
State Director
Alaska SBDC
University of Alaska/Anchorage
430 W. Seventh Ave., #110
Anchorage AK 99501
Tel: (907) 274-7232
Fax: (907) 274-9524

Arizona

Michael York
Acting State Director
Arizona SBDC
Maricopa County Community College
2411 W. 14th St.
Tempe AZ 85281
Tel: (602) 731-8720
Fax: (602) 731-8729

Arkansas

Janet Nye
State Director
Arkansas SBDC
University of Arkansas
Little Rock Technology Center Building
100 S. Main, #401
Little Rock AR 72201
Tel: (501) 324-9043
Fax: (501) 324-9049

California

Maria Morris
State Director
California SBDC
California Trade and Commerce
    Agency
801 K St., #1700
Sacramento CA 95814
Tel: (916) 324-5068
Fax: (916) 322-5084

Colorado

Rick Garcia
State Director
Colorado SBDC
Colorado Office of Business
    Development
1625 Broadway, #1710

Denver CO 80202
Tel: (303) 892-3809
Fax: (303) 892-3848

Connecticut

John P. O'Connor
State Director
Connecticut SBDC
University of Connecticut
368 Fairfield Rd.
Box U-41, Room 422
Storrs CT 06269-2041
Tel: (203) 486-4135
Fax: (203) 486-1576

Delaware

Clinton Tymes
State Director
Delaware SBDC
University of Delaware
Purnell Hall, #005
Newark DE 19711
Tel: (302) 831-2747
Fax: (302) 831-1423

District of Columbia

Woodrow McCutcheon
State Director
District of Columbia SBDC
Howard University
2600 Sixth St., Room 125
Washington DC 20059
Tel: (202) 806-1550
Fax: (202) 806-1777

Florida

Jerry G. Cartwright
State Director
Florida SBDC
University of West Florida
19 W. Garden St., Third Floor
Pensacola FL 32501
Tel: (904) 444-2060
Fax: (904) 444-2070

Georgia

Hank Logan Jr.
State Director
Georgia SBDC
University of Georgia
1180 E. Broad St., Chicopee Complex
Athens GA 30602
Tel: (706) 542-6762
Fax: (706) 542-6776

Hawaii

Darryl Mleynek
State Director
Hawaii SBDC
University of Hawaii at Hilo
523 W. Lanikaula St.
Hilo HI 96720-4091
Tel: (808) 933-3515
Fax: (808) 933-3683

Idaho

Jim Hogge
Acting State Director
Idaho SBDC
Boise State University
1910 University Dr.
Boise ID 83725
Tel: (208) 385-1640
Fax: (208) 385-3877

Illinois

Jeff Mitchell
State Director
Illinois SBDC
620 E. Adams St., Sixth Floor
Springfield IL 62701
Tel: (217) 524-5856
Fax: (217) 785-6328

Indiana

Stephen Thrash
State Director
Indiana SBDC
One North Capitol, #420
Indianapolis IN 46204

Tel: (317) 264-6871
Fax: (317) 264-3102

Iowa

Ronald A. Manning
State Director
Iowa SBDC
Iowa State University
137 Lynn Ave.
Ames IA 50010
Tel: (515) 292-6351
Fax: (515) 292-0020

Kansas

Tom Hull
State Director
Kansas SBDC
Wichita State University
1845 Fairmount
Wichita KS 67260-0148
Tel: (316) 689-3193
Fax: (316) 689-3647

Kentucky

Janet S. Holloway
State Director
Kentucky SBDC
University of Kentucky
College of Business and Economics
255 Business and Economics Building
Lexington KY 40506-0034
Tel: (606) 257-7668
Fax: (606) 258-1907

Louisiana

John P. Baker
State Director
Louisiana SBDC
Northeast Louisiana University
College of Business Administration
700 University Ave.
Monroe LA 71209-6435
Tel: (318) 342-5506
Fax: (318) 342-5510

Maine

Charles Davis
State Director
Maine SBDC
University of Southern Maine
96 Falmouth St.
Portland ME 04103
Tel: (207) 780-4420
Fax: (207) 780-4810

Maryland

Thomas McLamore
State Director
Maryland SBDC
Department of Economic and
    Employment Development
217 E. Redwood St., Ninth Floor
Baltimore MD 21202
Tel: (410) 333-6995
Fax: (410) 333-4460

Massachusetts

John F. Ciccarelli
State Director
Massachusetts SBDC
University of Massachusetts, Amherst
School of Management, #205
Amherst MA 01003
Tel: (413) 545-6301
Fax: (413) 545-1273

Michigan

Ron Hall
State Director
Michigan SBDC
Wayne State University
2727 Second Ave.
Detroit MI 48201
Tel: (313) 964-1798
Fax: (313) 964-3648

Minnesota

Mary Kruger
State Director
Minnesota SBDC

500 Metro Square
121 Seventh Pl. E.
St. Paul MN 55101-2146
Tel: (612) 297-5770
Fax: (612) 296-1290

Mississippi

Raleigh Byars
State Director
Mississippi SBDC
University of Mississippi
Old Chemistry Building, #216
University MS 38677
Tel: (601) 232-5001
Fax: (601) 232-5650

Missouri

Max E. Summers
State Director
Missouri SBDC
University of Missouri
300 University Pl., #300
Columbia MO 65211
Tel: (314) 882-0344
Fax: (314) 884-4297

Montana

Gene Marcille
State Director
Montana SBDC
Montana Department of Commerce
1424 Ninth Ave.
Helena MT 59620
Tel: (406) 444-4780
Fax: (406) 444-2808

Nebraska

Robert E. Bernier
State Director
Nebraska SBDC
University of Nebraska at Omaha
60th & Dodge Sts., CBA Room 407
Omaha NE 68182
Tel: (402) 554-2521
Fax: (402) 554-3747

Nevada

Sam Males
State Director
Nevada SBDC
University of Nevada in Reno
College of Business Administration,
  #411
Reno NV 89557-0100
Tel: (702) 784-1717
Fax: (702) 784-4337

New Hampshire

Elizabeth Lamoureux
State Director
New Hampshire SBDC
University of New Hampshire
108 McConnell Hall
Durham NH 03824
Tel: (603) 862-2200
Fax: (603) 862-4876

New Jersey

Brenda Hopper
State Director
New Jersey SBDC
Rutgers University Graduate School of
  Management
180 University St.
Ackerson Hall, Third Floor
Newark NJ 07102
Tel: (201) 648-5950
Fax: (201) 648-1110

New Mexico

Frank Hatstat
State Director
New Mexico SBDC
Santa Fe Community College
PO Box 4187
Santa Fe NM 87502-4187
Tel: (505) 438-1362
Fax: (505) 438-1237

New York

James L. King
State Director

New York State SBDC
State University of New York
SUNY Plaza, S-523
Albany NY 12246
Tel: (518) 443-5398
Fax: (518) 465-4992

North Carolina

Scott R. Daugherty
State Director
North Carolina SBDC
University of North Carolina
4509 Creedmoor Rd., #201
Raleigh NC 27612
Tel: (919) 571-4154
Fax: (919) 571-4161

North Dakota

Walter Kearns
State Director
North Dakota SBDC
University of North Dakota
Gamble Hall, University Station
Grand Forks ND 58202
Tel: (701) 777-3700
Fax: (701) 777-3225

Ohio

Holly Schick
State Director
Ohio SBDC
77 S. High St.
Columbus OH 43226
Tel: (614) 466-2711
Fax: (614) 466-0829

Oklahoma

Grady L. Pennington
State Director
Oklahoma SBDC
Southeastern Oklahoma State
    University
517 West University
PO Box 2584, Station A
Durant OK 74701

Tel: (405) 924-0277
Fax: (405) 920-7471

Oregon

Edward Cutler
State Director
Oregon SBDC
Lane Community College
44 W. Broadway, #501
Eugene OR 97401
Tel: (503) 726-2250
Fax: (503) 345-6006

Pennsylvania

Gregory L. Higgins
State Director
Pennsylvania SBDC
The Wharton School
University of Pennsylvania
444 Vance Hall
3733 Spruce St.
Philadelphia PA 19104
Tel: (215) 898-1219
Fax: (215) 573-2135

Puerto Rico

Mariluz Frontera
Acting Director
Puerto Rico SBDC
University of Puerto Rico
PO Box 5253, College Station
Building B
Mayaguez PR 00681
Tel: (809) 834-3590
Fax: (809) 834-3790

Rhode Island

Douglas H. Jobling
State Director
Rhode Island SBDC
Bryant College
1150 Douglas Pike
Smithfield RI 02917
Tel: (401) 232-6111
Fax: (401) 232-6416

South Carolina

John M. Lenti
State Director
South Carolina SBDC
University of South Carolina
College of Business Administration
1710 College St.
Columbia SC 29208
Tel: (803) 777-3130
Fax: (803) 777-4403

South Dakota

Robert Ashley Jr.
State Director
South Dakota SBDC
University of South Dakota
414 East Clark
Vermillion SD 57069
Tel: (605) 677-5498
Fax: (605) 677-5272

Tennessee

Kenneth J. Burns
State Director
Tennessee SBDC
University of Memphis
South Campus
Getwell Rd., Building 1
Memphis TN 38152
Tel: (901) 678-2500
Fax: (901) 678-4072

Texas

Elizabeth Klimback
Region Director
North Texas SBDC
Dallas County Community College
1402 Corinth St.
Dallas TX 75215
Tel: (214) 565-5833
Fax: (214) 565-5815

Elizabeth J. Gatewood
Region Director
University of Houston SBDC
1100 Louisiana, #500
Houston TX 77002

Tel: (713) 752-8444
Fax: (713) 756-1500

Craig Bean
Region Director
Northwest Texas SBDC
Texas Tech University
2579 S. Loop 289, #114
Lubbock TX 79423
Tel: (806) 745-3973
Fax: (806) 745-6207

Robert M. McKinley
Region Director
S. Texas-Border SBDC
University of Texas at San Antonio
Cypress Tower, #410
1222 N. Main St.
San Antonio TX 78212
Tel: (210) 558-2450
Fax: (210) 558-2464

Utah

David A. Nimkin
State Director
Utah SBDC
102 West 500 S.
Salt Lake City UT 84101
Tel: (801) 581-7905
Fax: (801) 581-7814

Vermont

Donald L. Kelpinski
Vermont SBDC
Vermont Technical College
PO Box 422
Randolph Center VT 05060
Tel: (802) 728-9101
Fax: (802) 728-3026

Virgin Islands

Chester Williams
Acting State Director
Virgin Islands SBDC
University of the Virgin Islands
8000 Nisky Center, #202
Charlotte Amalie, St. Thomas VI
00802-5804

Tel: (809) 776-3206
Fax: (809) 775-3756

Virginia

Robert D. Smith
State Director
Virginia SBDC
901 E. Byrd St., #1800
Richmond VA 23219
Tel: (804) 371-8258
Fax: (804) 225-3384

Washington

Carol Riesenberg
Acting State Director
Washington State University
135 Kruegel
Pullman WA 99164-4727
Tel: (509) 335-1576
Fax: (509) 335-0949

West Virginia

Hazel Kroesser
State Director

West Virginia SBDC
Governor's Office of Community and
  Industrial Development
950 Kanawha Blvd. E.
Charleston WV 25301
Tel: (304) 558-2960
Fax: (304) 558-0127

Wisconsin

William Pinkovitz
State Director
Wisconsin SBDC
University of Wisconsin
432 N. Lake St., #423
Madison WI 53706
Tel: (608) 263-7794
Fax: (608) 262-3878

Wyoming

David Mosely
State Director
Wyoming SBDC
University of Wyoming
Laramie WY 82071
Tel: (307) 766-3505
Fax: (307) 766-3406

APPENDIX B

Small-Business Brokers, Advisors, and Intermediaries

Alabama

Robert G. Newsome, Sr.
Newsome Properties and Investments
2231 Victory La., #600
Birmingham AL 35216
Tel: (205) 733-9700
Fax: (205) 733-9728

Dennis C. Mortimer, FCA
ABB—Associated Business Brokers, Inc.
107 St. Francis St., #1200
Mobile AL 36689
Tel: (334) 434-0030
Fax: (334) 434-0034

Alaska

Matthew Fink
Realty Center Inc.
8400 Hartzell Rd.
Anchorage AK
Tel: (907) 344-0501
Fax: (907) 349-6438

Arizona

Ann Pollock
Cave-Pollock Realty and Management Inc.
518 North Beaver St.
Flagstaff AZ 86001
Tel: (800) 658-5815

Richard L. Varner, CBI
BIZ-NET Brokers
21639 N. 12th Ave., #103
Phoenix AZ 85027
Tel: (602) 582-8778
Fax: (602) 482-8696

Clifford E. Bergstrom, CBI
Tucson Business Investments Inc.
440 S. Williams Blvd., #202
Tucson AZ 85711
Tel: (602) 750-1764
Fax: (602) 750-1769

Arkansas

Jerry Crowly, CBI
WABB Ltd.
2228 S. 57th St., #B
Fort Smith AR 72903
Tel: (501) 452-1313
Fax: (501) 452-3600

Daniel G. Bilek
Commercial Consultants
PO Box 15953
Little Rock AR 72231-5353
Tel: (501) 758-2802
Fax: (501) 758-1492

California

Charles Swift
Bottom Line Ink Inc.
1171 W. Shaw, #104
Fresno CA 93711
Tel: (209) 224-9465
Fax: (209) 224-6429

John J. Collins, CBI
Pioneer Business Brokers
9042 Garfield, #312

Huntington Beach CA 92646
Tel: (714) 964-7600
Fax: (714) 965-0480

Don Clearwater
Diamond Business Broker
Affiliated: Prudential Medley Realty
PO Box 990430
Redding CA 96099-0430
Tel: (916) 241-5380

John J. Quinn
Quinn Real Estate
6825 Magnolia Ave., #C
Riverside CA 92506
Tel: (909) 787-8812

Robert Mills
Abitir International Inc.
3111 Camino Del Rio N., #400
San Diego CA 92108
Tel: (619) 437-0204
Fax: (619) 297-7070

Larry Brown
Business Team Inc.
2950 Buskirk Ave., #160
Walnut Creek CA 94596
Tel: (510) 944-9009

Colorado

David W. Lewis
ProForma West Ltd.
7475 Dakin St., #600
Denver CO 80221-6926
Tel: (303) 427-0800
Fax: (303) 427-7707

Ken Mischel
Mischel and Company
2975 Broadmoor Valley Rd., #103
Colorado Springs CO 80906
Tel: (719) 576-6610

Fred M. Mehring
Business Acquisitions Ltd.
3900 E. Mexico, #970
Denver CO 80210
Tel: (303) 758-4600
Fax: (303) 692-0639

Connecticut

Richard Haskel, CBI
Country Business Inc.
PO Box 1867
Lakeville CT 06039
Tel: (203) 435-0678
Fax: (203) 435-2844

Delaware

Robert A. Pelletier, CBI
Stoltz Business Resources
1600 Pennsylvania Ave.
Wilmington DE 19806
Tel: (302) 658-6681
Fax: (302) 658-1434

District of Columbia (See Washington, D.C.)

Florida

Richard Read, CBI, CBD, LFBI
Corporate Investment International, Inc.
101 Wymore Rd., #225
Altamonte Springs FL 32714
Tel: (407) 682-9600
Fax: (407) 682-3676

Burton Engel
Stoltz-Leigh Business Resources Inc.
2650 N. Military Trail, #2304
Boca Raton FL 33431
Tel: (407) 998-4901
Fax: (407) 998-2966

Gerri Cosenza
Florida Business Group Inc.
24641 U.S. 19 N., #550
Clearwater FL 34623
Tel: (813) 791-4419
Fax: (813) 796-4092

Donald L. Cummins, CBI
Cummins and Associates
1500 Colonial Blvd., #222
Fort Myers FL 33907
Tel: (813) 278-4236
Fax: (813) 275-7437

M. B. "Ben" Ossi
Corporate Business Investments Inc.
6251 Phillips Highway, #5
Jacksonville FL 32216
Tel: (904) 739-2233
Fax: (904) 739-2646

Doug Baumwall
Collins and Collins Investments Inc.
8201 S.W. 124th St.
Miami FL 33156
Tel: (305) 235-4444

Jack Rush
Business Brokers of Northern Florida
1342 Timberlane Rd.
Tallahassee FL 32312
Tel: (904) 668-8001
Fax: (904) 668-8003

Georgia
Keith Henderson
The Keith Henderson Co.
1105 Tenth Ave., #3
Albany GA 31707
Tel: (912) 436-7384
Fax: (912) 436-7408

James H. Deitz
Southern Venture Services
365 Northridge Rd., #260
Atlanta GA 30350
Tel: (404) 587-2538
Fax: (404) 587-2538

Jim Baucom
Sunbelt Business Brokers
501 Greene St.
Augusta GA 30901
Tel: (706) 724-5005

Philip L. Taylor, CBI
Georgia Business Associates Inc.
2401 Lake Park Dr.
Smyrna GA 30080
Tel: (404) 319-6500

Hawaii
Eddie Flores, Jr., CBI
Sun Pacific Realty

100 N. Beretania St., #129-Q
Honolulu HI 96817
Tel: (808) 521-3044
Fax: (808) 521-3044

Idaho
William J. Laska
Arthur Berry and Co.
104 S. Capitol Blvd., #200
Boise ID 83702
Tel: (208) 336-8000
Fax: (208) 345-0609

Illinois
James Weir, CBI
Weir Realty Co.
5030 38th St.
Moline IL 61265
Tel: (309) 757-1111
Fax: (309) 764-2487

Glenn N. Haddad
G&N Venture Resource
40 Shuman Blvd., #264
Naperville IL 60563
Tel: (708) 355-1900
Fax: (708) 355-1910

Teri Pauly
Pauly Group
2937 Stanton Ave., #200
Springfield IL 62703
Tel: (217) 529-5400
Fax: (217) 529-5445

Indiana
William A. Ready
Markets USA Inc.
555 Forest Blvd.
Indianapolis IN 46240-2513
Tel: (317) 255-9721
Fax: (317) 255-6685

Iowa
Joy Jones
Hawkeye Business Brokerage Co.
6900 University Ave.

Des Moines IA 50311
Tel: (5l5) 279-1056
Fax: (515) 279-1209

Kansas

James R. O'Keeffe, CBI
O'Keeffe Inc.
6408 W. 107th St., #100
Overland Park KS 66212
Tel: (913) 648-0185
Fax: (913) 648-0188

Patrick J. Finn, CBI
Finn and Associates Inc.
545 North Woodlawn
Wichita KS 67208-3645
Tel: (316) 683-3466
Fax: (316) 683-4425

Kentucky

George E. Darling
Markets USA Inc.
233 W. Broadway, #507
Louisville KY 40101-2113
Tel: (502) 583-5408
Fax: (502) 585-1239

Richard L. Johnson
Venture Resource Business Brokers
    Inc.
1930 Bishop La., #110
Louisville KY 40218
Tel: (502) 458-2661
Fax: (502) 458-3036

Louisiana

Darrel L. Mills, CBI
C. J. Brown Inc.
7414 Perkins Rd.
Baton Rouge LA 70808
Tel: (504) 766-0000
Fax: (504) 767-7063

Nick Tusa
General Business Brokers
3 Williams Ave., #A
New Orleans LA 70121
Tel: (504) 834-4893

Maine

John A. Bonadio
Dawson Business and Commercial
    Brokers
417 Main St.
Bangor ME 04401
Tel: (207) 947-6788
Fax: (207) 941-9866

Philip L. Taylor, CBI
Country Business Inc.
36 Union Wharf
Portland ME 04101
Tel: (207) 773-1745
Fax: (207) 773-3183

Maryland

Robert C. Nettles
Abbot Associates Inc.
42 W. Chesapeake Ave.
Baltimore MD 21401-4801
Tel: (410) 337-6838
Fax: (410) 337-6839

Massachusetts

Robert Lucido
Vernon A. Martin Inc.
1 Corporate Place, #201
Danvers MA 01923-4001
Tel: (508) 774-0160
Fax: (508) 774-2579

Paul H. Boudo, CBI
Country Business Inc.
PO Box 983
West Springfield MA 01909-0983
Tel: (413) 739-4300
Fax: (413) 739-5690

Michigan

Jim Hines, CBI
Inexco Business Brokerage and
    Development
1568 Mt. Mercy N.W.
Grand Rapids MI 49504
Tel: (616) 949-4374
Fax: (616) 453-5160

Wade Montreif
Prime Business Brokers Inc.
1225 E. Eleven Mile Rd.
Royal Oak MI 48067-2049
Tel: (313) 399-7788
Fax: (313) 544-4261

Minnesota
Steven L. Berglund, CBI
Berglund and Co.
5500 Wayzata Blvd., #305
Minneapolis MN 55416
Tel: (612) 546-0220
Fax: (612) 546-1741

Bob Griesgraber
Opportunities in Business
3433 Broadway St. NE, #555
Minneapolis MN 55413
Tel: (612) 331-8392
Fax: (612) 331-8778

Mississippi
Rob Smith
Smith and Co. Inc.
1401 U.S. Highway 49 S.
Jackson MS 39218
Tel: (601) 939-8445

Dick Acker
Jackson Enterprise Center
931 Highway 80 W.
Jackson MS 39204
Tel: (601) 352-0957
Fax: (601) 948-3250

Missouri
Keith McLaughlin, CBI
America's Business Brokers
409 Vandiver, Bldg. 4, #200-B
Columbia MO 65202
Tel: (314) 443-4992
Fax: (314) 443-4995

Richard L. Laiben
American International Business
    Brokers
3173 Cresent Dr., #C

St. Louis MO 63129
Tel: (314) 991-5362

Montana
Cliff O. Jensen
Associate Realty
2409 Arnold La.
Billings MT 59102
Tel: (406) 656-2200

Tim Shay
Corporate Investment
101 E. Broadway, #316
Missoula MT 59802
Tel: (406) 549-5433
Fax: (406) 549-6140

Nebraska
James W. Otradosky
Real Estate Brokerage Co.
11717 Burt St.
Omaha NE 68154
Tel: (402) 333-3333

Nevada
Thomas T. Enerson
The Thomas Group
4218 W. Charleston
Las Vegas NV 89102-8839
Tel: (702) 870-4060
Fax: (702) 870-8839

Richard Bartholet
Pennington and Associates
495 Apple St., #205
Reno NV 89502
Tel: (702) 827-4661
Fax: (702) 827-0986

New Hampshire
Brij Prasad
Anvil Ventures
71 Spit Brook Rd. #407
Nashua NH 03060
Tel: (603) 891-0212, (508) 649-4110
Fax: (603) 891-0246

New Jersey

Mort Schrager, CBI
Broker One Inc.
14-25 Plaza Rd., #201
Fair Lawn NJ 07410
Tel: (201) 796-0303
Fax: (201) 796-0304

Stephen M. Steinberg
Execuserve Business Brokers Inc.
55 Schanck Rd., #A-1
Freehold NJ 07728
Tel: (908) 409-6288
Fax: (908) 409-6298

Steven Yeskel, CBI
Yeskel and Mirkin
746 State Highway 34, #5
Matawan NJ 07747
Tel: (908) 583-7400
Fax: (908) 583-8774

New Mexico

John P. Lastra
Hooten/Stahl Commercial Investments
2033 Wyoming Blvd. N.E.
Albuquerque NM 87112
Tel: (505) 262-3272

Sam Goldenberg
Advantage Financial Group Inc.
1850 Old Pecos Trail, #L
Santa Fe NM 87505
Tel: (505) 820-0163
Fax: (505) 820-0167

New York

Alfred S. Petty, CBI
Heritage Business Brokers
5 E. Genesee St.
PO Box 311
Baldwinsville NY 13027-0311
Tel: (315) 635-1372
Fax: (315) 635-1526

Ed Brandt
Country Business Inc.
Box 750

Lake Placid NY 12946
Tel: (518) 523-9953

Clifford Lemieux
United Business Associates Inc.
5872 Beattie Ave.
Lockport NY 14094
Tel: (716) 433-0100

Ross Brothers
19 W. 34th St.
New York NY 10001
Tel: (212) 563-7977

Michael Santomauro
Business Finders
250 W. 57th St., #1629
New York NY 10019
Tel: (212) 489-6943

Small and Landesman
1460 Broadway
New York 10036
Tel: (212) 730-7790

Bill Russell
Business Brokers Associates Inc.
8 Peachtree Dr.
Oyster Bay NY 11771
Tel: (516) 922-3130
Fax: (516) 922-6680

Murray Leffler
Business Sales Consultants Inc.
PO Box 203
Scarsdale NY 10538
Tel: (914) 472-6946
Fax: (914) 725-3039

Edward C. Telling, Jr., CBI
Telling Group Inc.
215 E. Water St.
Syracuse NY 13202
Tel: (315) 475-9300
Fax: (315) 475-9399

North Carolina

Ronald Clontz
Clontz Commercial Investments Inc.
1713 Cleveland Ave.
Charlotte NC 28203

Tel: (704) 374-0756
Fax: (704) 331-9805

Mark Fairchild
C. J. Harris and Co. Inc.
4208 Six Forks Rd., #334
Raleigh NC 27609
Tel: (919) 791-2448

North Dakota
Garry Pierce
Investment Realty Inc.
2910 E. Broadway, #33
Bismarck ND 58501
Tel: (701) 223-1226

Ohio
Vern Buckley
Buckley and Associates Inc.
33352 Lake Shore Blvd.
Cleveland OH 44095
Tel: (800) 821-7790, (216) 946-8200
Fax: (216) 953-1374

Jan Pieterse
Bauer Co.
1376 State Route 28, #H
Loveland OH 45140-8789
Tel: (513) 575-9400
Fax: (513) 575-7323

Oklahoma
Bill Robertson
ABM and Associates Inc.
4515 S. Yale, #115
Tulsa OK 74135
Tel: (918) 665-3301
Fax: (918) 664-5182

Oregon
Bob Butler, CBI
Bob Butler Business Brokers
1631 N.E. Second St.
Bend OR 97701
Tel: (503) 389-6001
Fax: (503) 389-9096

Samuel J. Burke, CBI
ARI Acquisitions Resource Inc.
399 E. Tenth Ave., #102
Eugene OR 97401
Tel: (503) 683-7042
Fax: (503) 683-6922

William L. Ingram
Business Brokers Inc.
1408 East Burnside St.
Portland OR 97214
Tel: (503) 238-7607

Pennsylvania
Fred S. Engle
The Summit Advisory Ltd.
275 Hess Blvd.
Lancaster PA 17601
Tel: (717) 560-0639
Fax: (717) 560-0639

John B. Bartling
Corporate Finance Associates
PO Box 15586
Pittsburgh PA 15244
Tel: (412) 787-2780
Fax: (412) 787-2786

Rhode Island
Rocco J. Pezza, CBI
New England Brokerge Corp.
225 Newman Ave.
East Providence RI 02916
Tel: (401) 438-2130
Fax: (401) 431-0555

South Carolina
Gordon W. Gillett, CBI
Gordon Gillett Business Realty Inc.
PO Box 6573
Hilton Head Island SC 29938
Tel: (803) 785-9555
Fax: (803) 686-8742

South Dakota
Rick Kahler
Kahler Financial Group

2020 W. Omaha St.
Rapid City SD 57702
Tel: (605) 343-7500

Henry Van Essen
ReMax Professionals
606 W. 33rd St.
Sioux Falls SD 57105
Tel: (605) 334-8585

Tennessee
Jim Heeren, CBI
Jay Investments Inc.
227 Third Ave. N.
Franklin TN 37064
Tel: (615) 791-1529
Fax: (615) 790-8964

Randy Tolley, CBI
American Business Group
2562 School Ave.
Memphis TN 38112
Tel: (901) 323-2300

Dale Pruett
American Business Center
631 Second Ave. S., #LL
Nashville TN 37210
Tel: (615) 259-0971
Fax: (615) 794-0706

Texas
Walter C. Emmett, CBI
The Emmett Group
2201 Civic Circle, #503
Amarillo TX 79109
Tel: (806) 358-8571
Fax: (806) 358-8572

Carl R. Monnin, BCB, CBI
Corporate Investment International
7320 N. Mopac Expressway, #305
Austin TX 78731
Tel: (512) 346-4444
Fax: (512) 346-4473

Maynard Clark, CBI
CIBB Group Inc.
4200 S. Hulen St., #600

Fort Worth TX 76109-4907
Tel: (817) 731-0622

Jerry F. Kroon, CBI
First Capital Business Group
1235 N. Loop W., #1120
Houston TX 77008
Tel: (713) 880-0606
Fax: (713) 880-1555

H. M. Hamilton
Hamilton and Associates
3222 Tanglewood
Odessa TX 79762
Tel: (915) 550-4610

Utah
William J. Tabar
VRUtah
349 S. 200 E., #370
Salt Lake City UT 84111
Tel: (801) 532-1530
Fax: (801) 532-1541

Vermont
Philip H. Steckler III, CBI
Country Business Inc.
PO Box 940
Brattleboro VT 05302
Tel: (802) 254-4504
Fax: (802) 254-4900

Virginia
David Gagen
Century 21 United States Realty Inc.
2930 W. Broad St.
Richmond VA 23230
Tel: (804) 359-1371

Washington
Don Tait
The Veritas Group
515-B 116th N.E., #170
Bellevue WA 98004
Tel: (206) 455-4626
Fax: (206) 455-5802

A. T. "Fred" Zirkle, CBI
Zirkle and Company
1121 N. Argonne Rd., #109
Spokane WA 99212
Tel: (509) 928-1737
Fax: (509) 926-1747

Washington, D.C. (District of Columbia)

George Muthara
GBS Realty
7600 Georgia Ave. NW
Washington DC 20012
Tel: (202) 291-9212

West Virginia

James P. Bazzle
Mercantile Financial Group
PO Box 3725
Charleston WV 25337
Tel: (304) 344-1335
Fax: (304) 346-8913

Wisconsin

David E. Meiers, CBI
First Commerce Business Group Inc.
1345 W. Mason St.
Green Bay WI 54303
Tel: (414) 494-3122
Fax: (414) 494-3122

Michael S. Hoesly, CBI
Hoesly and Co. Inc.
4510 Regent St.
Madison WI 53705
Tel: (608) 231-2050
Fax: (608) 231-2583

Wyoming

Sandra R. Adams
Business Brokerage West
805 E. Second St., #5
Casper WY 82601
Tel: (307) 234-6553

APPENDIX C

Further Reading

Anthony, Joseph. *Kiplinger's Working for Yourself*, Kiplinger Books, Washington DC, 1993.

Applegate, Jane. *Succeeding in Small Business: The 101 Toughest Problems and How to Solve Them*, Penguin Books, New York NY, 1992.

Arden, Lynie. *The Work-at-Home Sourcebook*, Revised and Expanded Fifth Edition, Live Oak Publications, Boulder CO, 1994.

Bade, Nicholas E. *Marketing without Money*, NTC Business Books, Lincolnwood IL, 1994.

Barrow, Colin. *The Essence of Small Business*, Prentice Hall, Englewood Cliffs NJ, 1992.

Benson, Richard V. *Secrets of Successful Direct Mail*, NTC Business Books, Lincolnwood IL, 1991.

Berle, Gustav. *The Do-It-Yourself Business Book*, John Wiley & Sons, New York NY, 1989.

Berle, Gustav. *The Green Entrepreneur: Business Opportunities That Can Save the Earth and Make You Money*, Prentice Hall, Englewood Cliffs NJ, 1991.

Blum, Laurie. *Free Money for Small Businesses and Entrepreneurs*, John Wiley & Sons, New York NY, 1992.

Bond, William J. *Home-Based Mail Order: A Success Guide for Entrepreneurs*, McGraw Hill, New York NY, 1990.

Bond, William J. *Home-Based Catalog Marketing: A Success Guide for Entrepreneurs*, McGraw Hill, New York NY, 1993.

Boyan, Lee. *Successful Cold Call Selling*, Amacom, New York NY, 1989.

Brabec, Barbara. *Homemade Money*, Fifth Edition, Better Way Books, Cincinnati OH, 1994.

Brown, Peter C. *Jumping the Job Track: Security, Satisfaction and Success as an Independent Consultant*, Crown, New York NY, 1994.

Burstiner, Irving. *Mail Order Selling: How to Market Almost Anything by Mail*, Simon and Schuster, New York NY, 1993.

Burstiner, Irving. *Start and Run Your Own Profitable Service Business*, Prentice Hall, Englewood Cliffs NJ, 1993.

Burstiner, Irving. *The Small Business Handbook: A Comprehensive Guide to Starting and Running Your Own Business*, Updated and Revised Edition, Simon & Schuster (Fireside), New York NY, 1994.

Chant, Ben, and Melissa Morgan. *How to Start a Service Business*, Avon Books, New York NY, 1994.

Clark, Scott A. *Beating the Odds: 10 Smart Steps to Small Business Success*, Amacom, New York NY, 1991.

Cohen, William A. *The Entrepreneur and Small Business Problem Solver: An Encyclopedic Reference and Guide*, John Wiley & Sons, New York NY, 1990.

Coleman, Bob. *The New Small Business Survival Guide*, Norton, New York NY, 1991.

Cook, Mel. *Home Business, Big Business*, Collier, New York NY, 1992.

Dominguez, Joe, and Vicki Robin. *Your Money or Your Life: Transforming Your Relationship with Money and Achieving Financial Independence*, Penguin, New York NY, 1992.

Edwards, Paul, and Sarah Edwards. *Making It on Your Own*, Tarcher/Putnam, New York NY, 1991.

Edwards, Paul, and Sarah Edwards. *Working from Home*, Fourth Edition, Tarcher/Putnam, New York NY, 1994.

Edwards, Paul, Sarah Edwards, and Laura Clampitt Douglas. *Getting Business to Come to You*, Tarcher/Putnam, New York NY, 1991.

Godfrey, Joline. *Our Wildest Dreams: Women Entrepreneurs Making Money, Having Fun, Doing Good*, HarperCollins, New York NY, 1992.

Gordon, Kim T. *Growing Your Home-Based Business: A Complete Guide to Proven Sales and Marketing Strategies*, Prentice Hall, Englewood Cliffs NJ, 1992.

Hahn, Fred E. *Do-It-Yourself Advertising: How to Produce Great Ads, Brochures, Catalogs, Direct Mail and Much More*, John Wiley & Sons, New York NY, 1993.

Halloran, James W. *Why Entrepreneurs Fail: Avoid the 20 Fatal Pitfalls of Running Your Business*, Liberty Hall Press, Blue Ridge Summit PA, 1991.

Harper, Stephen C. *The McGraw-Hill Guide to Starting Your Own Business*, McGraw-Hill, New York NY, 1991.

Hausman, Carl. *Moonlighting: 148 Great Ways to Make Money on the Side*, Avon, New York NY, 1989.

Hawken, Paul. *Growing a Business*, Simon & Schuster, New York NY, 1988.

Holtz, Herman. *The Complete Work-at-Home Companion*, Revised and Expanded Second Edition, Prima, Rocklin CA, 1994.

Kamoroff, Bernard. *Small-Time Operator: How to Start Your Own Small Business, Keep Your Books, Pay Your Taxes, and Stay Out of Trouble*, Bell Springs Publishing, Laytonville CA, 1992.

Kirk, Randy W. *When Friday Isn't Payday: A Complete Guide to Starting, Running—and Surviving in—a Very Small Business*, Warner, New York, NY, 1993.

Kirsch, M. M. *How to Get Off the Fast Track and Live a Life Money Can't Buy*, HarperPaperbacks, New York NY, 1991.

Kishel, Gregory F., and Patricia Gunter Kishel. *How to Start, Run and Stay in Business*, John Wiley & Sons, New York NY, 1993.

Lonier, Terri. *Working Solo: The Real Guide to Freedom and Financial Success with Your Own Business*, Portico Press, New Paltz NY, 1994.

Mancuso, Joseph R. *How to Start, Finance and Manage Your Own Small Business*, Simon & Schuster, New York NY, 1992.

Mancuso, Joseph, and Donald Boroian. *How to Buy and Manage a Franchise*, Simon & Schuster, New York NY, 1993.

Matthews, John R. *The Beginning Entrepreneur: Starting Your Own Business . . . and Making It Work!*, VGM Career Horizons, Lincolnwood IL, 1994.

Matusky, Gregory, and the Philip Lief Group. *The Best Home-Based Franchises*, Doubleday, New York NY, 1992.

Nykiel, Ronald A. *You Can't Lose If the Customer Wins: 10 Steps to Growth and Profit*, Berkley Books, New York NY, 1994.

Perry, Robert L. *The 50 Best Low-Investment, High-Profit Franchises*, Second Edition, Prentice Hall, Englewood Cliffs NJ, 1994.

Peterson, C. D. *How to Leave Your Job and Buy a Business of Your Own*, McGraw-Hill, New York NY, 1988.

Pinchot, Gifford, III. *Intrapreneuring*, Harper & Row, New York NY, 1985.

Pino, Laurence J. *Finding Your Niche: A Personal Guide for Entrepreneurs*, Berkley Books, New York NY, 1994.

Price, Courtney. *Answers the Most-Asked Questions from Entrepreneurs*, McGraw-Hill, New York NY, 1994.

Rapp, Stan, and Tom Collins. *Maxi-Marketing: The New Direction in Advertising, Promotion and Marketing Strategy*, McGraw-Hill, New York NY, 1988.

Rapp, Stan, and Tom Collins. *The Great Marketing Turnaround: The Age of the Individual—and How to Profit from It*, Plume, New York NY, 1992.

Saltzman, Amy. *Down-Shifting: Reinventing Success on a Slower Track*, Harper-Perennial, New York NY, 1991.

Seglin, Jeffrey L. *Financing Your Small Business*, McGraw-Hill, New York NY, 1990.

Shenson, Howard L. *The Contract and Fee-Setting Guide for Consultants and Professionals*, John Wiley & Sons, New York NY, 1990.

Sherman, Andrew J., and Donna Tozzi Cavanagh. *The Best Nonfranchise Business Opportunities*, Henry Holt, New York NY, 1993.

Slutsky, Jeff, with Marc Slutsky. *Street Smart Marketing*, John Wiley & Sons, New York NY, 1989.

Slutsky, Jeff, with Marc Slutsky. *How to Get Clients*, Warner Books, New York NY, 1992.

Stockwell, John, and Henry Shaw. *Direct Marketing Checklists: 99 Proven Checklists to Save Time, Cut Costs and Boost Direct Response*, NTC Business Books, Lincolnwood IL, 1993.

Tomzack, Mary E. *Tips and Traps When Buying a Franchise*, McGraw-Hill, New York NY, 1994.

Tuller, Lawrence W. *Financing the Small Business*, Prentice Hall, Englewood Cliffs NJ, 1991.

Wagner, Stephen, and the Editors of *Income Opportunities* Magazine. *Mind Your Own Business: The Best Businesses You Can Start Today for Under $500*, Bob Adams Inc., Holbrook MA, 1992.

Weiss, Alan. *Million Dollar Consulting: The Professional's Guide to Growing a Practice*, McGraw-Hill, New York NY, 1992.

Weitzen, H. Skip. *Infopreneurs: Turning Data into Dollars*, John Wiley & Sons, New York NY, 1991.

Whitmeyer, Claude, and Salli Rasberry. *Running a One-Person Business*, Ten-Speed Press, Berkeley CA, 1994.

Wilson, Sandi. *Be the Boss: Start and Run Your Own Business*, Avon, New York NY, 1985.

Wood, Robert M. *Home Office Money and Tax Guide*, Probus Publishing, Chicago IL, 1992.

Yale, David R. *The Publicity Handbook: How to Maximize Publicity for Products, Services and Organizations*, NTC Business Books, Lincolnwood IL, 1993.

Index

About the Authors

Noted author and small-business expert **Glenn Desmond** brings almost 40 years of experience to *The Ideal Entrepreneurial Business for You*. He has been a professional business consultant for more than 35 years, specializing in assisting business owners and potential buyers, especially regarding the best ways to build value and enhance marketability. He has founded several companies, including a publishing company, a seminar firm, and national appraisal firms. He consults regularly with both small businesses and large corporations as well as the U.S. Department of Justice, the Internal Revenue Service, the General Services Administration, and other federal, state, and local public agencies.

Glenn holds several memberships and professional senior designations in associations including the Appraisal Institute, American Society of Appraisers, International Right of Way Association, and others. He has qualified as an expert witness on business and real estate in hundreds of court cases from Hawaii to Maine. A nationally recognized lecturer, he has conducted hundreds of seminars throughout the United States for professionals and nonprofessionals on a wide range of business subjects, including what the best businesses are and how much businesses are worth.

He is the author of several books on business subjects, including the *Business Valuation Handbook, How to Value Professional Practices*, the *Handbook of Small Business Valuation Formulas and Rules of Thumb*, and now *The Ideal Entrepreneurial Business for You*.

He hopes this new book will be an indispensable guide for anyone who has ever dreamed of taking the plunge into the world of entrepreneurship either as a buyer or as a seller.

Editor and writer **Monica Faulkner** has worked with dozens of authors on books ranging from business to Buddhism. She has also been an editor and publishing consultant in Hong Kong and China. Her editing consultancy, Book Doctors, is based in Los Angeles.